IMAGES
of America

PORTSMOUTH
RHODE ISLAND

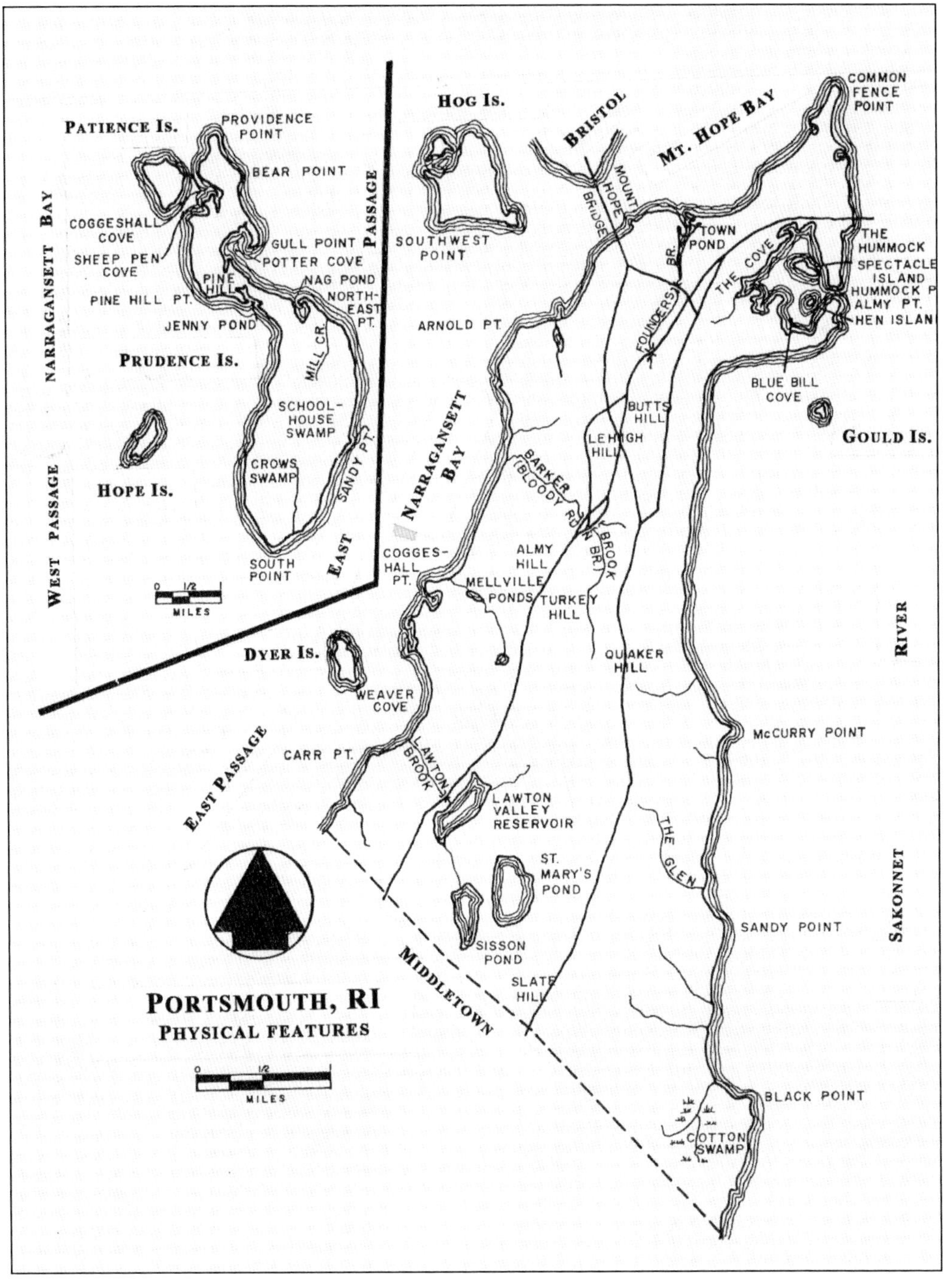
PORTSMOUTH, RI
PHYSICAL FEATURES
MILES
PATIENCE IS.
PROVIDENCE POINT
BEAR POINT
NARRAGANSETT BAY
COGGESHALL COVE
SHEEP PEN COVE
PINE HILL
PINE HILL PT.
GULL POINT
POTTER COVE
NAG POND
NORTH-EAST PT.
JENNY POND
PRUDENCE IS.
MILL CR.
SCHOOL-HOUSE SWAMP
CROWS SWAMP
SANDY PT.
HOPE IS.
WEST PASSAGE
SOUTH POINT
EAST PASSAGE
HOG IS.
SOUTHWEST POINT
BRISTOL
MT. HOPE BAY
MOUNT HOPE BRIDGE
COMMON FENCE POINT
TOWN POND
BR.
THE COVE
THE HUMMOCK
SPECTACLE ISLAND
HUMMOCK P
ALMY PT.
HEN ISLAN
FOUNDERS
ARNOLD PT.
BLUE BILL COVE
GOULD IS.
BUTTS HILL
LEHIGH HILL
NARRAGANSETT BAY
BARKER (BLOODY RUN BROOK BR.)
COGGES-HALL PT.
ALMY HILL
MELLVILLE PONDS
TURKEY HILL
DYER IS.
QUAKER HILL
WEAVER COVE
CARR PT.
LAWTON BROOK
McCURRY POINT
EAST PASSAGE
LAWTON VALLEY RESERVOIR
THE GLEN
ST. MARY'S POND
SISSON POND
SANDY POINT
SAKONNET
RIVER
MIDDLETOWN
SLATE HILL
BLACK POINT
COTTON SWAMP

IMAGES
of America

PORTSMOUTH
RHODE ISLAND

Nancy Jensen Devin and Richard V. Simpson

ARCADIA
PUBLISHING

ISBN 978-0-7385-9018-9

Published by Arcadia Publishing
Charleston, South Carolina

Printed in the United States of America

For all general information contact Arcadia Publishing at:
Telephone 843-853-2070
Fax 843-853-0044
E-mail sales@arcadiapublishing.com
For customer service and orders:
Toll-Free 1-888-313-2665

Visit us on the Internet at www.arcadiapublishing.com

Dedicated to the Aboriginal People of Aquidneck Island,
the Narragansett

Other Publications by R.V. Simpson

Crown of Gold: A History of the Italian-Roman Catholic Church in Bristol, RI (1967)

Independence Day: How the Day is Celebrated in Bristol, RI (1989)

Old St. Mary's: Mother Church in Bristol, RI (1994)

Bristol, Rhode Island: In the Mount Hope Lands of King Philip (1996)

Contents

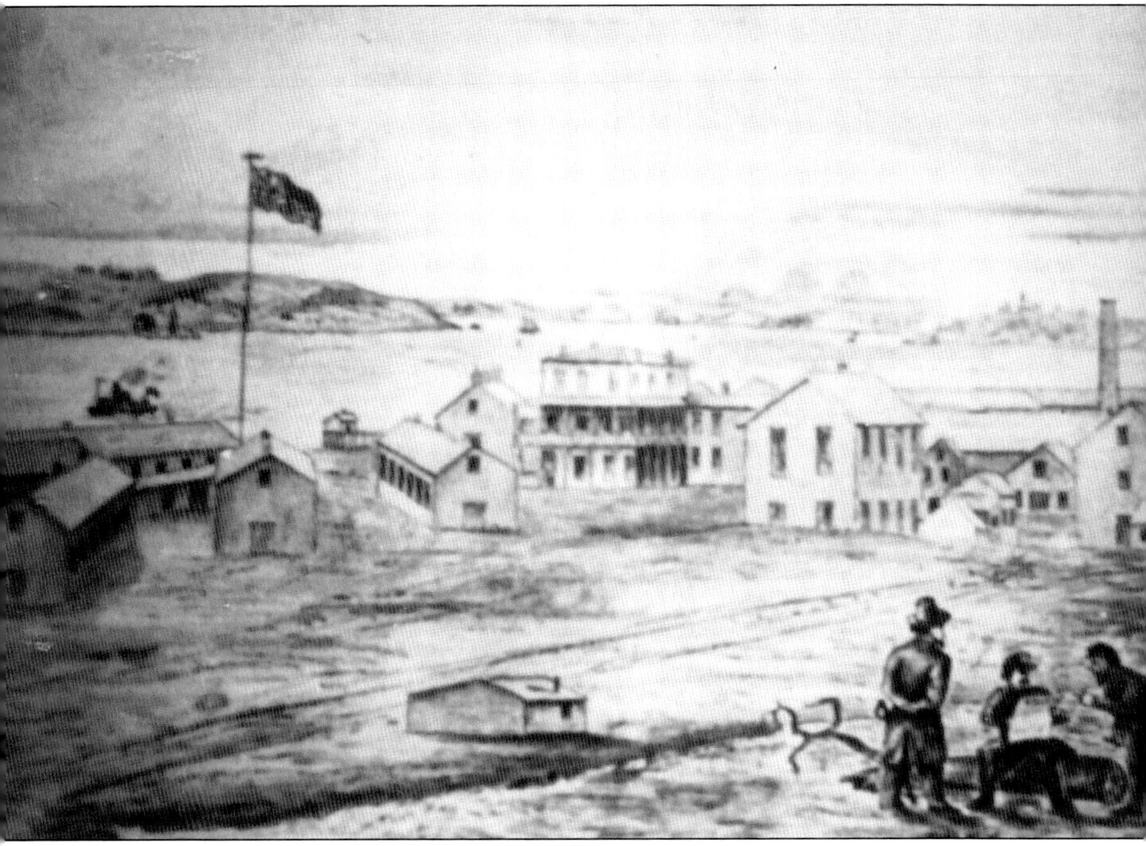

Lovell Hospital, opened at Portsmouth Grove, in the area now called Melville, in 1862. Lovell operated for three years caring for wounded Union and captured Confederate soldiers. In a June 1927 article, the *Fall River Herald* reported that steamer and train excursions were organized from Providence, Newport, New Bedford, Taunton, and Fall River to visit Portsmouth Grove, hopefully to "catch sight" of the Rebels and wounded Union men. The article told of pleasant summer Sundays when families would flock to the grove carrying, "cakes, pies, and dainties of all kinds" not only for the Union sick and wounded, but also for the Confederate prisoners. William Moran of Fall River, who as a child visited Lovell, recalled a Confederate Army captain who picked him up and held him in his arms. The captain said, "My little lad, I left in Georgia another such lad as you, and my fondest wish on earth is that I may see him once again." Moran vividly remembered the man's tear-stained cheek, though at the time he did not understand why the man was crying.

Introduction

The main portion of the town of Portsmouth, Rhode Island, is on the north end of Aquidneck Island. Its land mass includes seven small islands to the east and west: Prudence, Patience, and Hog Islands are inhabited in Narragansett Bay, while the islands of Hope, Despair, and Dyer are not; on the Sakonnet River, the small uninhabited dumpling-shaped island called Gould is also part of Portsmouth. The town is bounded on the north by Mt. Hope Bay, the south by Middletown, the east by the Sakonnet River, and the west by Narragansett Bay.

In 1524, Giovanni de Verrazzano sailed up Narragansett Bay and spent some time exploring Aquidneck Island and exchanging greetings with the natives who lived here. His journal contains praise for the fertile land and its indigenous people. By 1614, Dutch navigators and trappers were exploring the island and trading with the native population.

When Roger Williams arrived at what is now Providence, in 1636, Canonicus and Miantonomi were sachems (chiefs) of the peaceful, prosperous, and powerful Narragansett people. The tribe occupied Aquidneck Island and the mainland, west to Charlestown and beyond. In 1638, when the outspoken and charismatic Anne Hutchinson and her family were banished from the Massachusetts Bay Colony, her friends approached Williams hoping to find a place for Anne and her family and followers to settle. Williams met with the sachems and proposed to purchase the island. The price: 40 fathoms of white beads, 10 coats, and 20 hoes.

In the spring of 1638, the first permanent white settlement established a beachhead on Aquidneck Island. Following the example set by the settlers of Plymouth Colony, the Aquidneck colonists drafted and signed the Portsmouth Compact, the first document of its kind that swears allegiance to no earthly monarch.

The Narragansett's name for the site of the first white settlement is Pocasset; in the summer of 1639, the colonists changed the name to Portsmouth. The original settlement centered around Town Pond at the north end of the island. In those days, Town Pond was of sufficient size for small vessels to navigate; it was a sheltered harbor with access to Mt. Hope Bay. As the pond silted up, the channel to Mt. Hope Bay disappeared. Today, the pond is a marsh northeast of Route 24 and Boyd's Lane, near the hotel. Founder's Brook is behind the Mello's farm vegetable stand off Boyd's Lane.

As a part of the original settlement, the area known as Common Fence Point got its name because of the fence built as a barrier across that narrow neck of land, in the area used by citizens as common grazing pasture.

In 1647, Portsmouth was the site of the greater colony's most important legislative meeting. In May of that year, Portsmouth, Newport, and Providence adopted the Charter of Providence Plantations; at the same meeting the colony incorporated the anchor as part of its official seal, and the council adapted the ". . . laws of the Province of Providence Plantations in Narragansett Bay."

By the mid-1730s, after the Town Pond silted up, popular sentiment was that the original settlement was getting overcrowded. A site on a gently sloping hill, now the Water Street area, became the new village center. Here, the town began to flourish as new businesses established residence and homes were constructed. By the late eighteenth century, several mercantile stores, a livery, a wood shop, a blacksmith, two churches, a market, and a music hall thrived.

The advent of American trade with China sparked a flurry of Portsmouth shipbuilding. Captain Benjamin Tallman, one of New England's most respected shipbuilders, was responsible for the design and construction of a large number of fast sailing ships destined for the China Sea. One of these ships, the *Ann and Hope*, built for the Browns of Providence, became the most celebrated of American clipper ships.

The British began their occupation of Newport in December 1776 with 8,000 troops, and their presence influenced the entire island. Colonists not loyal to the crown had their freedom restricted to immediate surroundings; some others were taken prisoner and locked up on board prison ships. In August 1778, the British filled in all Portsmouth wells. Finally, when the British left in October 1779, not a tree was left standing on the island, half of the houses were burned, all public works were destroyed, and the countryside was generally devastated.

The local Americans did not take all this abuse lying down. The most notable of their counter-attacks was the daring mid-night capture of British General Richard Prescott at his quarters at Overing Farm (Prescott Farm).

Although not decisive, the Battle of Rhode Island, fought in August 1778, was the only major land battle fought in the colony. It provided an opportunity for the members of the First Rhode Island Regiment (otherwise known as the Black Regiment) to prove their valor, which they did, and the British were driven from the colony's shores. Other less spectacular, but important, events took place in Portsmouth during the Revolution. Because of its isolation and many hidden coves, it was a pocket of rebel resistance and underground activity.

During the seventeenth and eighteenth centuries, sheep farming was the mainstay of the community. When the land recovered from the rigors of the war, dairy farming and agriculture became the population's principle occupations. By the end of the 1800s, no fewer than twenty windmills were busy grinding meal from the grain produced on the town's farms.

Portsmouth did have some industry in the early 1800s. In Lawton's Valley two mills operated. One manufactured a type of cloth called "negro" and the other was a "carding and fulling" mill. In 1809, the discovery of coal near Bristol Ferry, below Willow Lane on land now owned by the Kaiser Aluminum Company, was the grist for a whole new industry. The mining of Portsmouth coal proceeded on and off for more than a century; it came to an end in the mid-1930s.

In a non-belligerent way, Portsmouth became involved in the Civil War. In July 1862, the Lovell General Hospital opened at Portsmouth Grove, in the area known as Melville. The hospital cared for Union and captured Confederate soldiers. At its peak there were 1,724 patients in residence, including about 70 Confederates. The Newport Artillery Company guarded the facility.

With the granting of a right-of-way in December 1897 to the Newport & Fall River Street Railway Company, and the beginning of its service at the turn of the century, the entire island could be traversed by rapid transit. The trolleys enabled everyone to travel inexpensively, for business or pleasure. Thus, the Island Park region began to develop as a seaside recreation area. In due time, an amusement center featuring rides, games of chance, and a dine and dance pavilion became a popular place for family outings. Sadly, the area was devastated by the Hurricane of 1938, and it never regained its former stature as an amusement park.

Early in 1987, as the town began planning its 350th anniversary celebration, retired Police Chief John Pierce made an exciting discovery. Pierce recognized that a framed copy of the Declaration of Independence hanging in Town Hall (always accepted by others to be a reproduction) was an original. Upon expert analysis, the document proved to be one of only eight authentic originals in existence.

Today, Portsmouth is a thriving suburban community that is a pleasant blend of new and old. Most of the great estates of wealthy merchants and the large dairy farms of old-line Yankees are now housing developments. Still remaining, however, are many eighteenth-century homes that retain ancient stone fences outlining sprawling verdant meadows. Historic cemeteries dot the landscape, their crumbling markers giving silent testament; reminders of how our way of life, based on liberty and self-rule, was instituted (won) by the founders and patriots who lived and died here in another time.

One

Roots to Rebellion

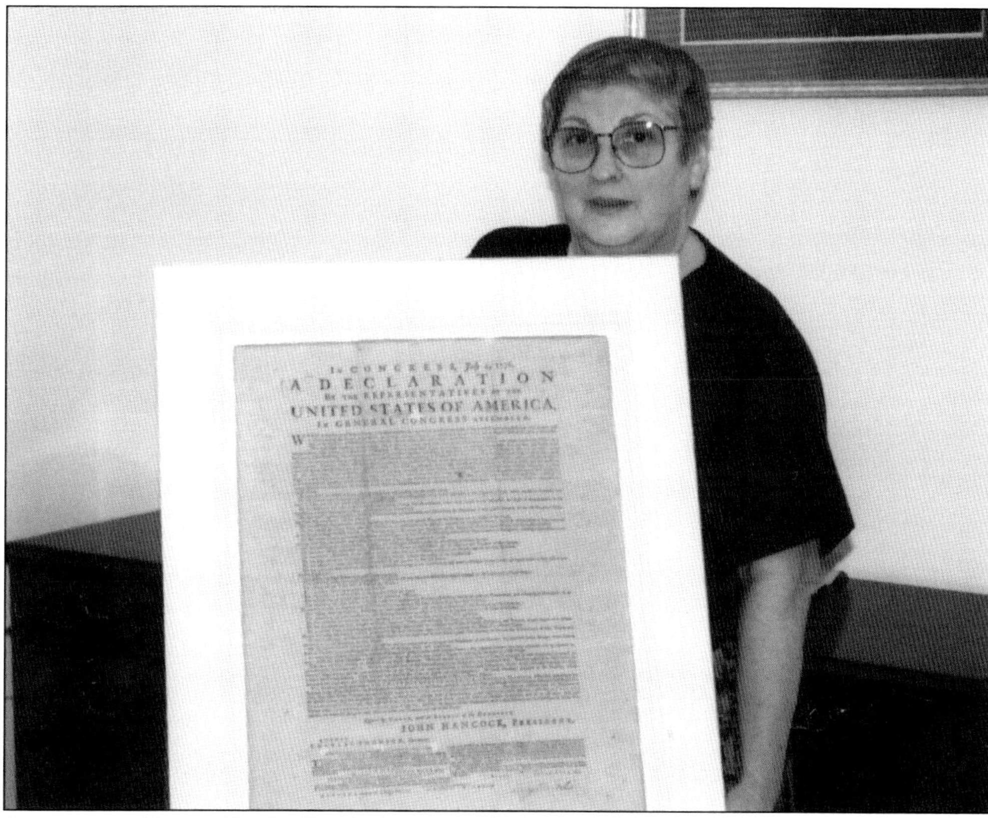

Portsmouth Town Clerk Carol Zinno with Portsmouth's copy of the Declaration of Independence. The document is the same one sent to Portsmouth Town Clerk John Thurston in 1776 by the Rhode Island General Assembly. While the Portsmouth copy is not one of the twenty-two surviving July 4, 1776 printings of the document by Philadelphia printer John Dunlap, it is only the eighth copy known to exist of the Declaration printed on July 13, 1776, by Newport printer Solomon Southwick. It is supposed that Southwick printed between two and three dozen of them from a copy of Dunlap's, and then they were distributed to each city or town clerk in Rhode Island to be read or posted.

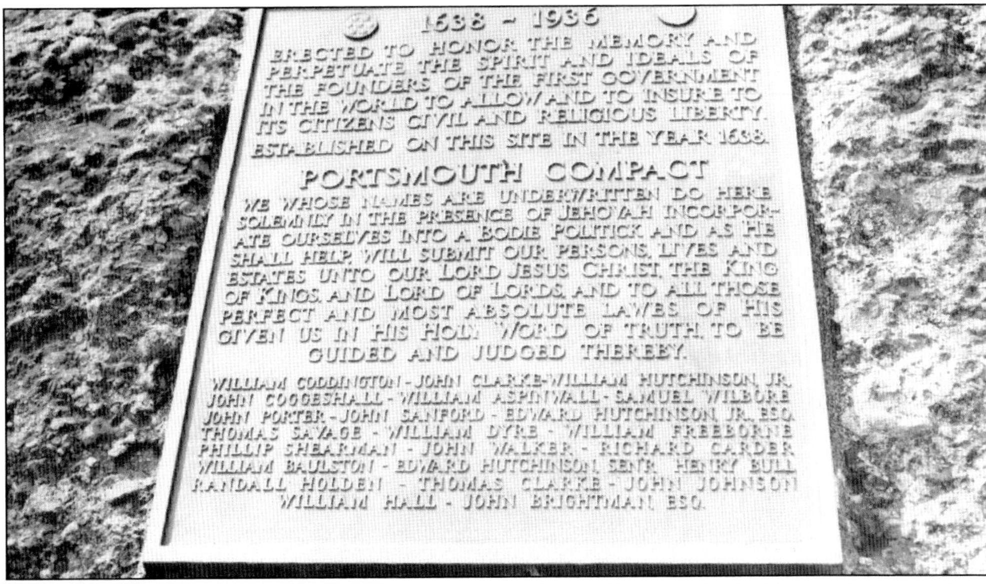

The Portsmouth Compact (modeled after the Mayflower Compact), the first authentic written guarantee of civil and religious liberty in the world. The bronze plaque commemorating the historic document was dedicated on the occasion of the 300th anniversary of its signing.

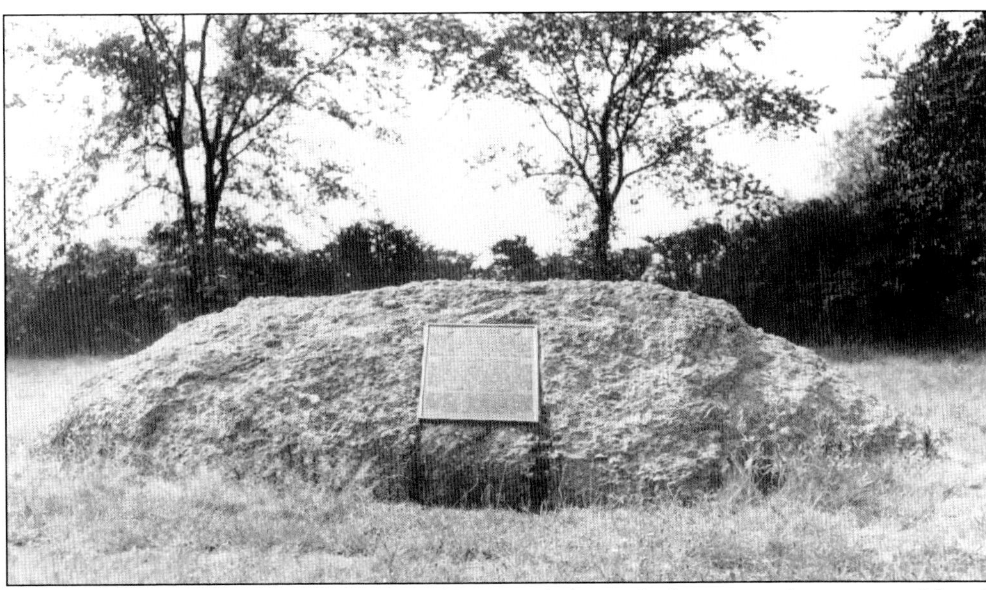
The Portsmouth Compact plaque and Pudding Rock, located adjacent to the spring and brook at what was the center of the original 1638 settlement.

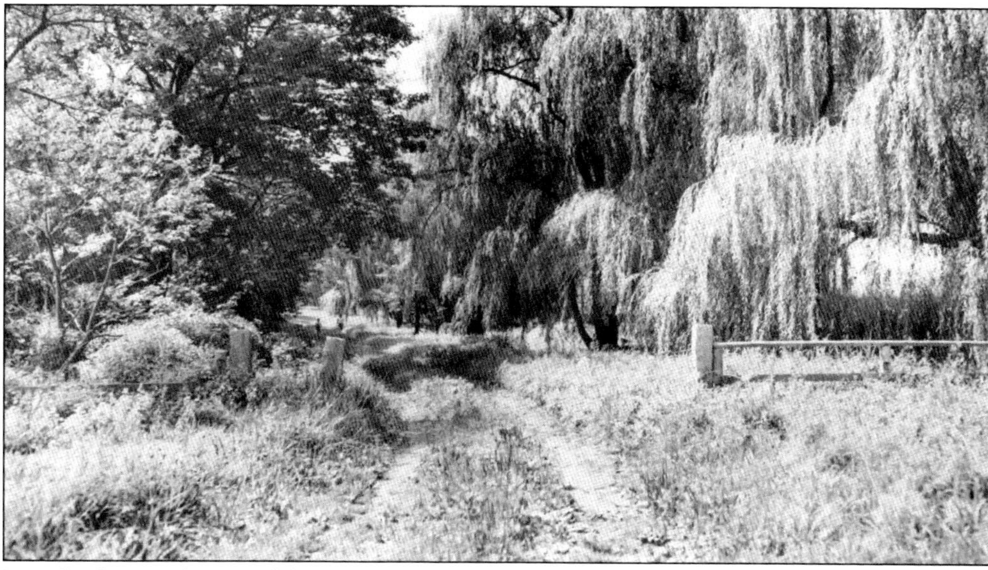

Lane leading to the site of the Memorial Boulder, adjacent to the spring source of the so-called Founder's Brook.

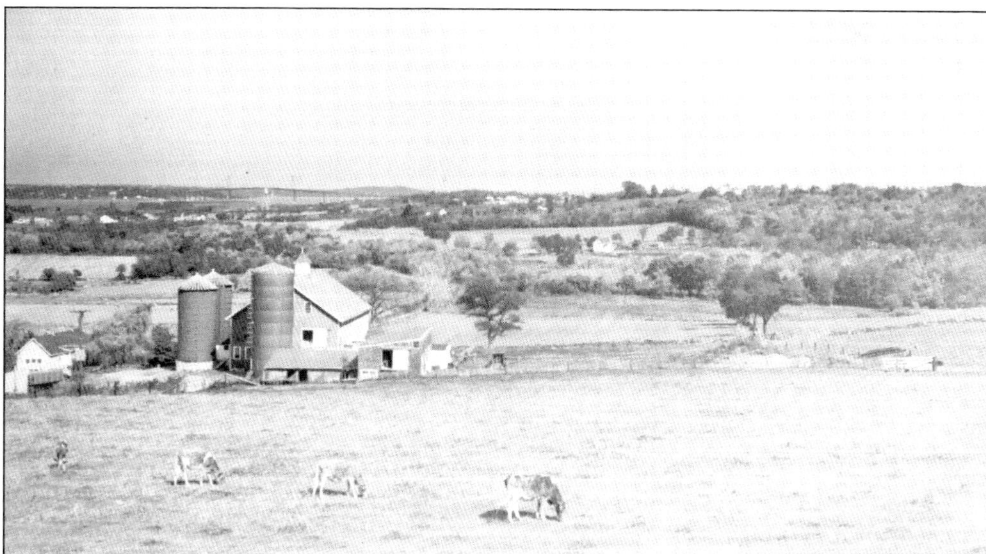

View from Almy Hill, c. 1930, of the northeastern part of Portsmouth, toward Lehigh Hill, the site of major fighting in the Battle of Rhode Island, August 29, 1778. Mount Hope and the Mount Hope Bridge are visible in the left background.

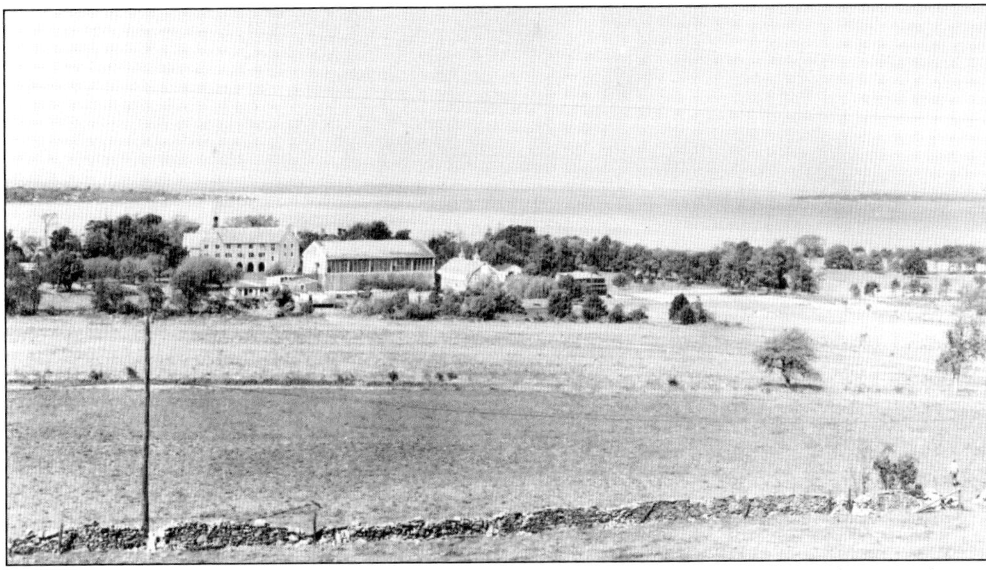

Panorama of the general area of the Battle of Rhode Island. In the distance is the Benedictine Priory and the School of St. Gregory, with Narragansett Bay beyond.

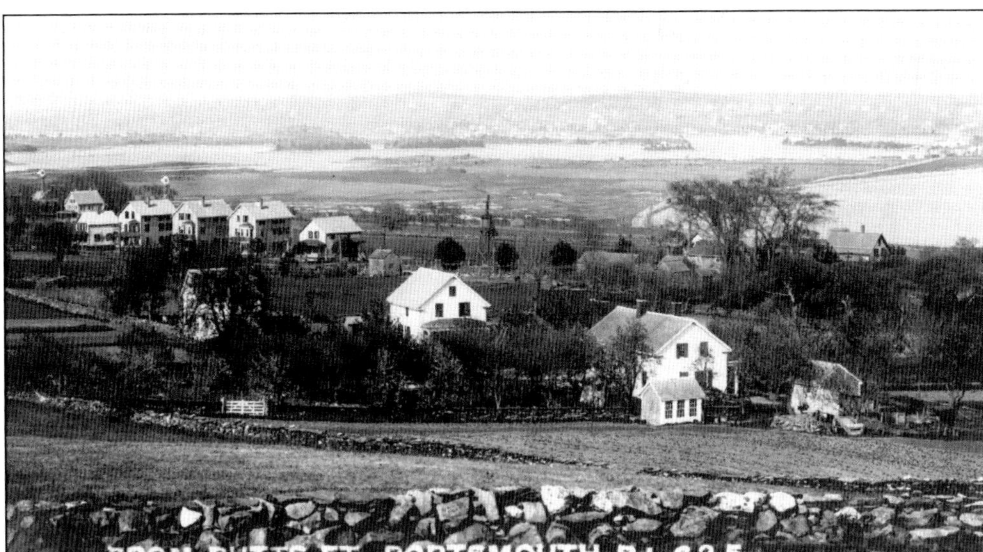

Excellent overview afforded of Portsmouth's eastern flank and the Sakonnet River from Butts Hill, site of Fort Butts, from a c. 1906 postcard. On August 8, 1778, the British withdrew from Fort Butts to new positions at Coddington Cove. American General John Sullivan, crossing from Tiverton at Howland Ferry, discovered the British had evacuated the northern end of the island, and ordered his troops to occupy Fort Butts and all other former British positions.

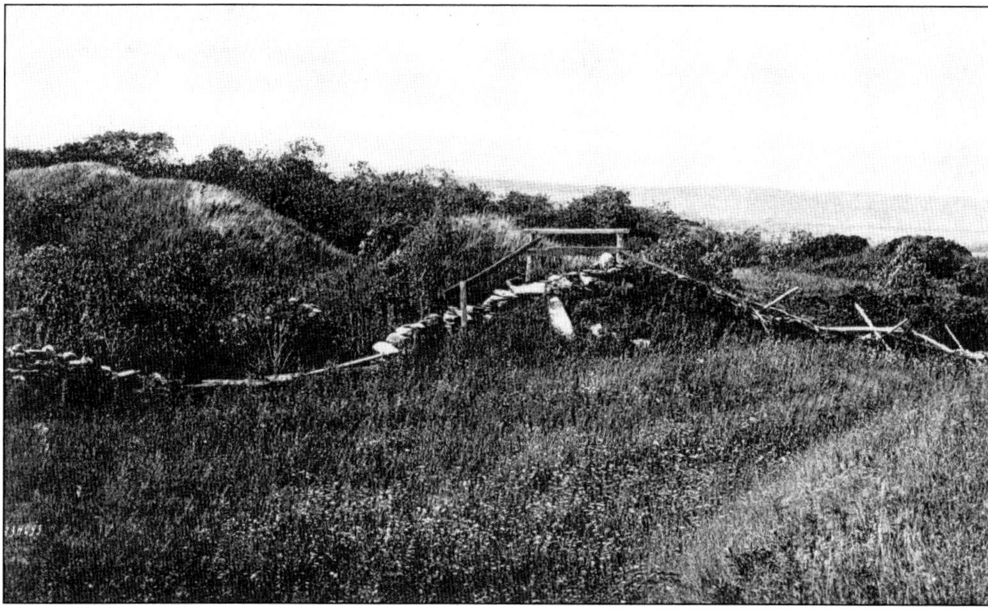

Remains of Fort Butts earth and stone works, *c.* early 1910s. During the Battle of Rhode Island, this site provided the Americans with a strategic position. American lines, centered at this point, were about one mile north of the British and Hessian lines extending across the island. The valley between Butts Hill and the British-held Quaker, Turkey, and Almy Hills soon became the scene of Rhode Island's only land battle.

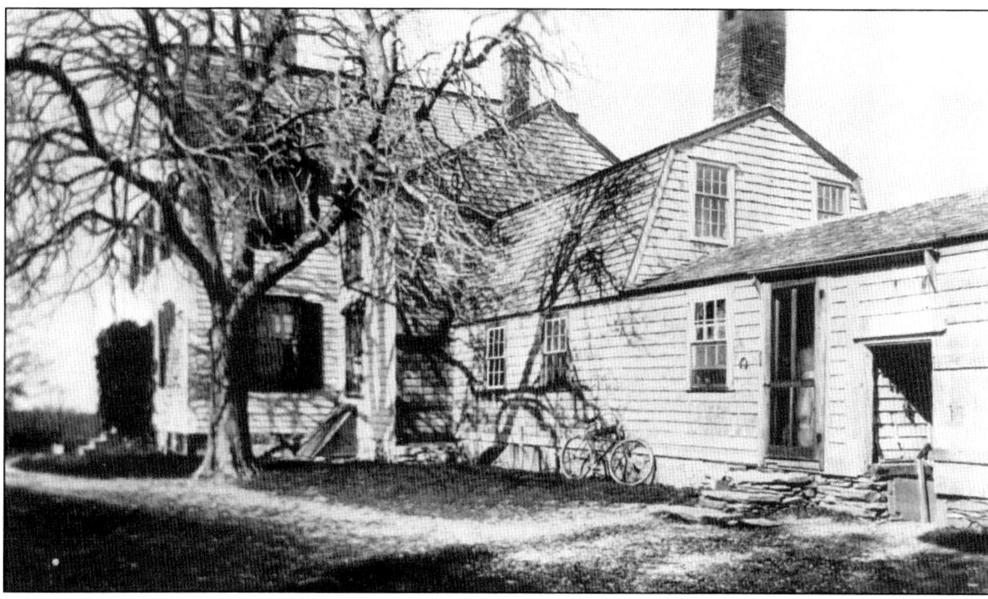

British General Prescott's Portsmouth headquarters at Overing Farm. This is a view of the south face of the house as it appeared in the 1930s, before restoration.

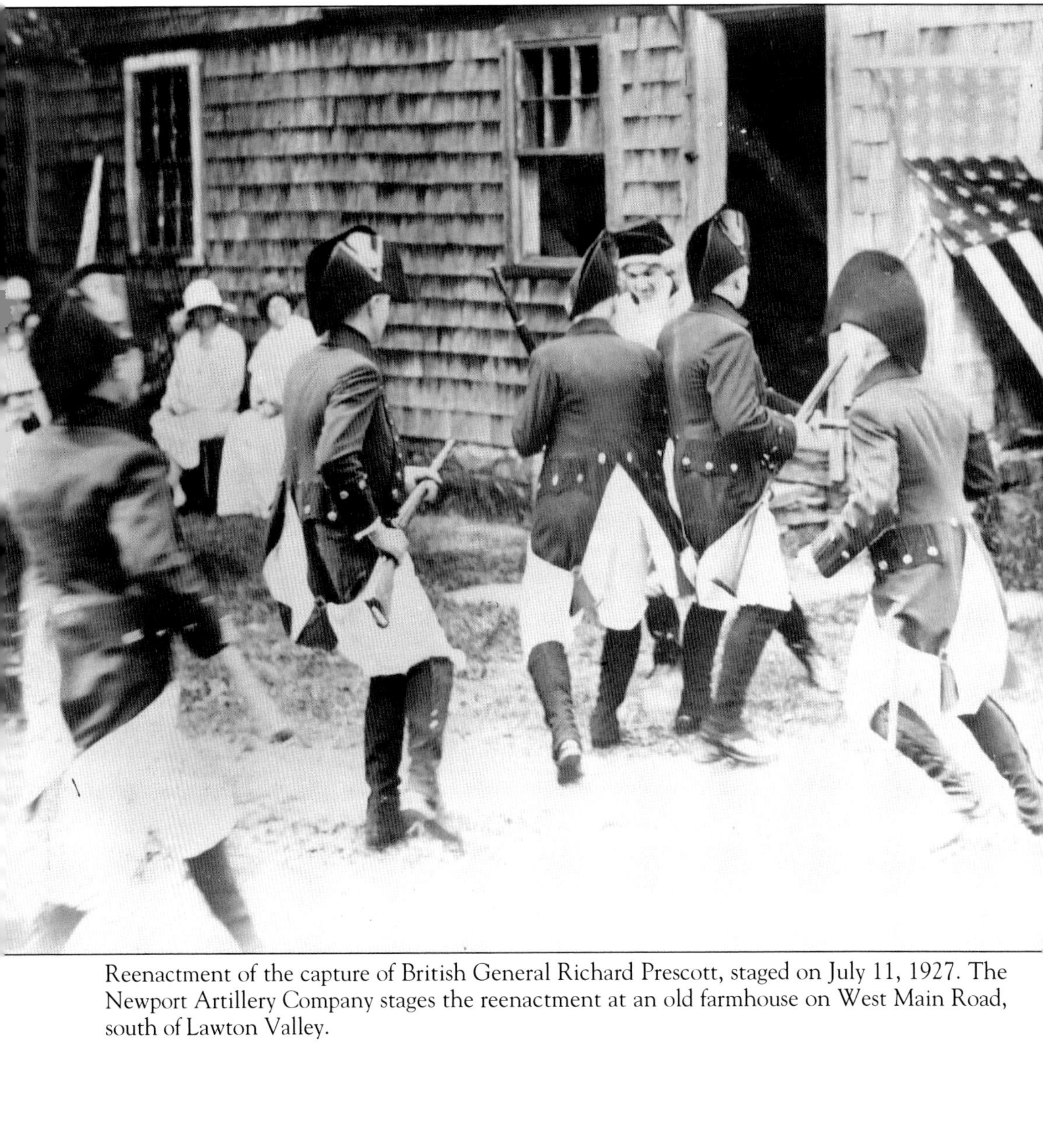

Reenactment of the capture of British General Richard Prescott, staged on July 11, 1927. The Newport Artillery Company stages the reenactment at an old farmhouse on West Main Road, south of Lawton Valley.

American soldiers outside Prescott's quarters. These troops stand "guard" while others discharge the daring act of capturing the hated British general.

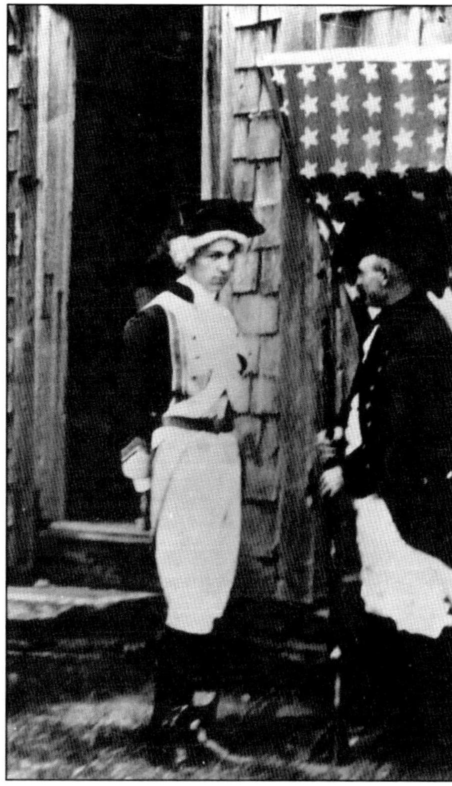

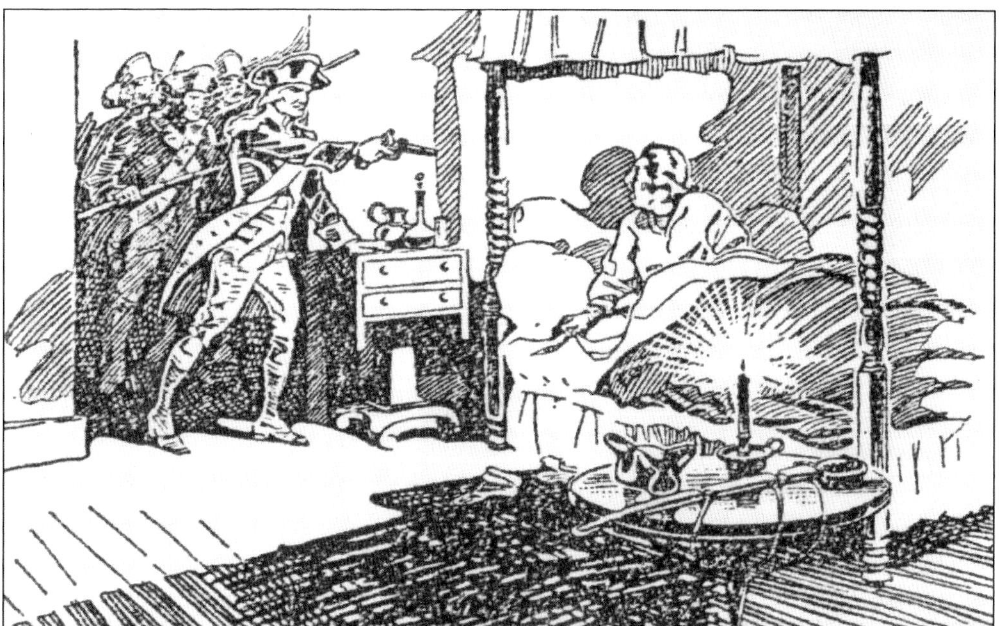

The capture of General Prescott. At gun point, the general is rousted from his bed and taken prisoner in his nightshirt. Later, before Prescott was taken to Providence from Warwick, to save him embarrassment, a servant was allowed to fetch his uniform, wig, and toiletries. This illustration is from p. 67 of the *Old Stone Bank History of Rhode Island* (1929).

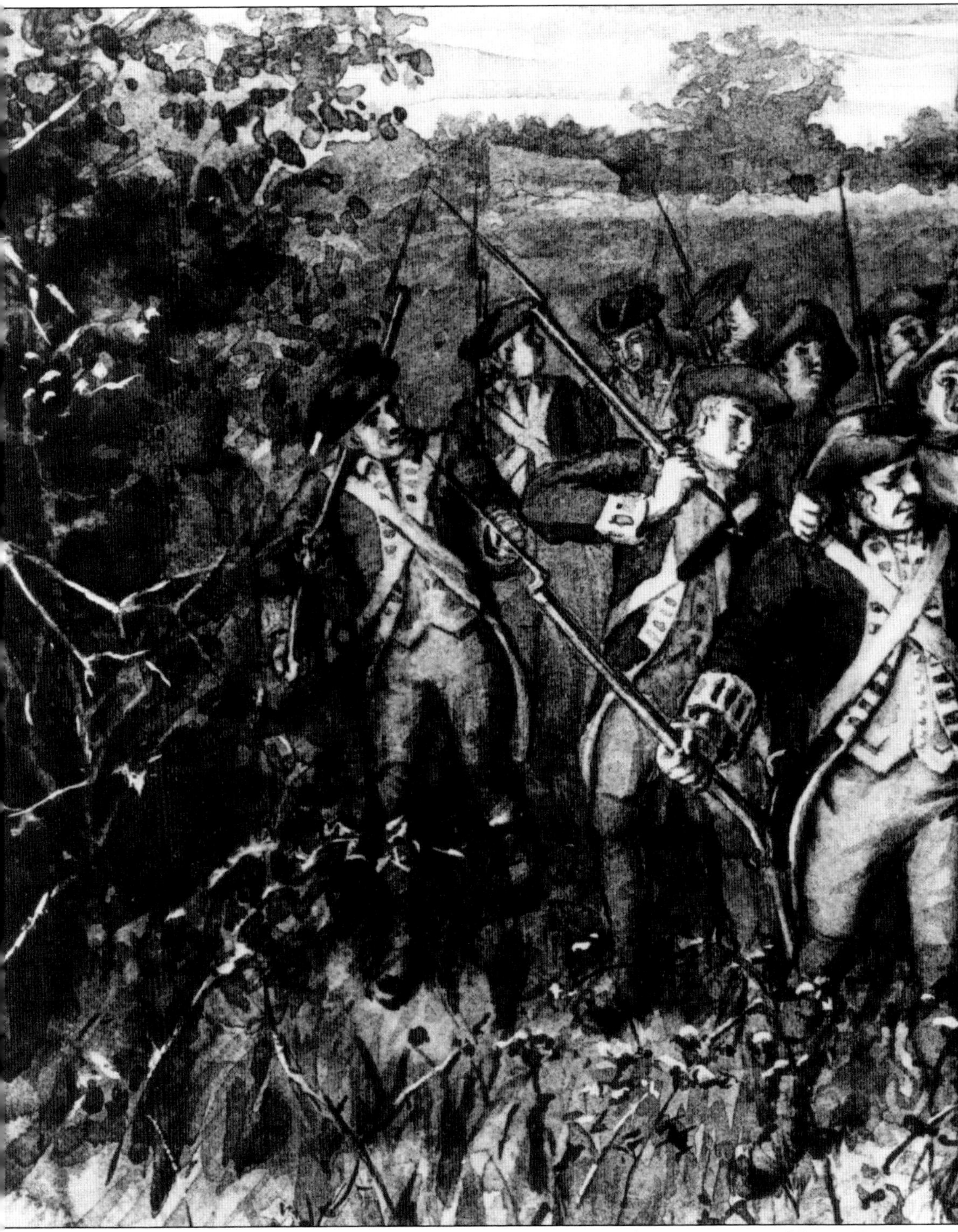

Painting by M.F. Richards depicting Prescott's capture by American soldiers. Twenty-nine-year-old Lieutenant Colonel William Barton hatched the plan and led the squad of raiders on the daring deed, which General Lafayette said was the boldest of the war. In the

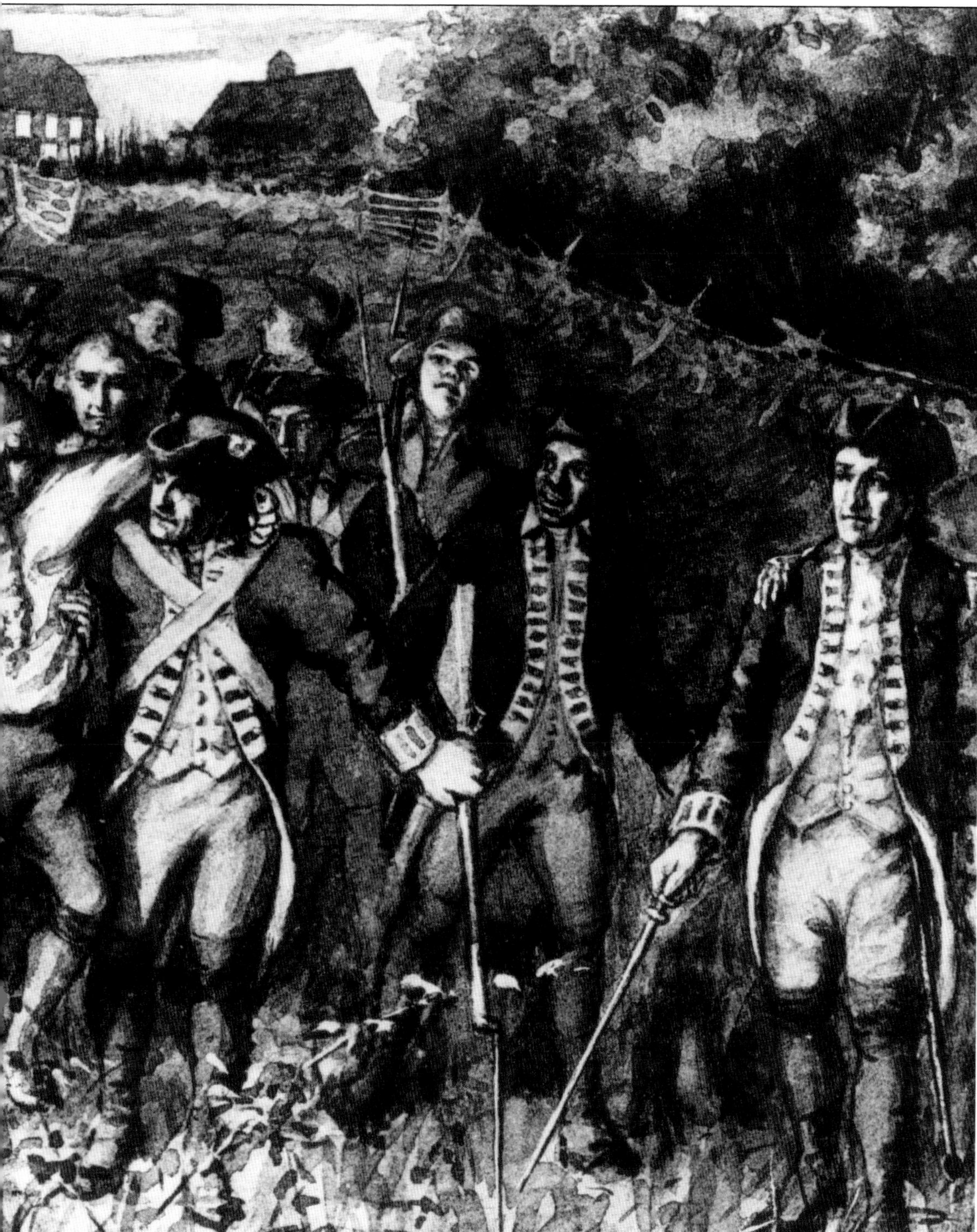

background is the Overing Farmhouse that is now the centerpiece of the Prescott Farm historic restoration. (Photograph courtesy of the Rhode Island Historical Society.)

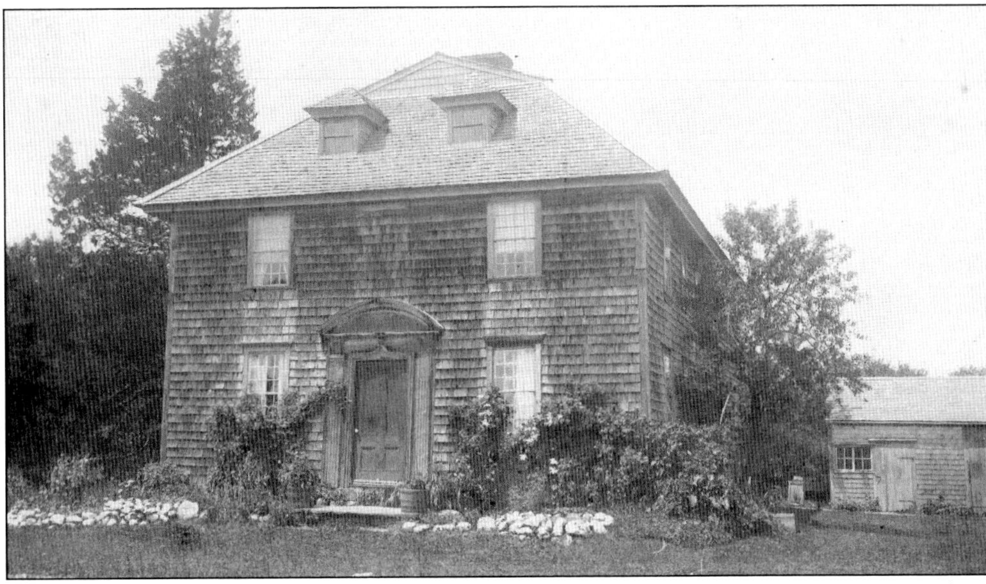

Residence of Metcalf Bowler on Wapping Road. Bowler, a wealthy and enterprising merchant of Newport, bought a 70-acre farm in Portsmouth and established his country seat there. Active in Rhode Island politics, he supported the Revolution and was a signer of the Rhode Island Renunciation of Allegiance. He served in the state General Assembly for nineteen years; eventually he became Chief Justice of the Rhode Island Supreme Court.

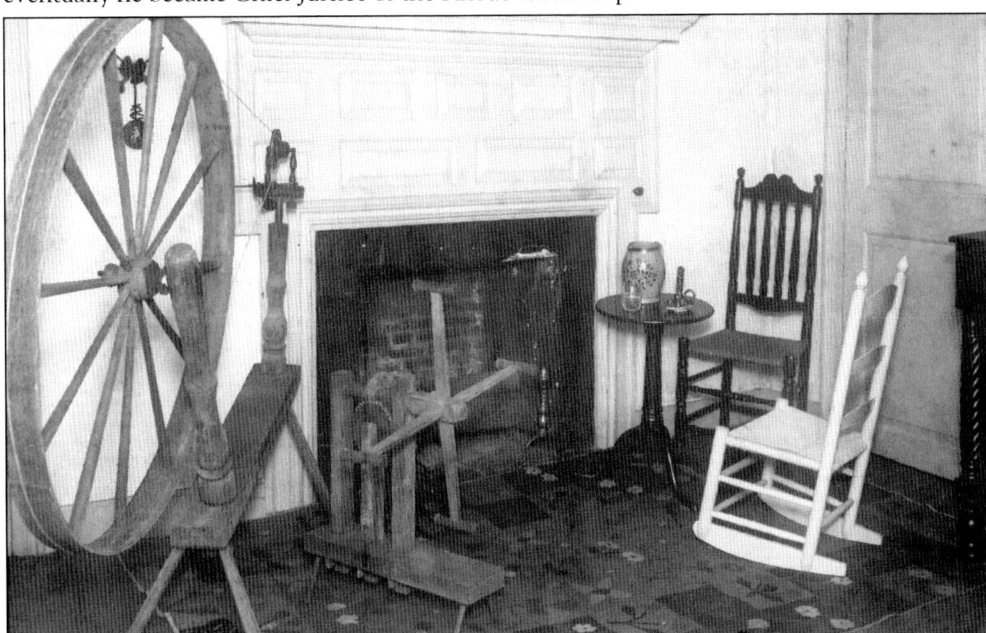

Room in Bowler's home where he entertained such dignitaries as Washington and Lafayette. In the early-1900s Bowler's house was beyond repair and was pulled down; paneling from the house survives, however, in the New York Metropolitan Museum of Art. In 1930 it was discovered that Bowler never gave up his loyalty to the King. To protect his estate, he placed himself under protection of the King's troops, corresponding with Sir Henry Clinton under the pseudonym Rusticus.

Two

Bristol Ferry Landing

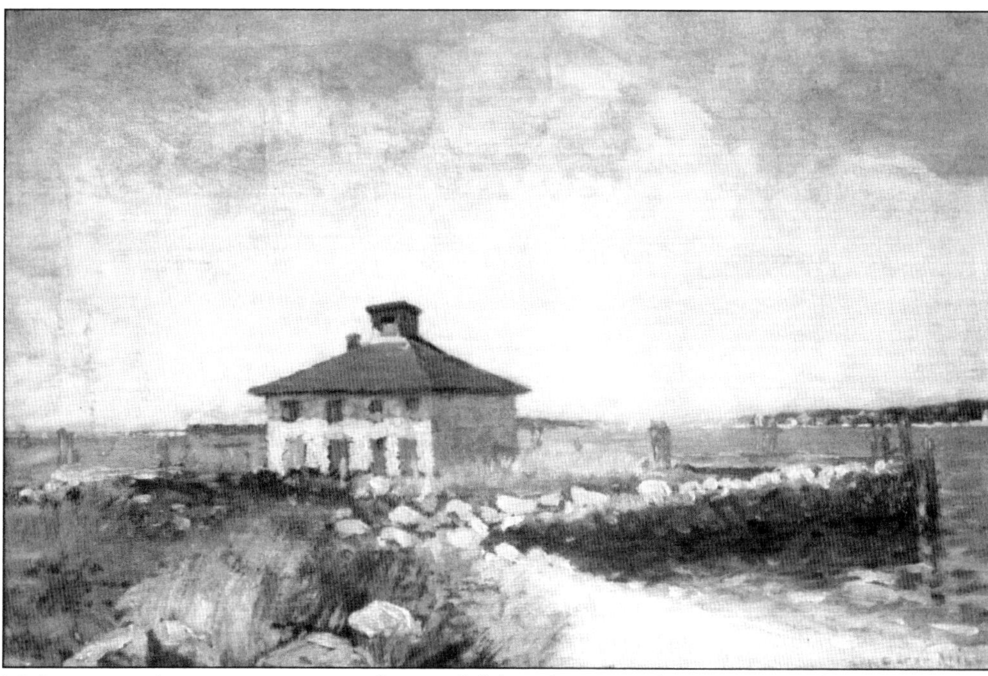

Mid-nineteenth-century two-story, hip-roofed ferry house, with a square cupola and two small brick chimneys. Oscar Miller, a celebrated Rhode Island Impressionist painter, created this image around the turn of the century. Miller lived and worked at his Brownell family homestead and studio at Bristol Ferry and Porter Street.

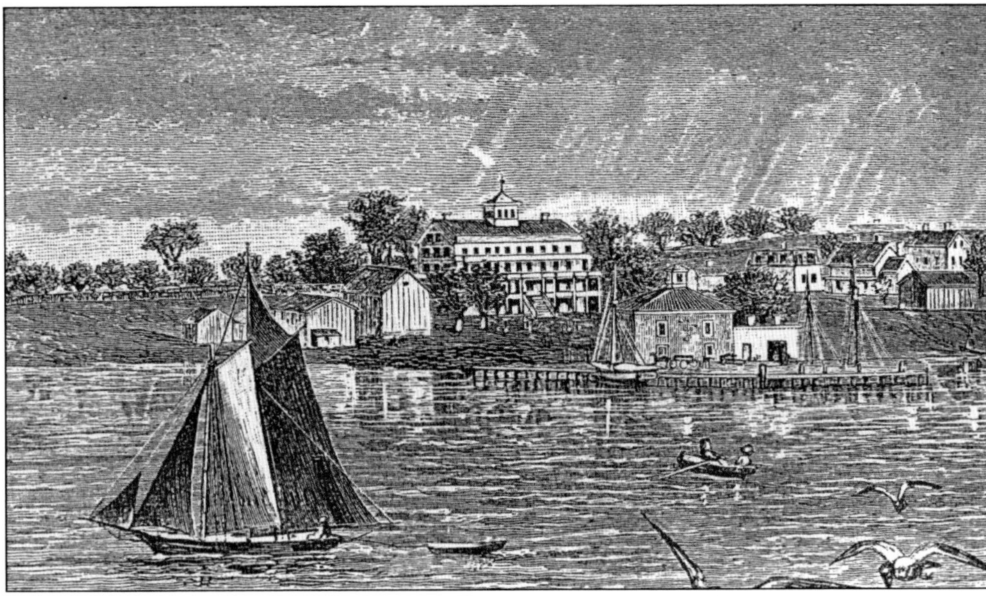

Etching from *Providence Plantations for 250 Years* (1886), showing the Portsmouth shore, ferry dockage, and the large hotel with facilities for fifty. During the Revolutionary War, a British battery was located near the ferry landing. This contemporary view of the Mount Hope Marina House and Bristol Ferry landing affords the observer a unique mid-passage perspective.

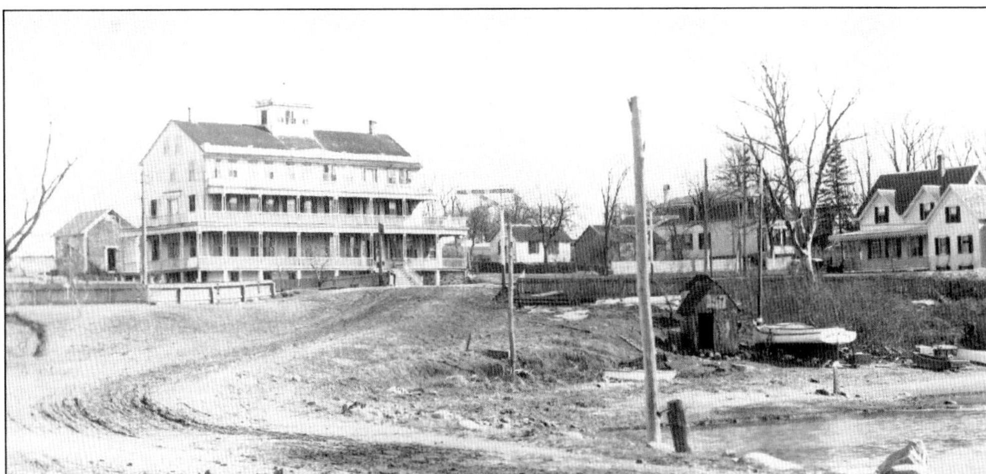

Bristol Ferry Inn (c. 1850). Since 1680, when a ferry began to transverse the narrows between Portsmouth and Bristol, public accommodations were available on the Portsmouth shore. The Bristol Ferry Inn, a three-and-one-half-story building, was largely destroyed by fire sometime in the first quarter of this century. Partly salvaged and rebuilt as a one-story building, it is now the clubhouse for the Pocasset Country Club. With the opening of the Mount Hope Bridge in 1929, ferry service discontinued. After the Bristol Ferry Inn fire, Portsmouth's Bristol Ferry district became a quiet, suburban residential community.

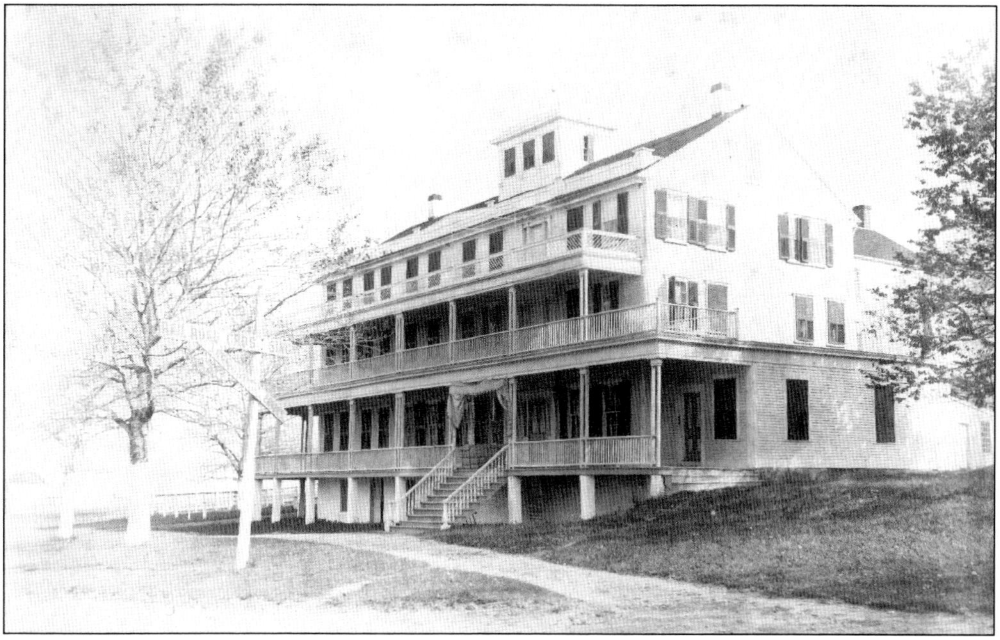

Bristol Ferry Inn at the turn of the century. Elegant accommodations awaited weary travelers at the well-appointed Bristol Ferry Inn. Note the railroad crossing warning and the convenient location of the inn to the depot and ferry.

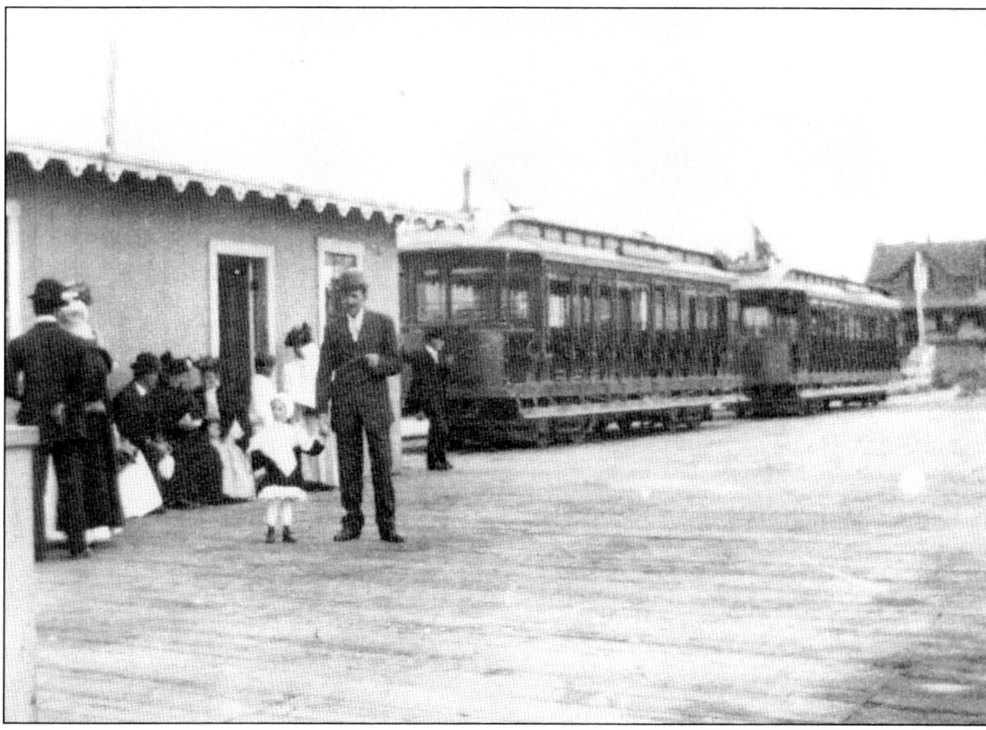

Travelers' waiting station and broad-board concourse at Bristol Ferry landing. At the turn of the century, electric street trolley cars of the Newport & Fall River Street Railway Company made several daily trips to Bristol Ferry and Island Park.

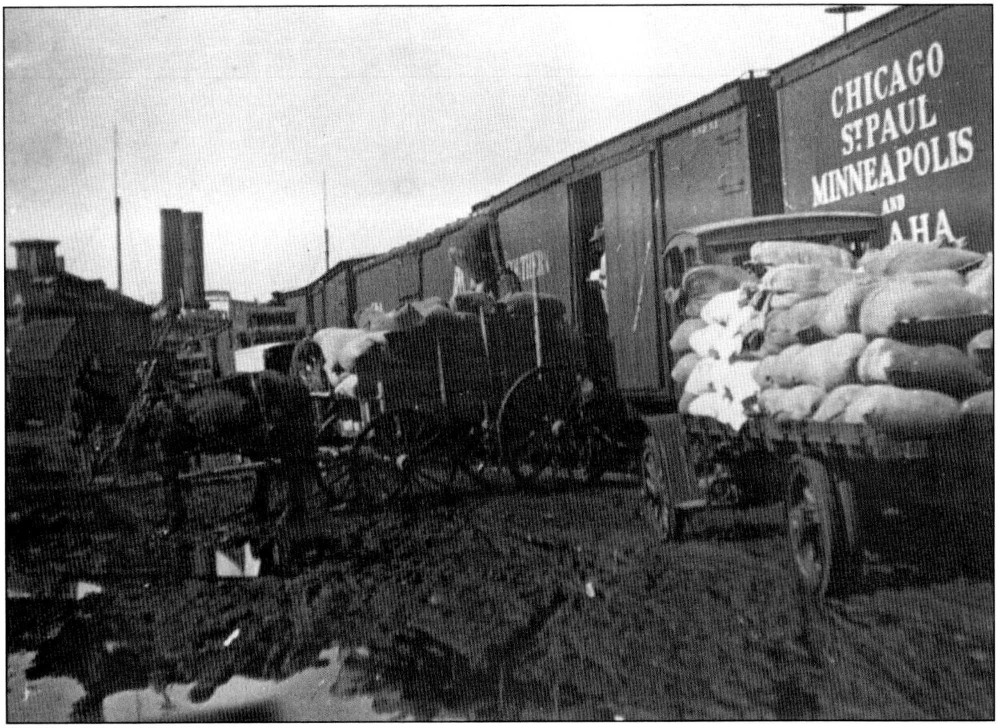

Muddy Bristol Ferry freight yard. Railroad freight cars load Portsmouth grain from a variety of farmers' vehicles. Note the ferry station's square cupola and the twin smoke stacks of a docked Narragansett Bay steamer in upper-left section of the photograph.

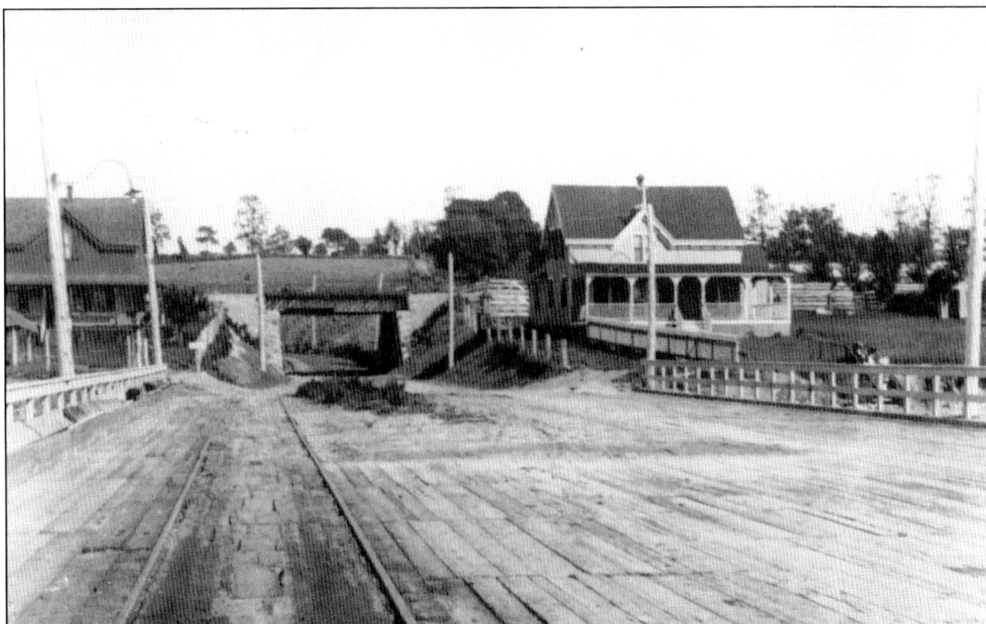

Street rail tracks and the wood concourse, c. 1926, looking east off the Bristol Ferry landing. Ferries first began service to this landing from Bristol in 1676. The last ferry ceased to run after the Mount Hope Bridge opened in 1929.

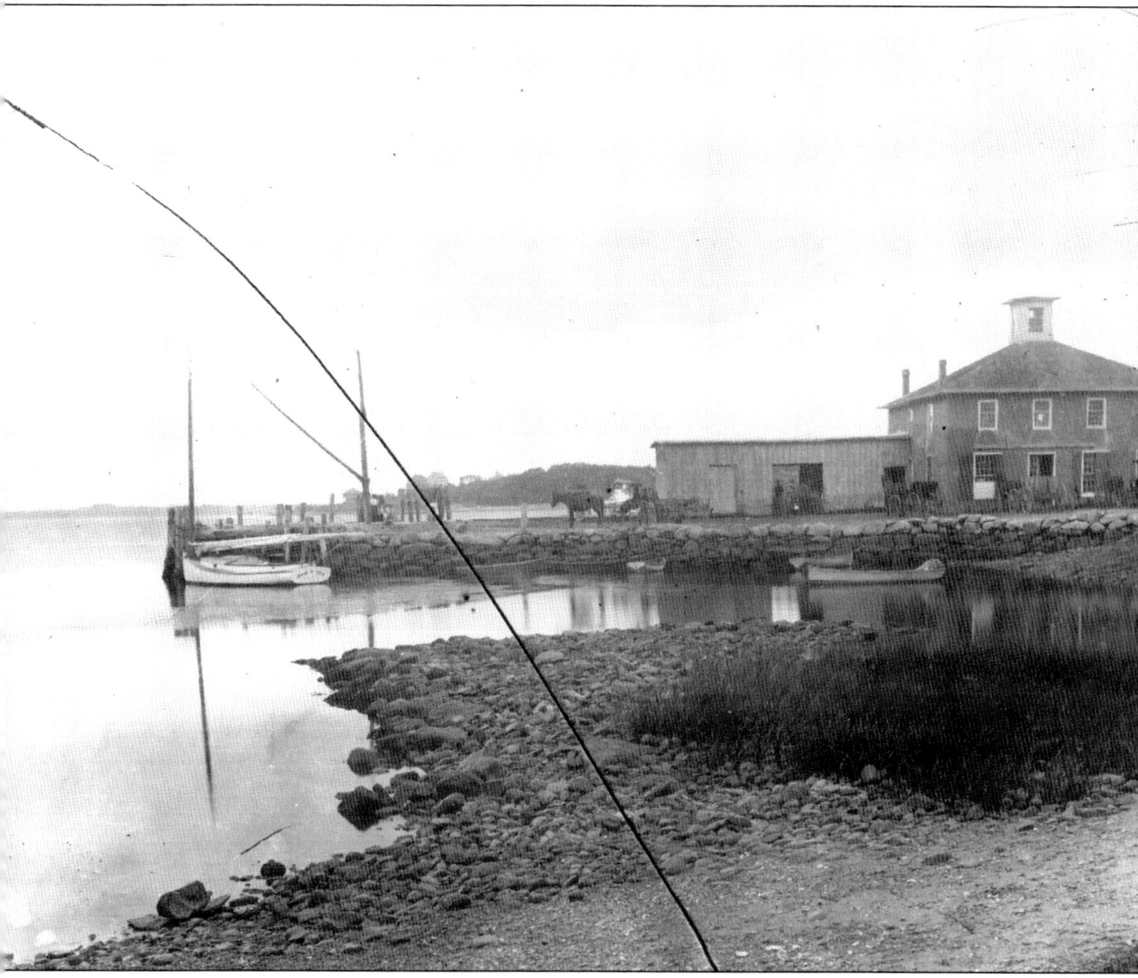

Excellent turn-of-the-century view looking east at sunset, after a busy day at the ferry landing. Judging by the waiting carriages and coach, the last ferry of the day was expected to arrive at any moment. The original stone and rubble-filled pier was later extended, covering the still water basin in the foreground.

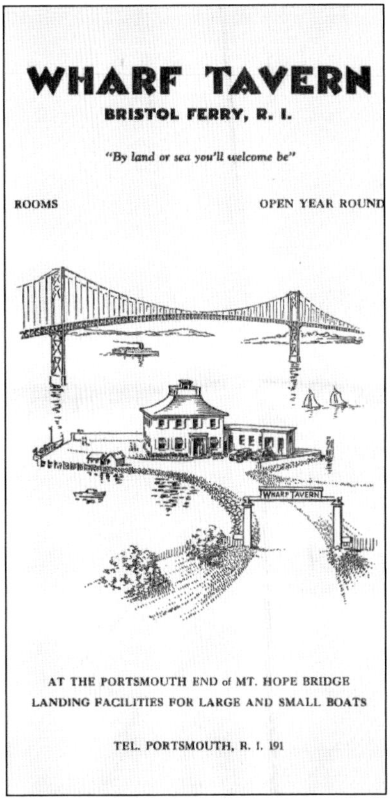

Marina House Restaurant, *c.* 1950. Long after ferry service became a nostalgic memory, and the railroad and the Bristol Ferry Inn no longer solicited patrons, the old ferry station found new life as a gourmet restaurant. Viewed from the Mount Hope Bridge span, the Marina House Restaurant, where dinner guests could marvel at Mount Hope Bay's natural beauty, sits in its splendid isolation.

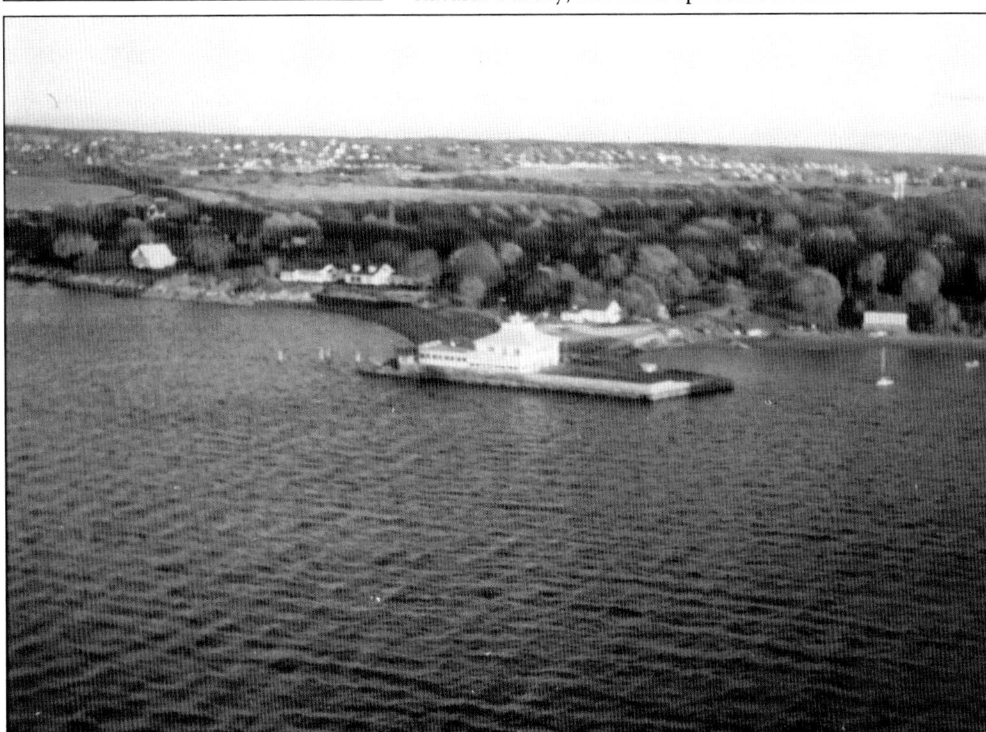

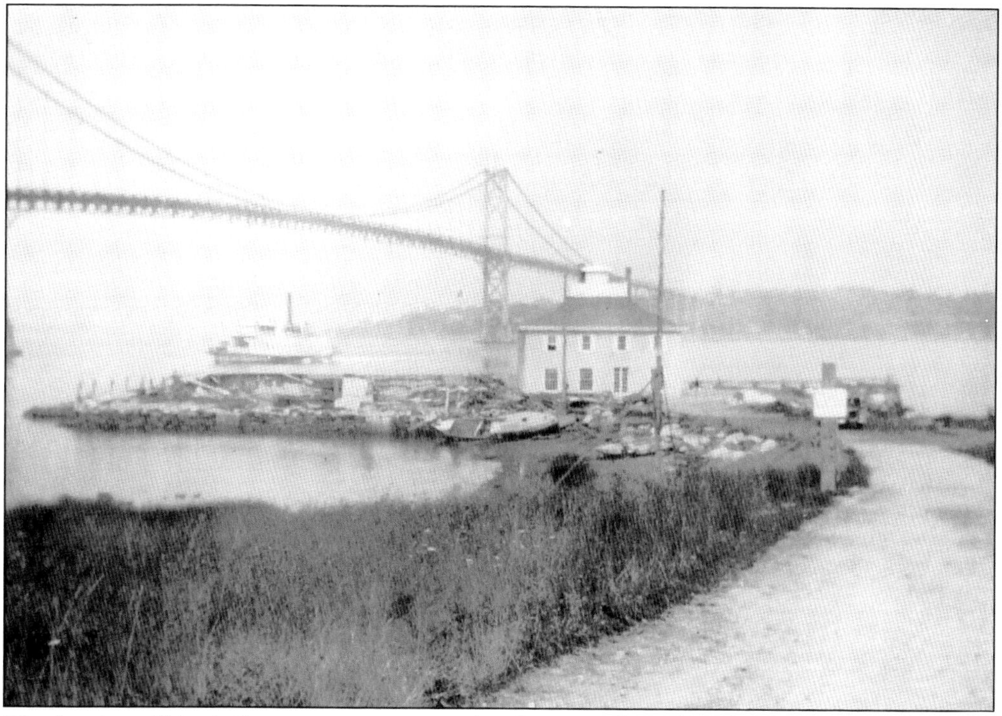

The ferryboat *Bristol*. One era passes, as another begins; eclipsed by the opening of the Mount Hope Bridge, the ferryboat *Bristol* makes one of her last passages across Mount Hope Bay.

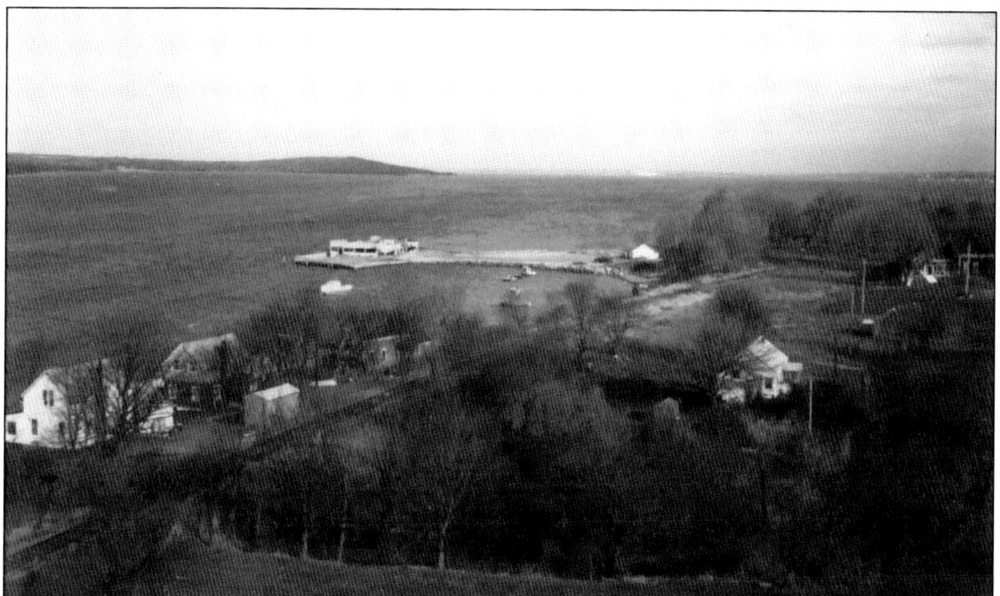

Mount Hope, the bay, and the Bristol ferry house. The apparent serenity of this scene is deceiving. The 150-year-old building, vacant for two years—torched by vandals in 1985—is a fire-ravaged shell. This elevated view is from the bridge approach.

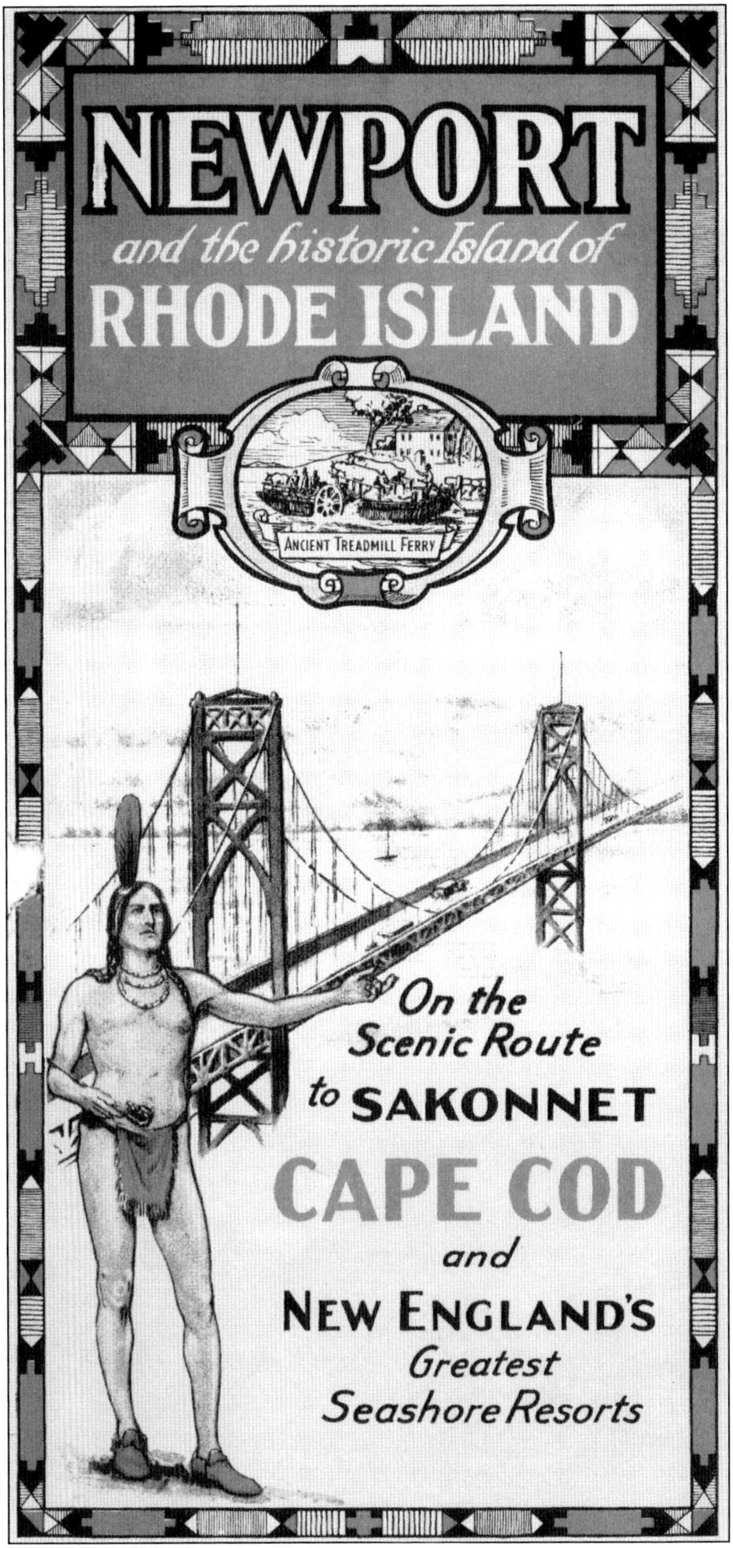

Southeastern New England road map, produced in 1939 by the Mount Hope Bridge Corporation of Bristol. The bridge owners found it advantageous to promote Newport and Rhode Island (Aquidneck Island) as a summer resort, so motorists would use the modern suspension bridge for a modest toll. Note the small inset illustration of the 1680s two-horse treadmill ferry.

Three

All Around the Town

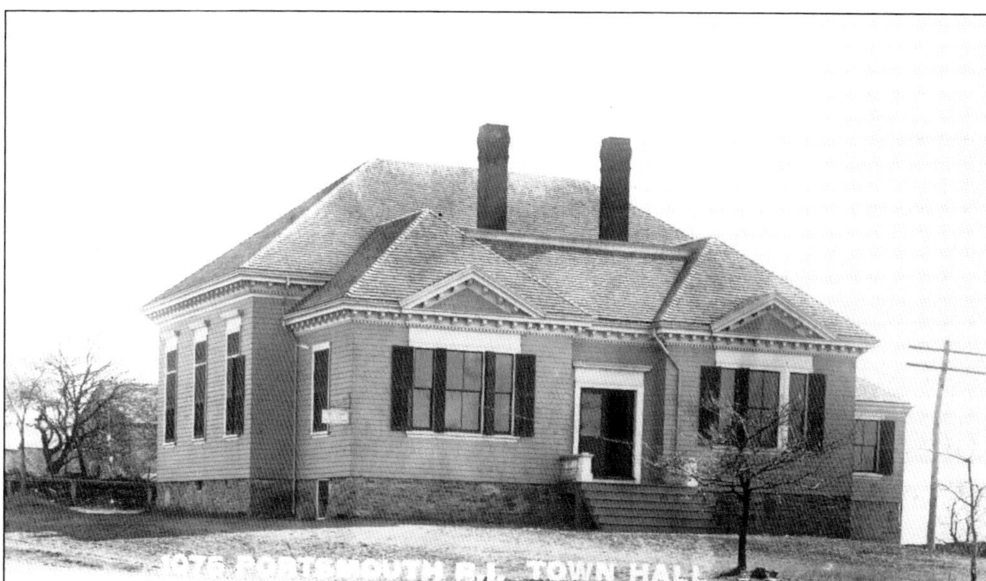

Portsmouth Town Hall (1895). This two-story, hip-roofed structure, with modillion and dental courses at the cornice, has a wing on the west side and a central double-door entry portico flanked by pavilions. The building is complemented by two interior brick chimneys.

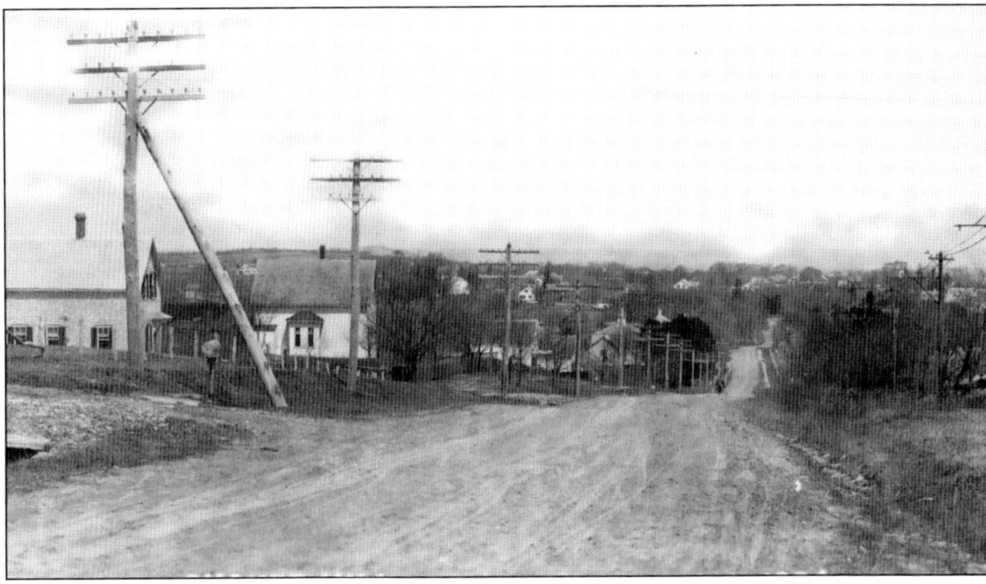

Commanding view from the top of Quaker Hill, near the intersection of Middle Road, about the area of the police/fire station, *c.* 1905. The Portsmouth-Newtown Historic District, along East Main Road, consists of mostly early to mid-nineteenth-century structures. Modern twentieth-century commercial development has been unsympathetic to historic preservation.

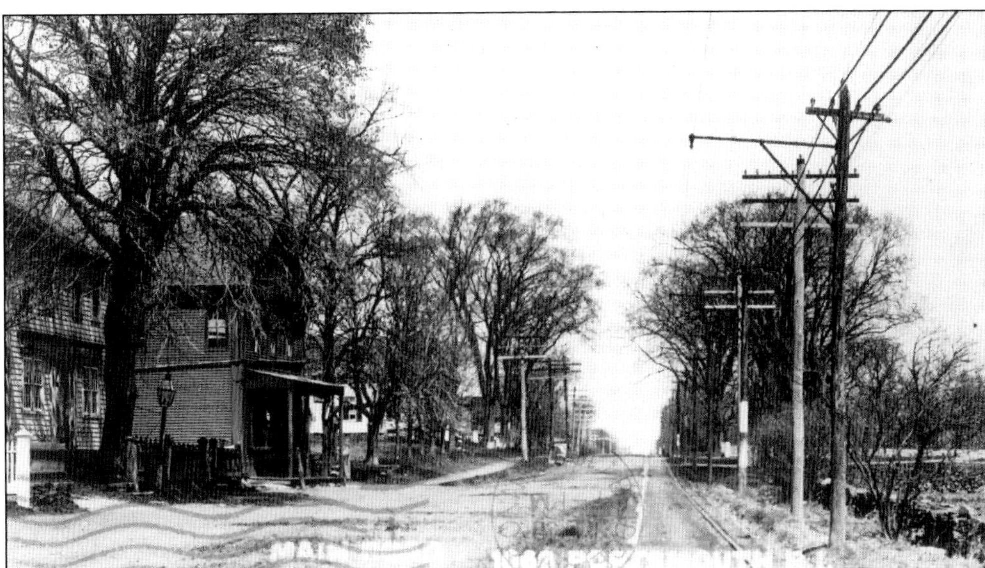

East Main Road. As seen in this 1906 postcard photograph, some areas of the East Main Road streetscape still retained much of the provincial charm into the early decades of the twentieth century. Note the trolley tracks on the right (east) side of the road.

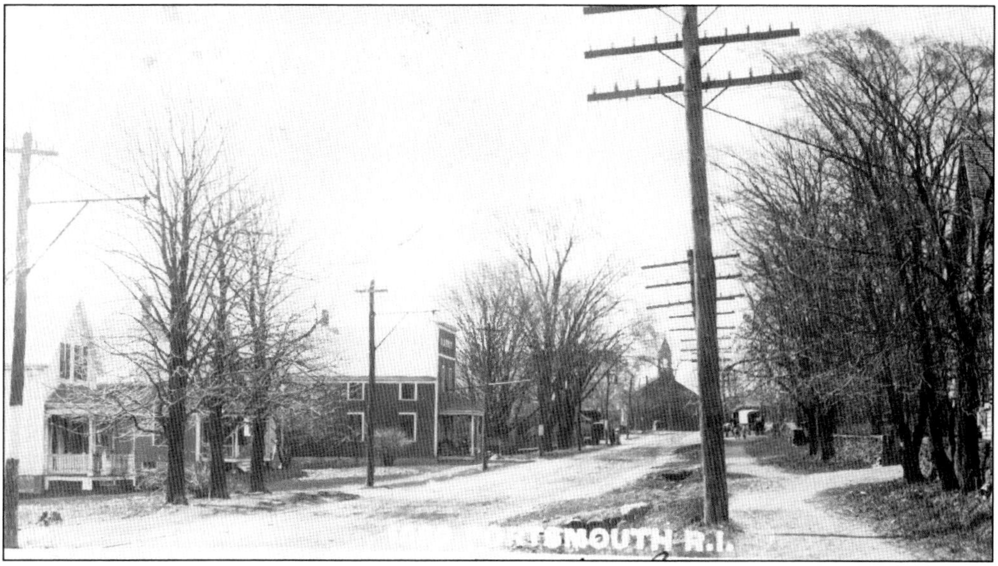

East Main Road in the Newtown Historic District looking south toward St. Paul's Church, c. 1907. This section still continues its function as the town center. In this view and the one below, an open drainage ditch on the west side of the street is plainly visible.

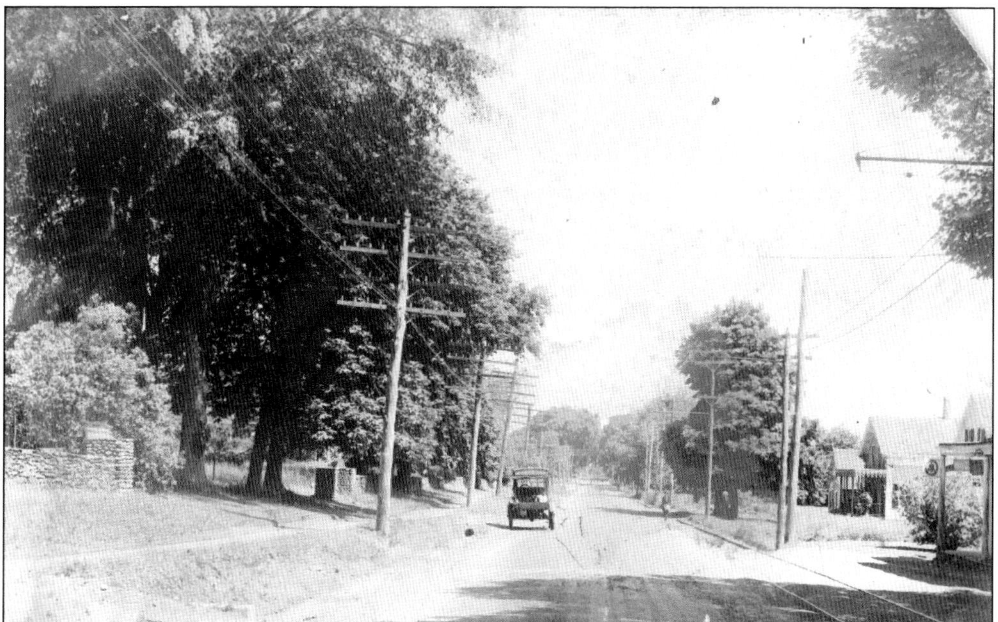

Looking north on East Main Road, in the Newtown District. It's believed the store on the right is the Chase & Co. Store. The round Bell Telephone sign attached to the store's porch post, and the trolley tracks, date this photograph to the 1910s. Interestingly, the driverless pickup truck is facing north in the eastbound lane.

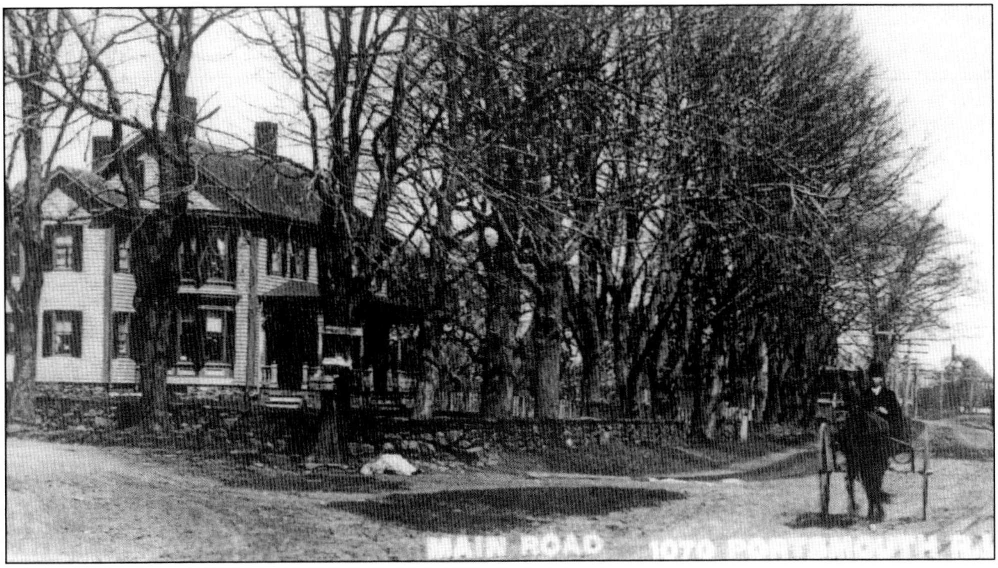

Tree-lined section of East Main Road looking north, c. 1907. This was certainly a transitional period for commuting citizens; note the southbound trolley bearing down on the horse-drawn buggy.

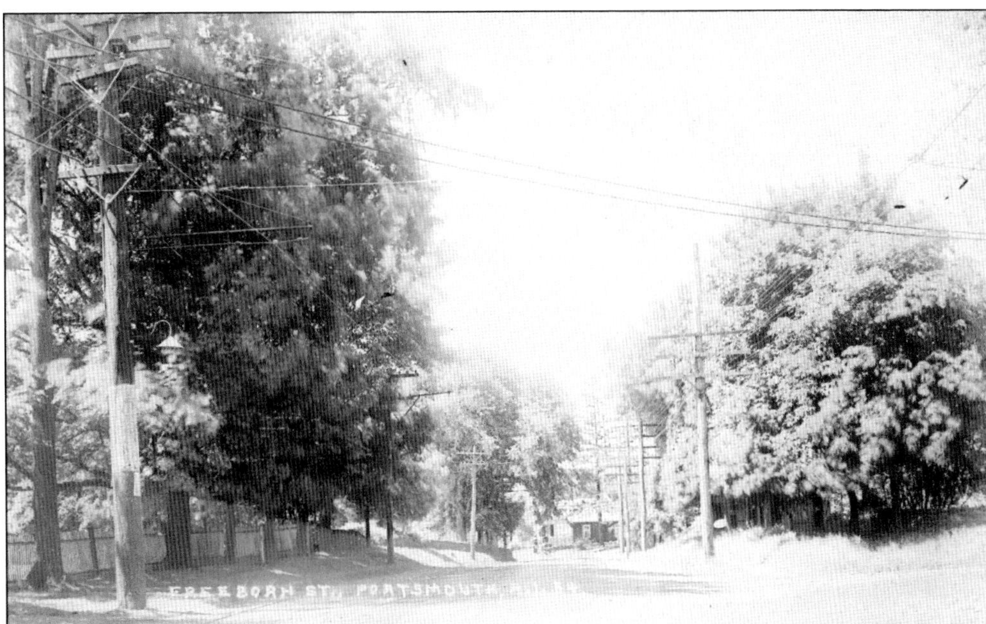

Freeborn Street. A mix of first and second growth of mature and healthy trees flank the road.

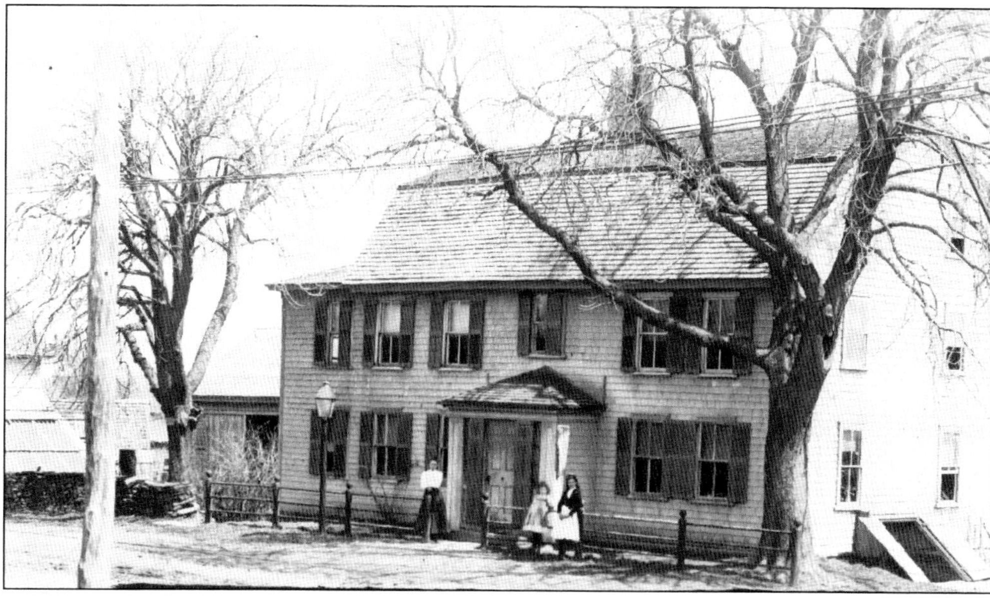

Dennis House, 2851 East Main Road, *c.* 1760. This house, a two-and-one-half-story, gambrel-roofed dwelling with a small brick chimney, served as General Lafayette's headquarters prior to the Battle of Rhode Island. The building's main architectural features include a central enclosed entry in a five-bay facade; a two-story hip-roofed wing at the north side; and a small addition at the rear.

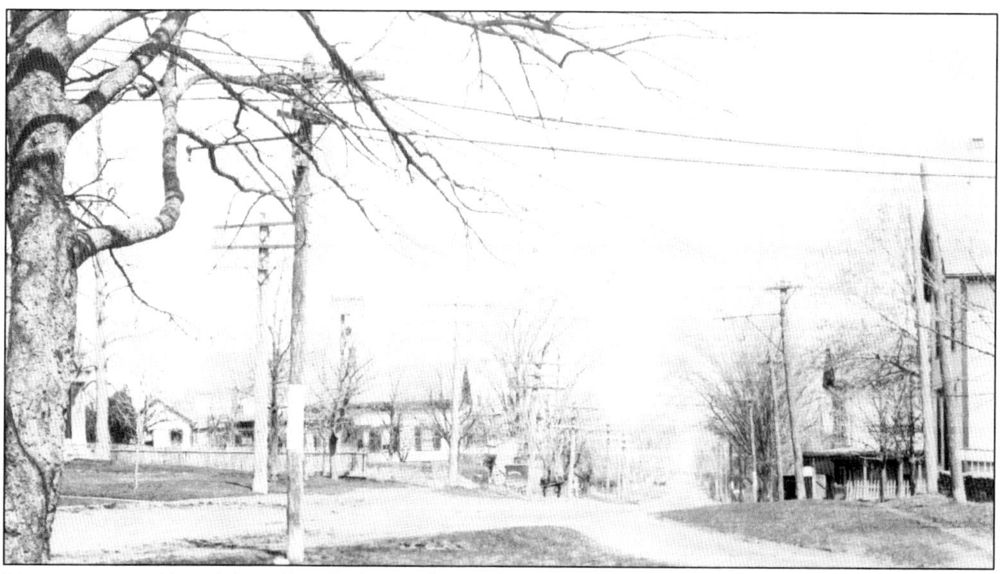

View east on East Main Road, from about the front of St. Paul's Episcopal Church. The Portsmouth Methodist Church tower can be seen center-left.

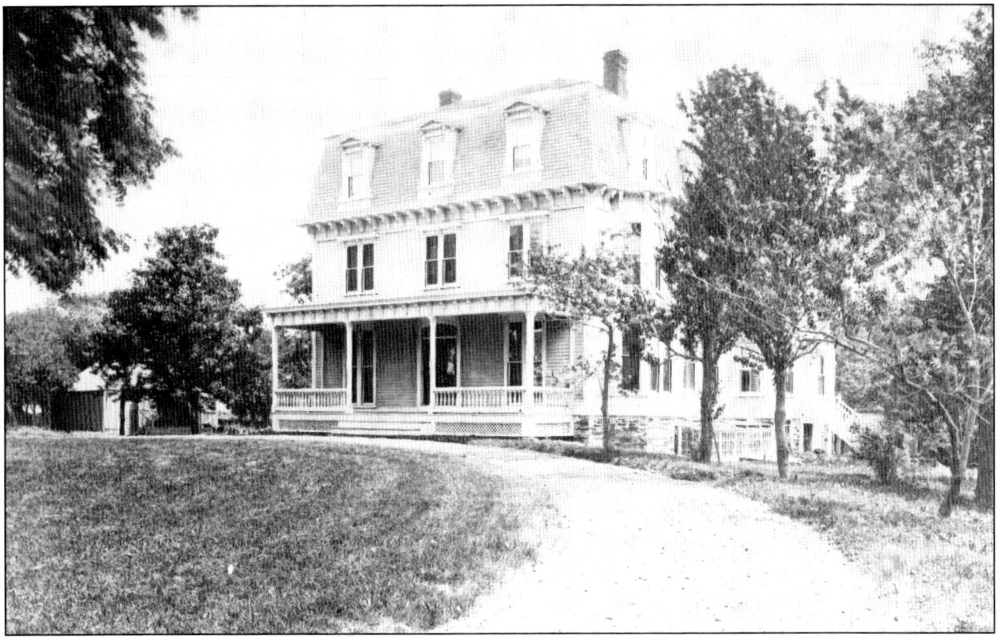

John L. Borden House (1885), 2951 East Main Road. This is a two-and-one-half-story, late Victorian house with a mansard roof and bracketed pediment dormers with a three-bay facade. A central entry with double doors in an open porch dominates the front. The right side of the building features a two-story bay window.

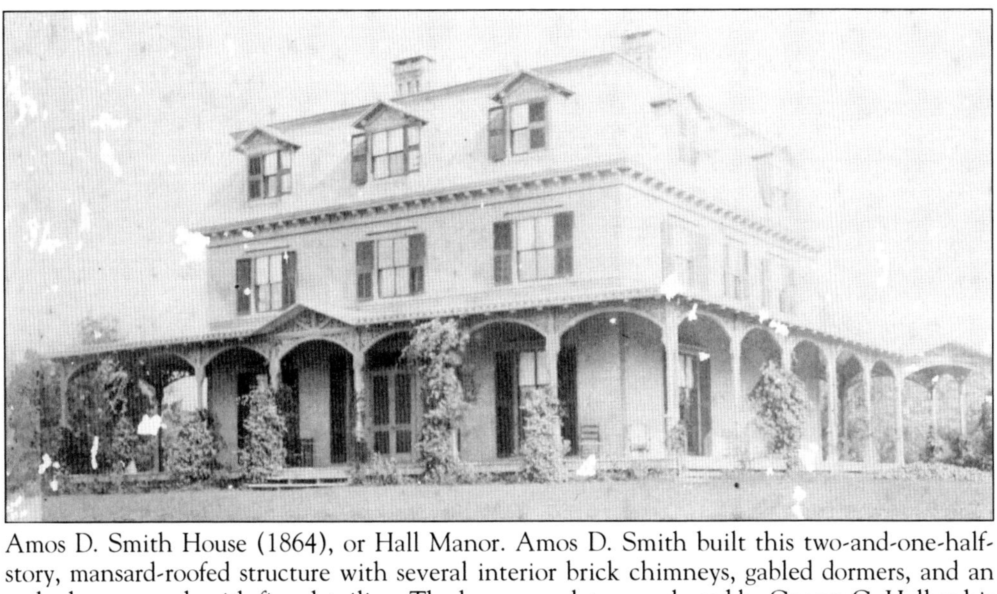

Amos D. Smith House (1864), or Hall Manor. Amos D. Smith built this two-and-one-half-story, mansard-roofed structure with several interior brick chimneys, gabled dormers, and an arched open porch with fine detailing. The house was later purchased by George G. Hall as his summer place. In 1918, the property, on Narragansett Bay, was purchased by the Order of St. Benedictine and is now part of the Portsmouth Abbey School.

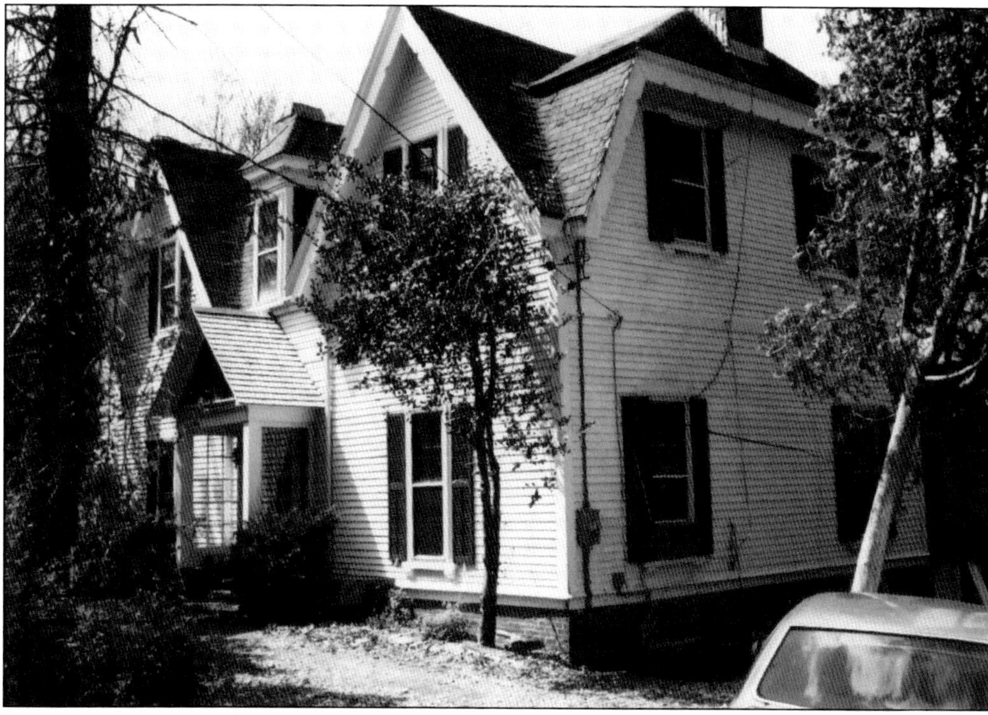

Contemporary view of Oak Glen, Julia Ward Howe House (*c.* 1870), 745 Union Street. When Dr. Samuel Howe bought the property in 1850, he had a small cottage moved to the site. The cottage became the rear ell of the present two-and-one-half-story Victorian gambrel-roofed structure, which features a central pediment portico in a three-bay facade and several brick chimneys. A historical burying ground, containing members of the Lawton and Sisson families, is on the property.

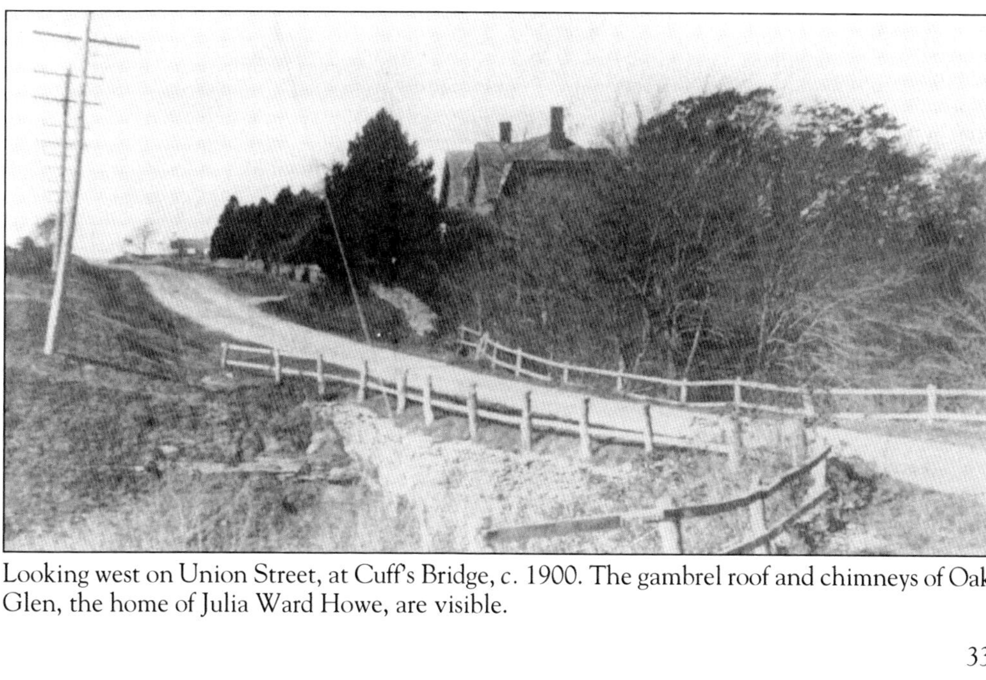

Looking west on Union Street, at Cuff's Bridge, *c.* 1900. The gambrel roof and chimneys of Oak Glen, the home of Julia Ward Howe, are visible.

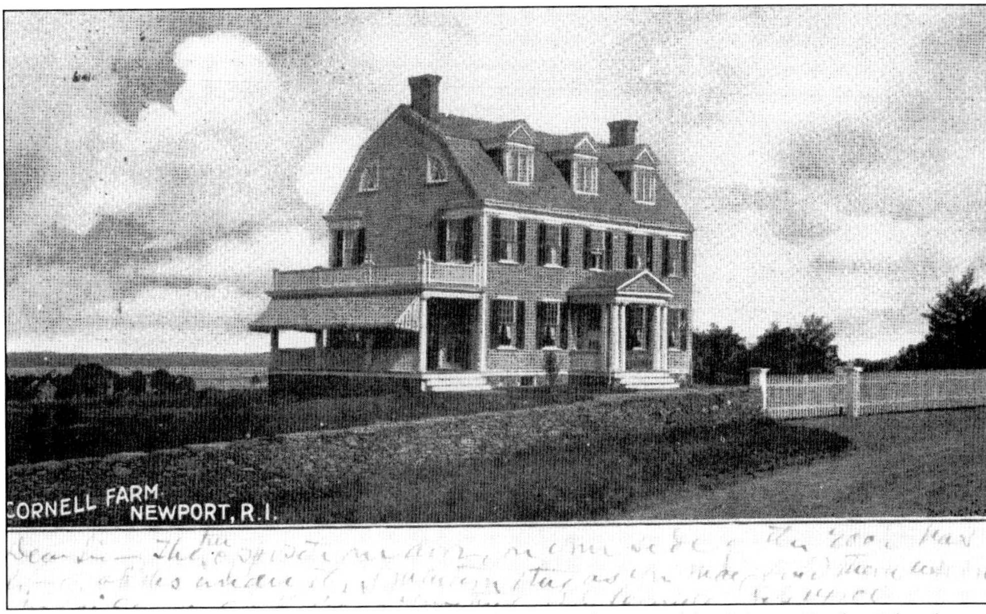

Valley Inn of Newport, 2431 West Main Road, currently owned by Mario Occhi. The former Cornell Farm mansion is a two-and-one-half-story, late Victorian residence that features a gambrel roof, three gabled front dormers, and an enclosed central portico in a five-bay facade. Interior features include several large fireplaces of brick and stone, and ornate Federal-style mantles. The handwritten message on this September 14, 1906 postcard is that of John Cornell.

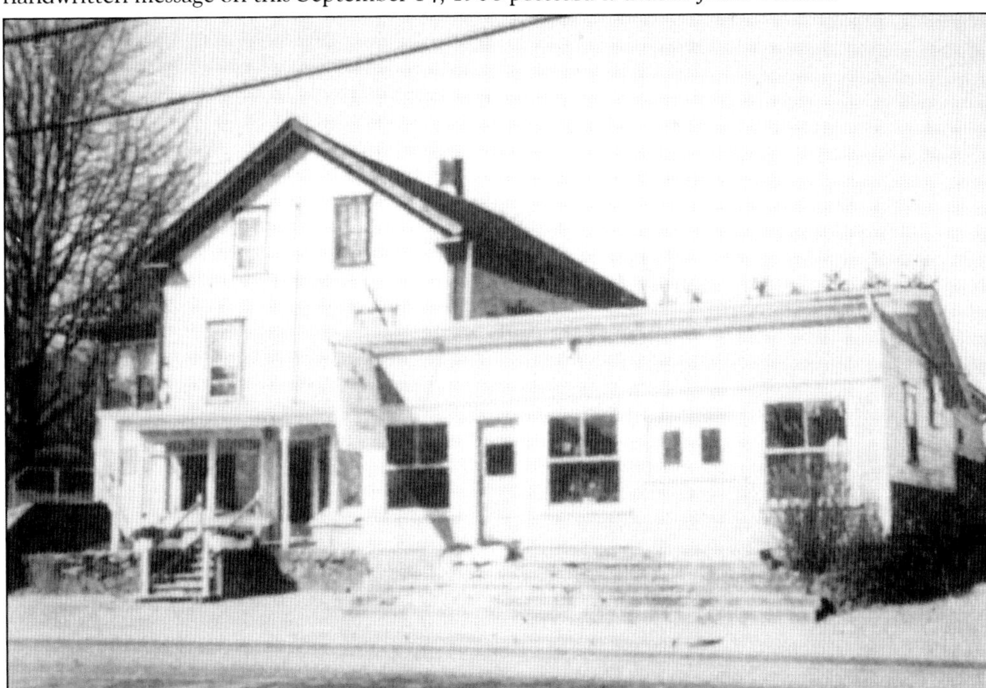

Chase Store on East Main Road, south of St. Anthony's Church. The store portion of the structure was razed when the dwelling part was moved to Union Street, c. 1990. Restored, with the addition of a garage, the house is again a residence.

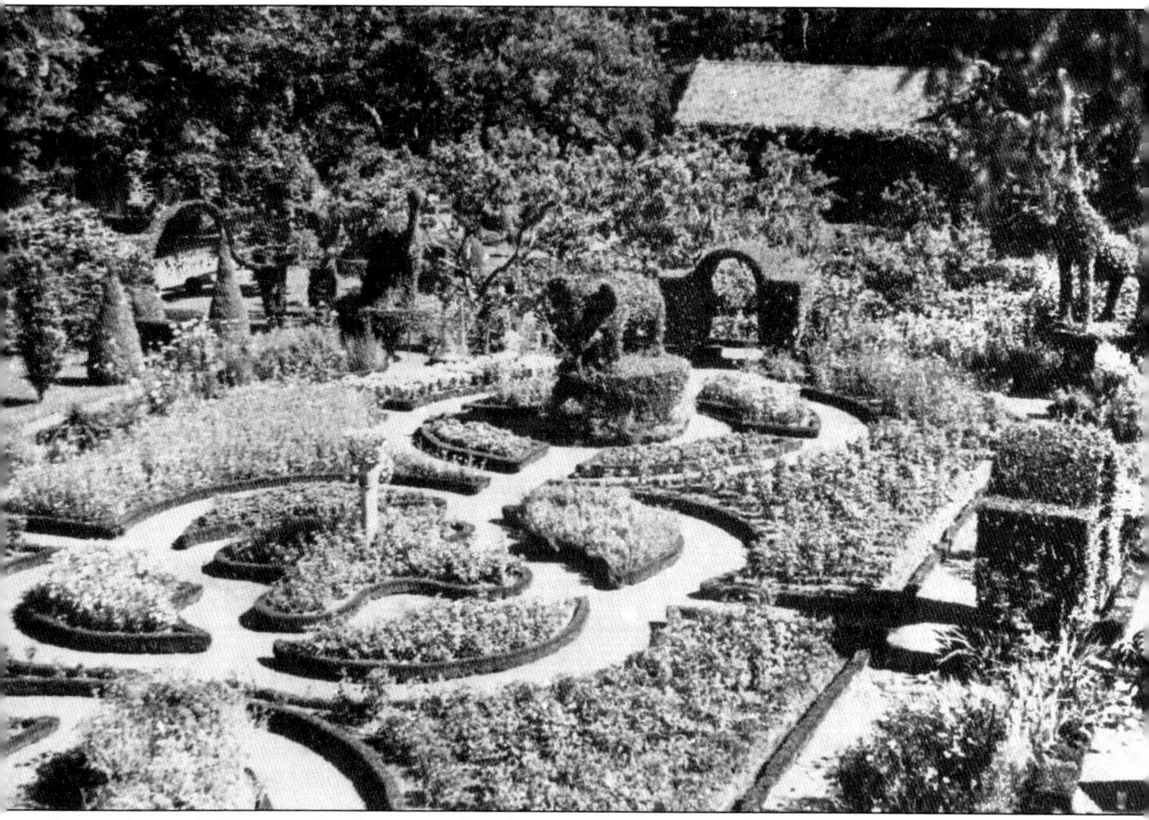

Green Animals Topiary Garden, completed in 1919, located behind the Brayton house. The garden plan, conceived by Thomas Brayton, was executed by his superintendent, Joseph Carreiro. It consists of professionally maintained formal gardens and an extensive topiary of eighty-five California privets, golden boxwoods, and American boxwoods trimmed in intricate geometric and ornamental designs of animals and birds. The gardens, at the end of Cory Lane, are open to the public; they are now the property of the Preservation Society of Newport.

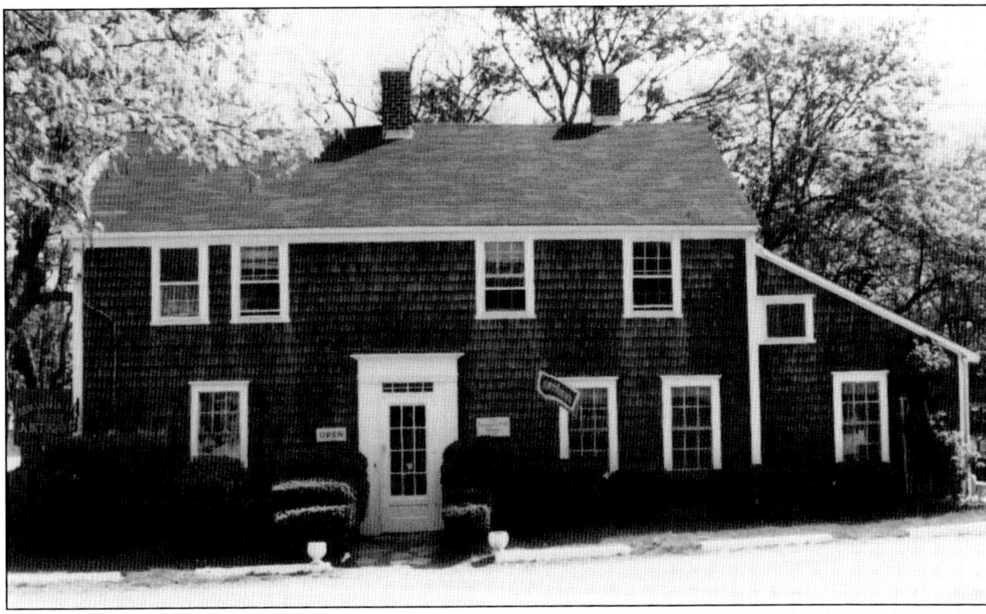

Benjamin Fish House (*c*. 1798), 934 East Main Road, currently owned by Charles and Caroline Crouch. The house is a two-and-one-half-story structure, with two interior brick chimneys, an off-center entry at each flanking side, an asymmetrical four-bay facade, and a shed-roof addition at the rear.

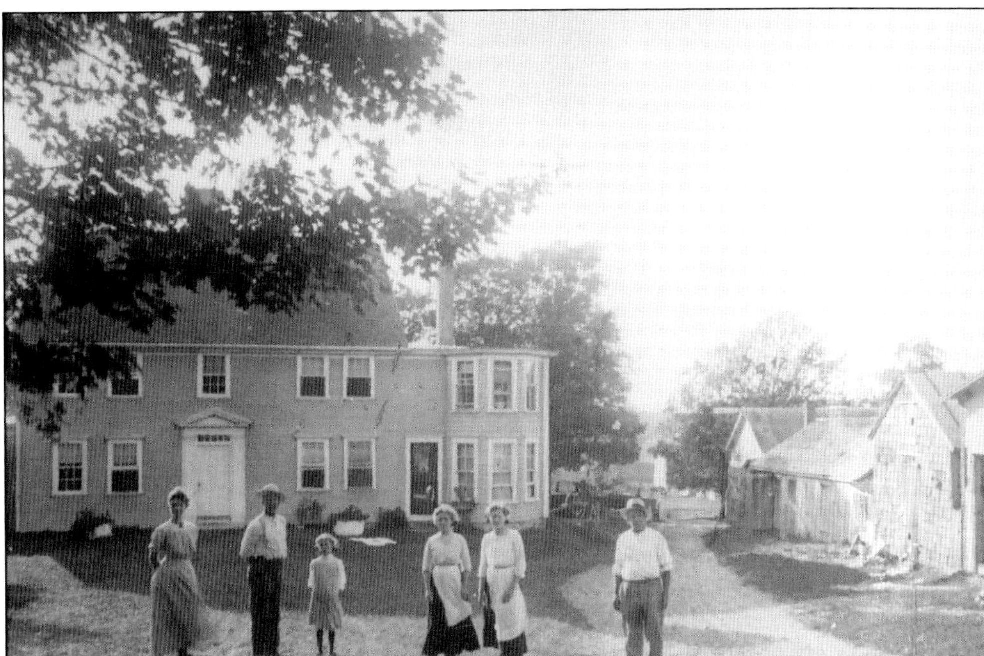

Coggeshall Farm, on the west side of West Main Road at the Middletown-Portsmouth town line. This house was destroyed by fire in 1917. The following are shown here, from left to right: Edith Frances Coggeshall (Mrs. Whitney Warren Child); Edith's father, William Sisson Coggeshall; Edith Coggeshall Chase (Mrs. Alvin G. Reise); two German servants; and Joseph Rogers Coggeshall.

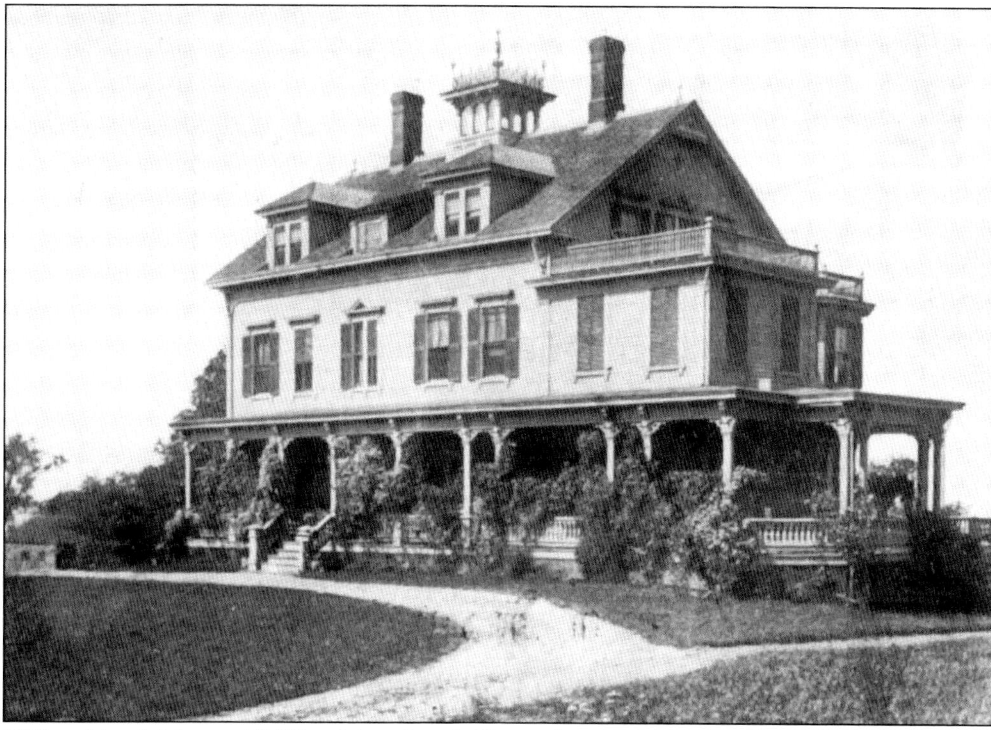

Willow Brook Manor, 55 West Main Road. Shown here in 1907, this two-and-one-half-story early Victorian residence was built *c.* 1850 by D. Anthony. The house features three dormers in front, with a pair of tall interior brick chimneys and a two-story flat-roof addition at the north side. Entry is off-set in an open bracketed porch that runs the length of the front and the north side.

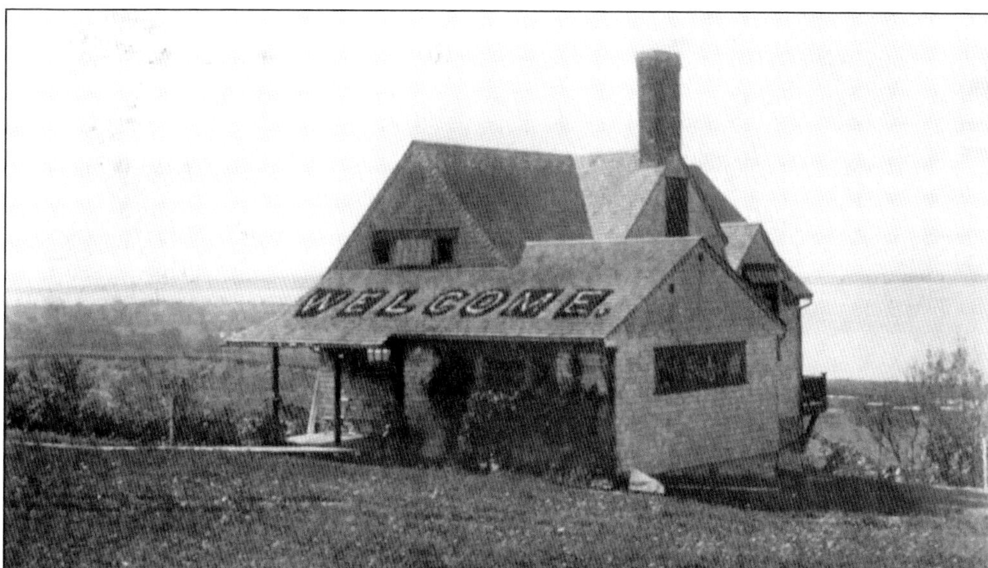

Social Studio, founded in the spirit of American philosopher, writer, and craftsman Elbert Hubbard (1856–1915). Hubbard founded the "Roycrofters" and the American Arts & Crafts Movement.

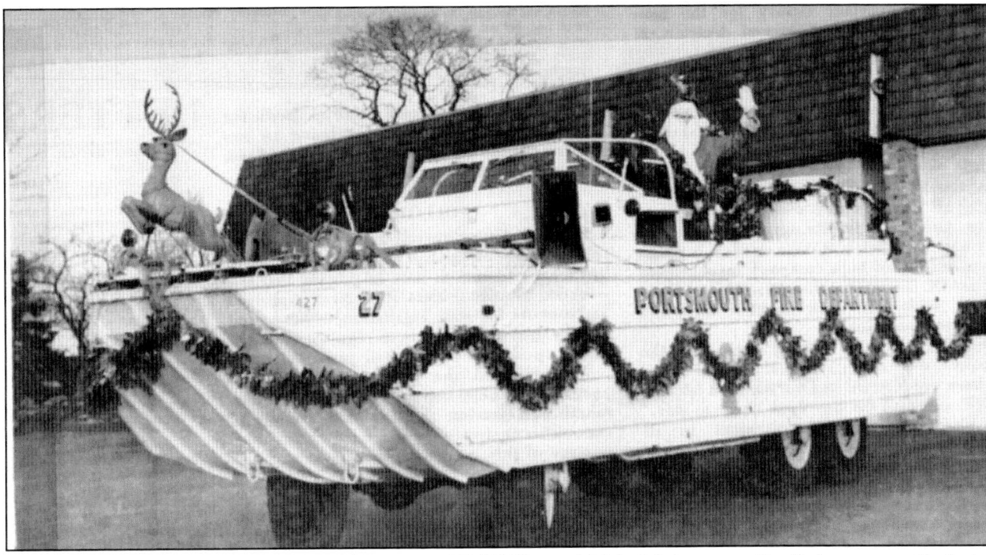

Portsmouth Fire Department's Christmas DUWK, *c.* 1964. Volunteer firefighters readied the DUWK to bring Santa and Christmas cheer to the town's children. Santa's volunteers included Ronald Costic (pictured), Paul Valente, Paul Rogers, Henry Silvia, Alex Cote, Bill Gerlich, Larry Faryniarz, and Town Councilmen Paul Poirier and Gardner Seveney.

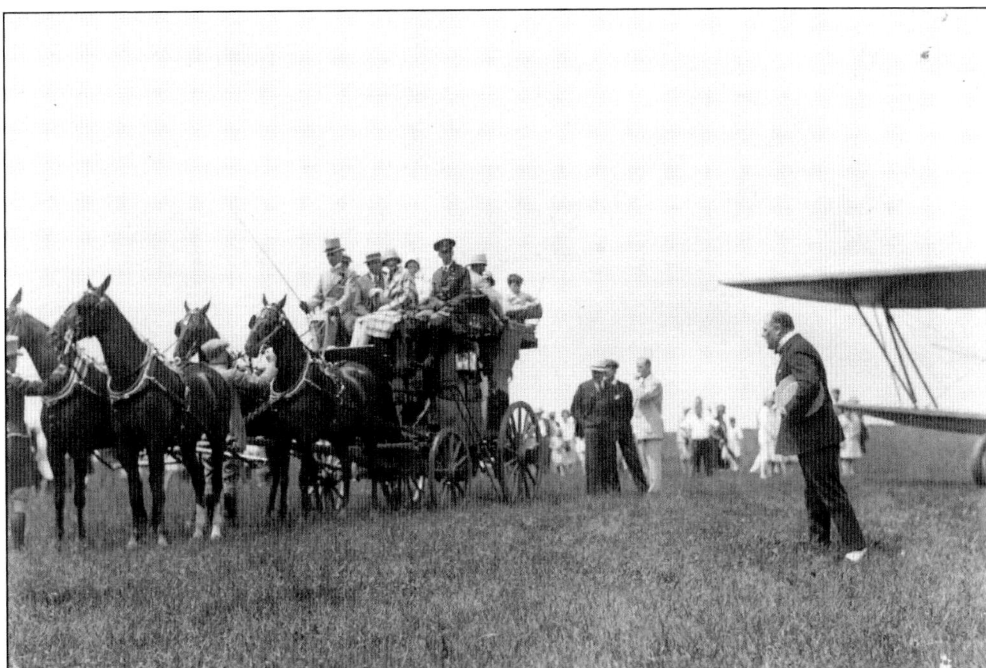

Outing at the fairgrounds. During the 1920s, outings at the fairgrounds included rides on horse-drawn coaches and demonstrations of airplane flights. Judging by the participants' dress, we may assume this was a Vanderbilt-sponsored affair.

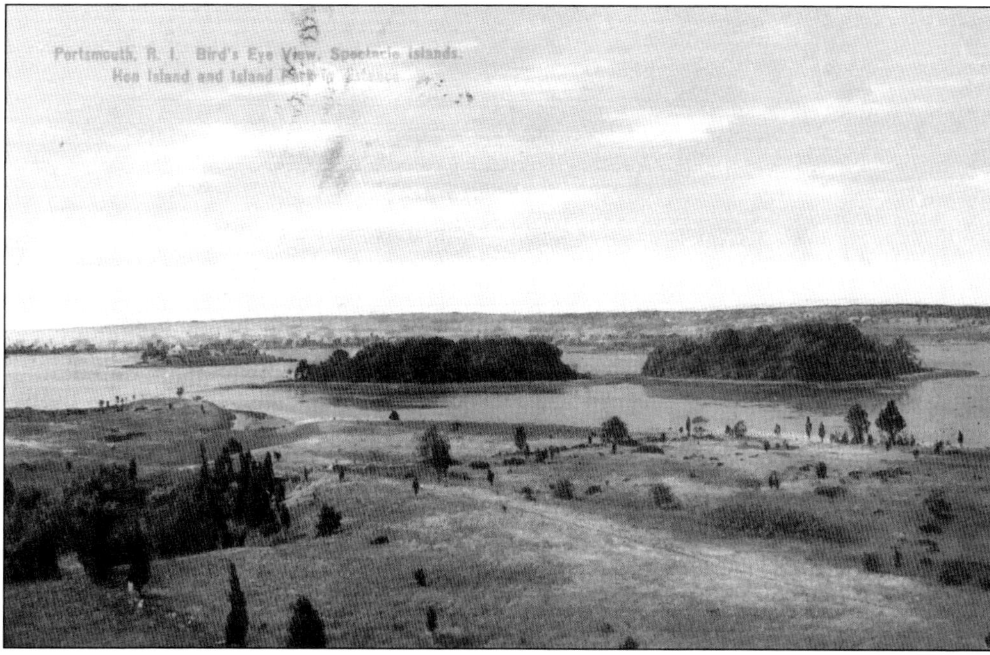

Turn-of-the-century view of the Spectacle Islands, from the area of Bluebill Cove. These islands, each about one acre in area, are named Spectacle, Hen, and Tom's. This cove is the Great Cove of colonial days; one that silted over. It got its contemporary name because of the large number of Bluebill ducks that once gathered here. In the far background is the Tiverton shore.

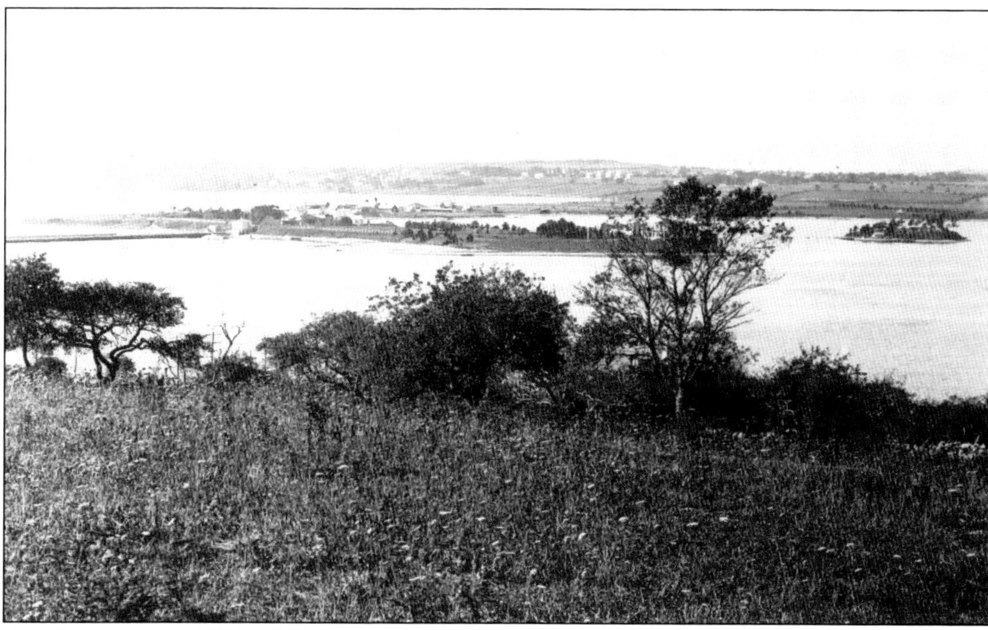

Another view, *c.* 1907, of the same general Spectacle Island group, with the developed Island Park in the background. The islands of the cove are now inhabited and connected by a causeway. This view is from the Tiverton Baptist Church; the Portsmouth shore is in the far background.

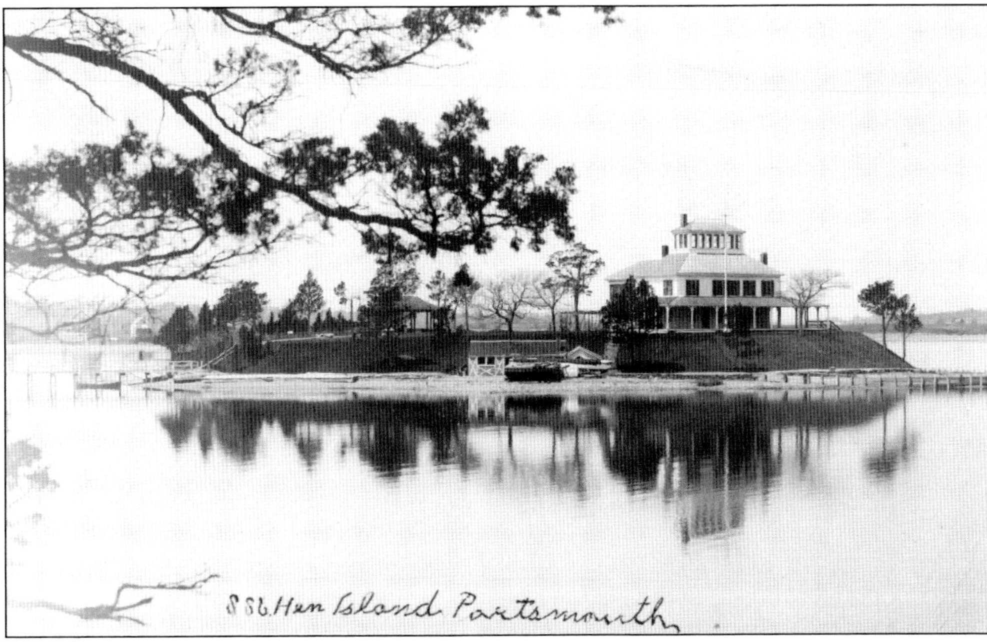

Postcard sent by E.S. Sisson. The message on this 1909 postcard reads, "Haffenreffer, the brewer of Fall River has built a new house here, it looks very nice." The Haffenreffer family owned Hen Island from about the turn of the century until 1912; it is the birthplace of Carl W. Haffenreffer (1906). The building was vandalized and destroyed by fire in 1944.

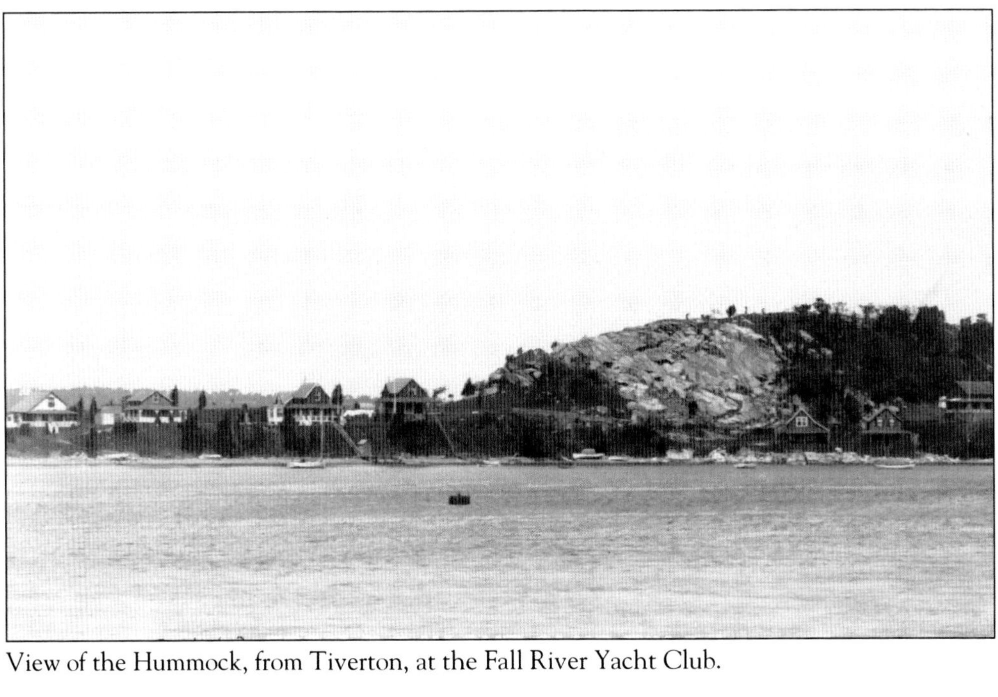

View of the Hummock, from Tiverton, at the Fall River Yacht Club.

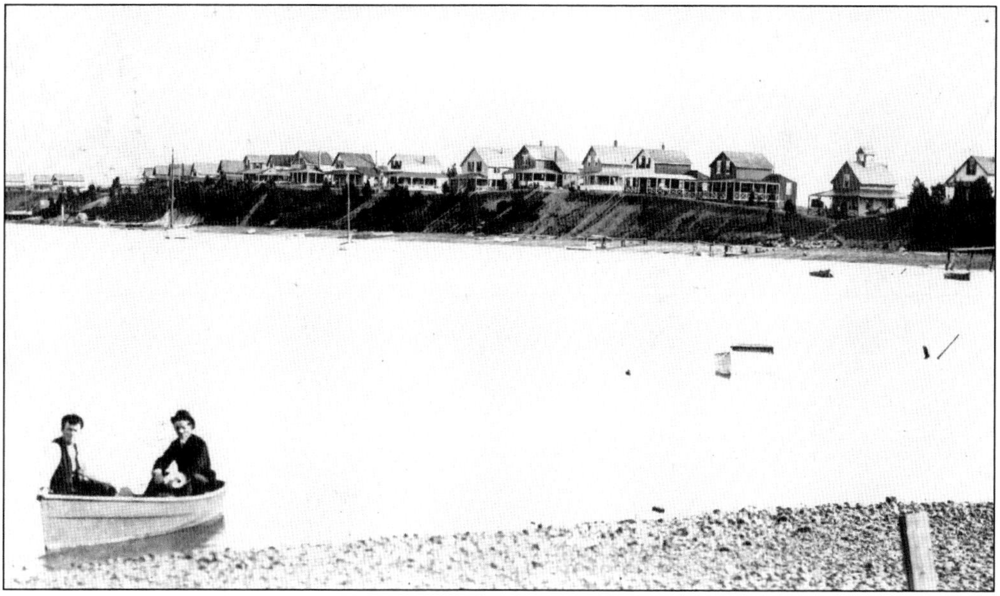

Summer cottages at Hummock Point in 1909, from a sandy beach cove near the Hummock.

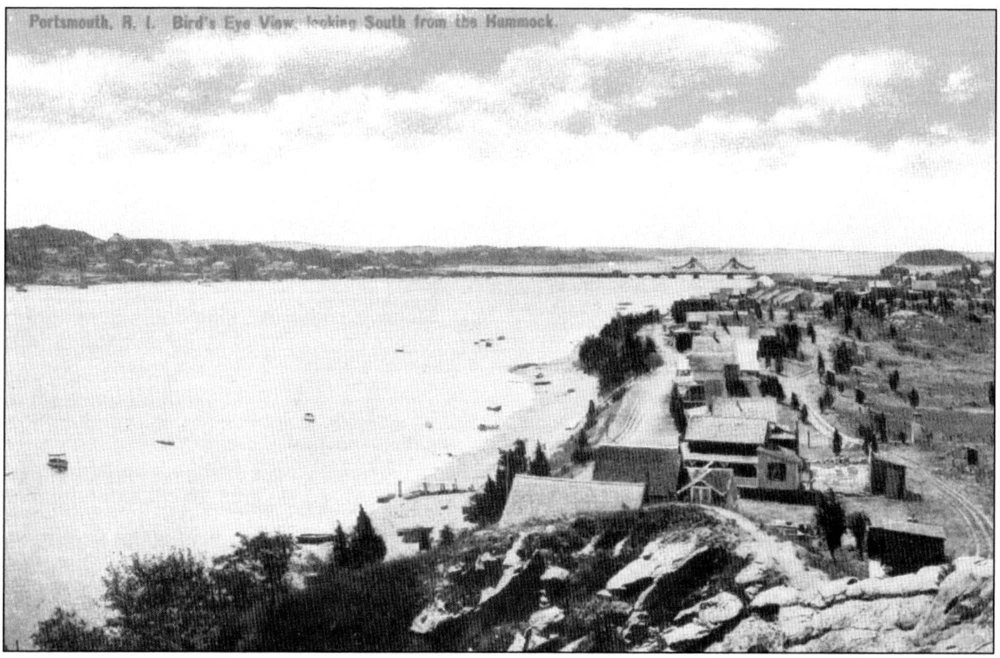

Sakonnet River, the far Tiverton shore, and the Stone Bridge in a 1913 bird's-eye view looking south from the Hummock. Gould Island is in the skyline to the far right.

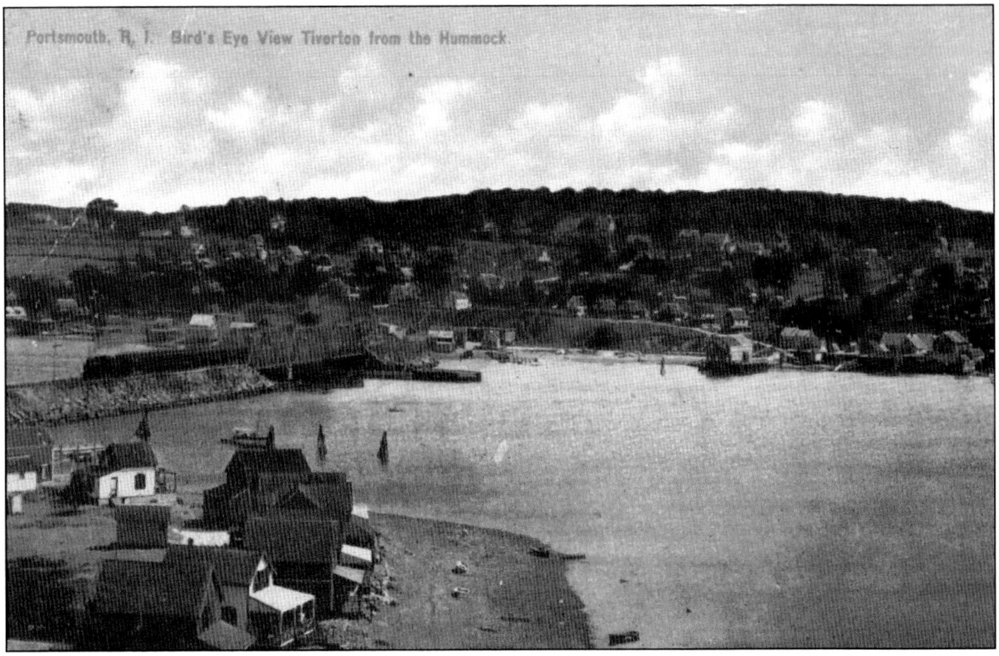

View of the Tiverton shore from the Portsmouth Hummock, 1913. This so-called Hummock was started as a summer resort by people from Tiverton around 1900. The place was physically separated from Island Park until a bridge was built in 1961.

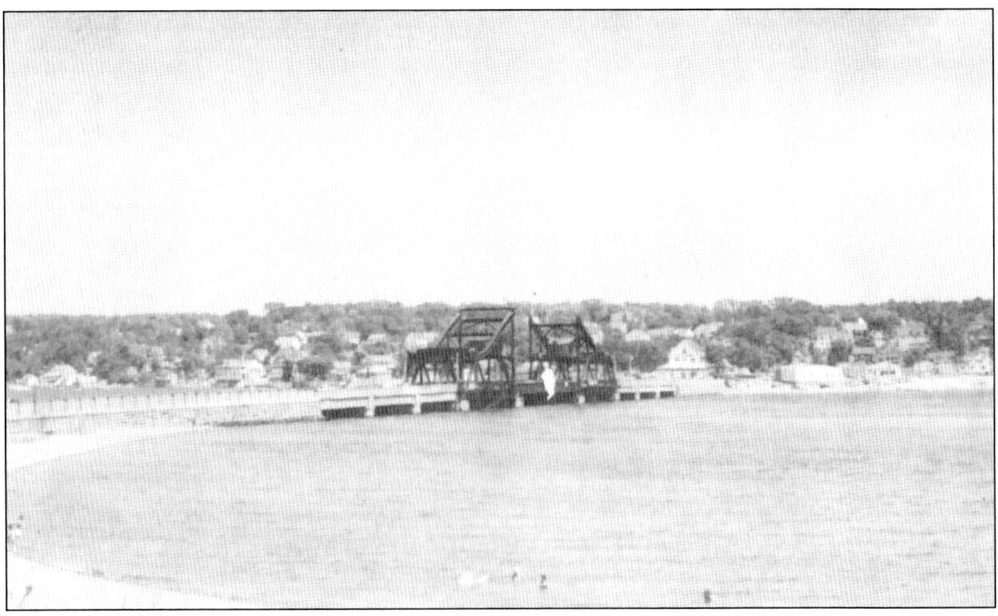

Sakonnet River Railroad Bridge. This approximately 220-foot bridge is a modified Baltimore through-truss span and a cantilevered assembly, composed of two identical trusses. The circular track on which the bridge pivots is mounted on a central pier, in mid-river. The original 1864 bridge was severely storm-damaged in 1898 and replaced with the bridge pictured here. Passenger service was discontinued in 1937.

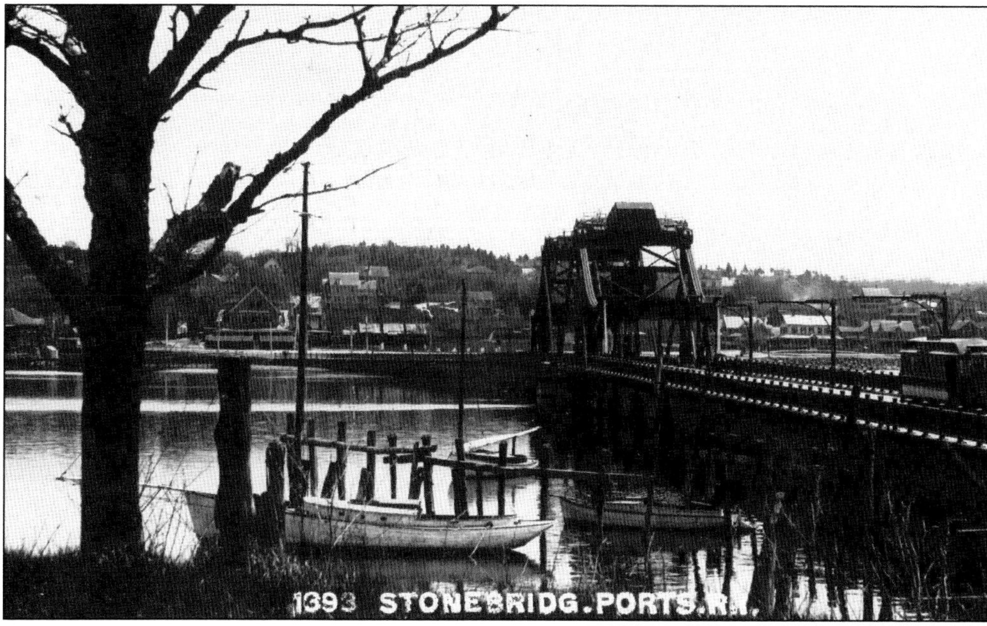

Trolley on the Stone Bridge, *c.* 1908. An engine house mounted on top of the central span encloses a steam engine that supplies the power to swing the bridge and allow boats to pass the structure. The stone causeway and drawbridge to the north is similar to the railroad bridge.

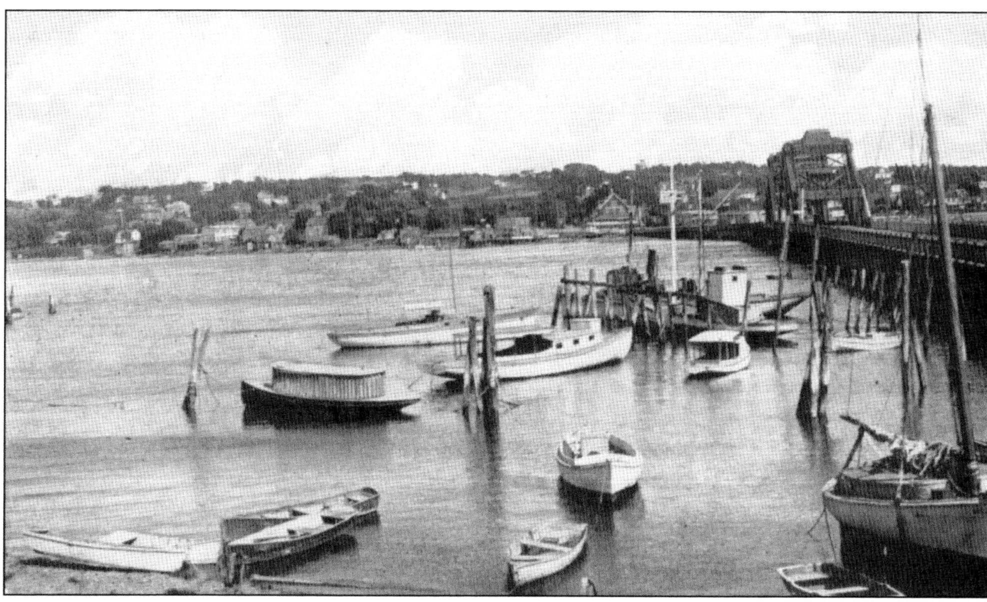

Stone Bridge, in the same general area as above, *c.* 1926. When the bridge became electrified, the steam engine previously used to swing the bridge was abandoned.

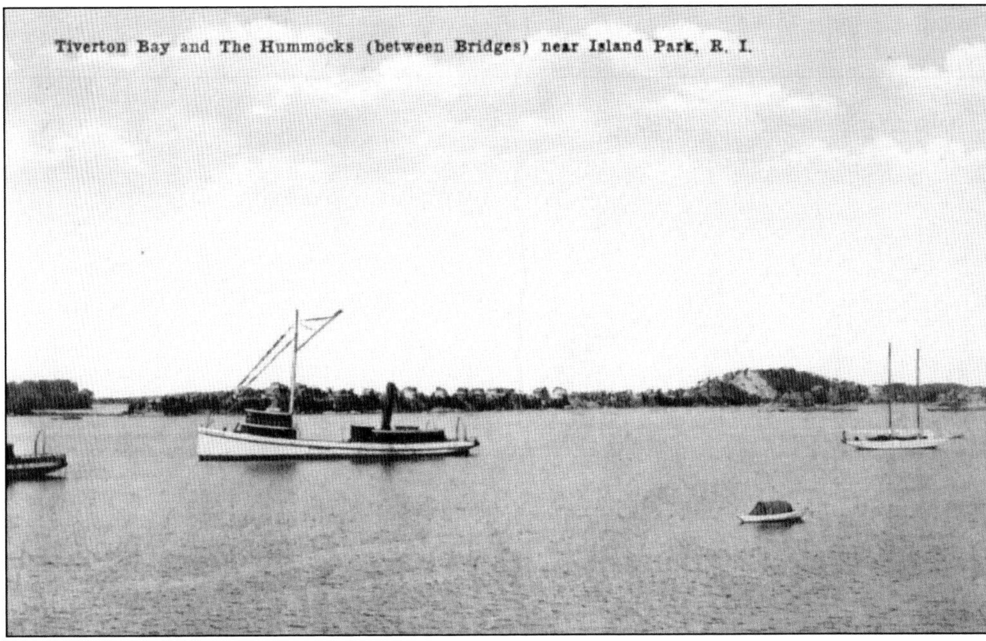

Sakonnet River and Portsmouth Hummock. By these two postcards' messages, we may assume the Tiverton-Portsmouth area must have been the place for young people to meet. A girl named "Sadie" sent this postcard, dated July 3, 1908, to a Fall River address. Sadie writes, ". . . I am having a wild time."

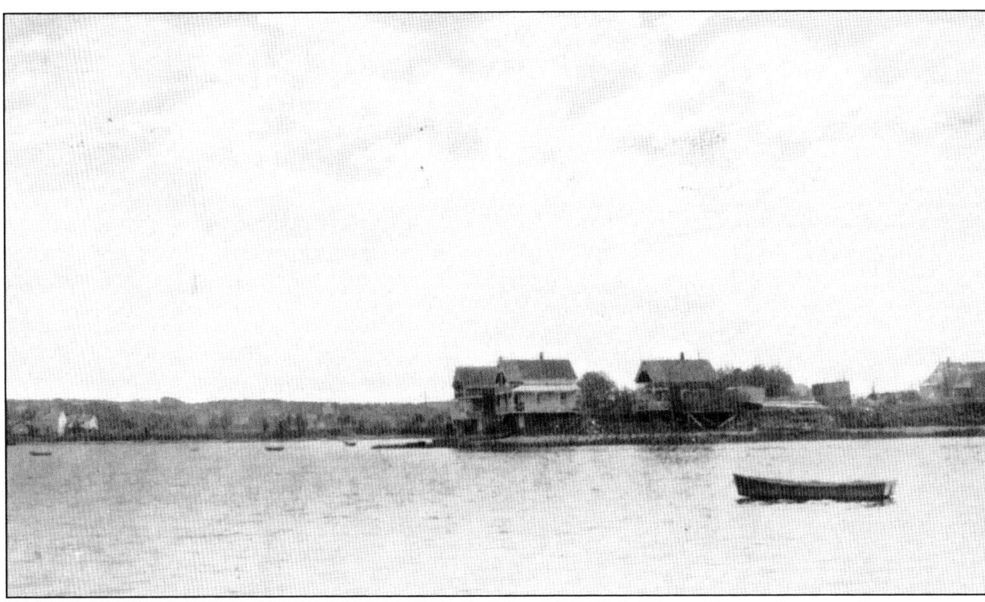

Summer cottages at Barker Point, along Island Park's Sakonnet River shore. This postcard, sent on July 28, 1906, to an Elmhurst, NY address, carries a Fall River postmark. The message from "Mark" reads in part, ". . . we have met plenty of French girls."

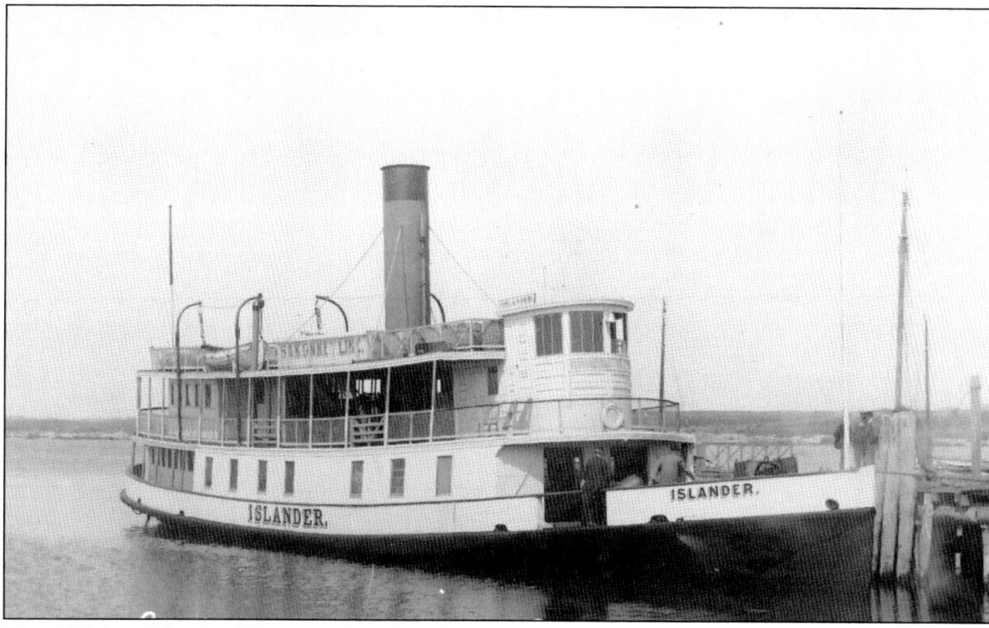

The 106-foot *Islander*. This vessel replaced the *Awashonks*, which burned in 1901. Beginning in 1886, the Seaconnet Steamboat Co. of Little Compton, RI, operated between Providence and Sakonnet Point; stops included Bristol Ferry, Stone Bridge, Newtown, and Fogland Point. The run continued each summer until 1919.

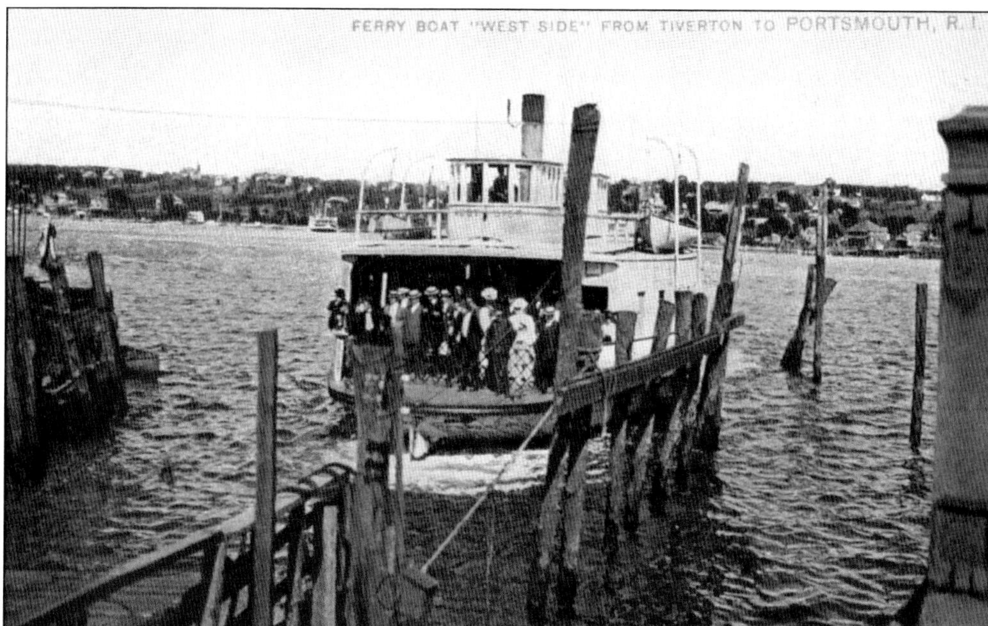

The ferry boat *West Side*. Passengers and vehicles were shuttled by the *West Side* across the Sakonnet River from Tiverton to Portsmouth, and back again.

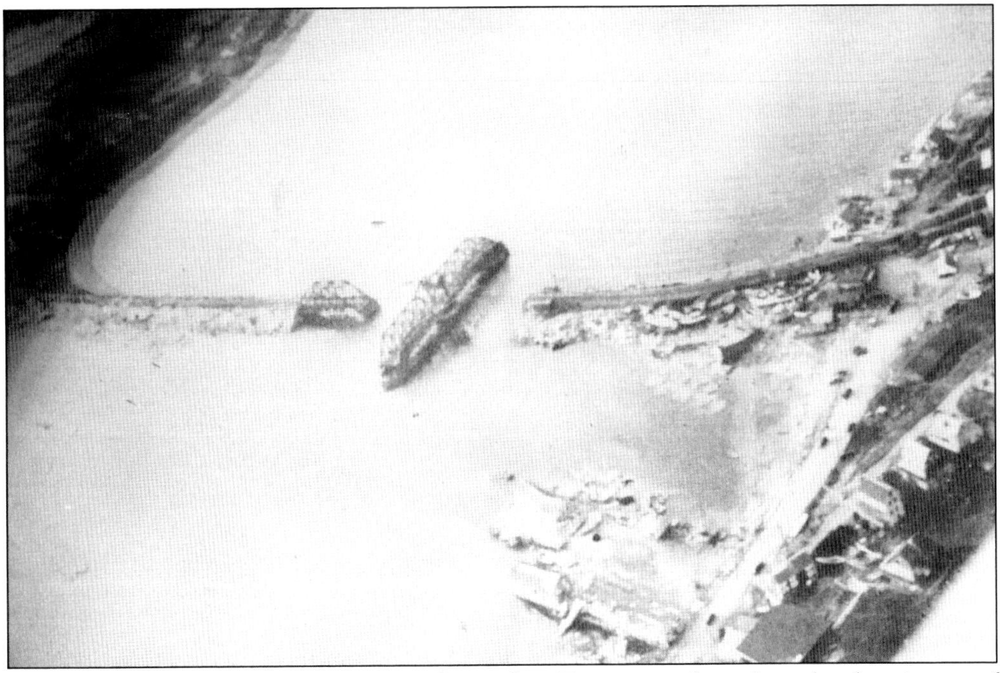

Railroad Bridge, in an aerial view from the Tiverton side, after the hurricane of September 21, 1938.

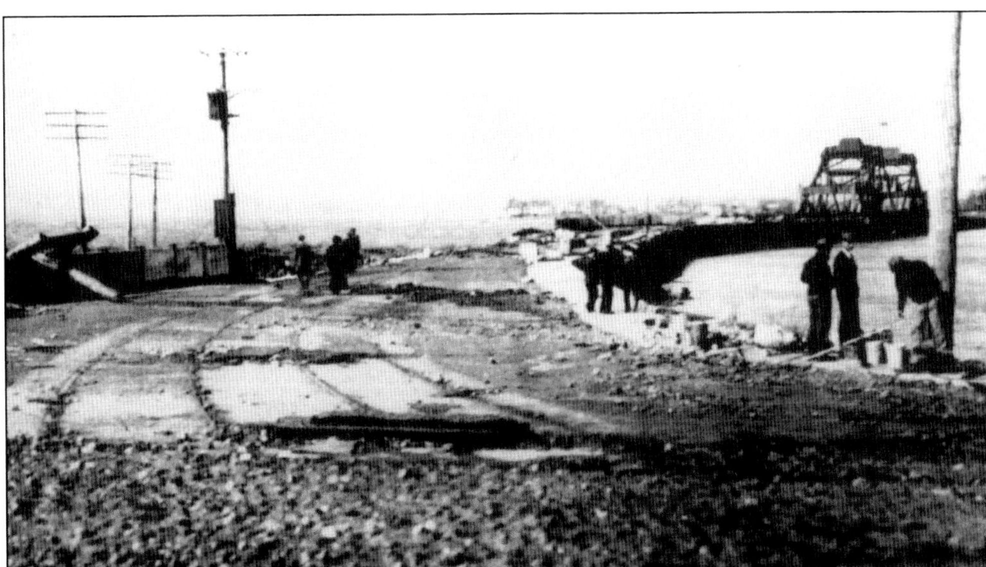

Old Stone Bridge. The roadway and walls of the old Stone Bridge felt the full fury of the September 21, 1938 storm.

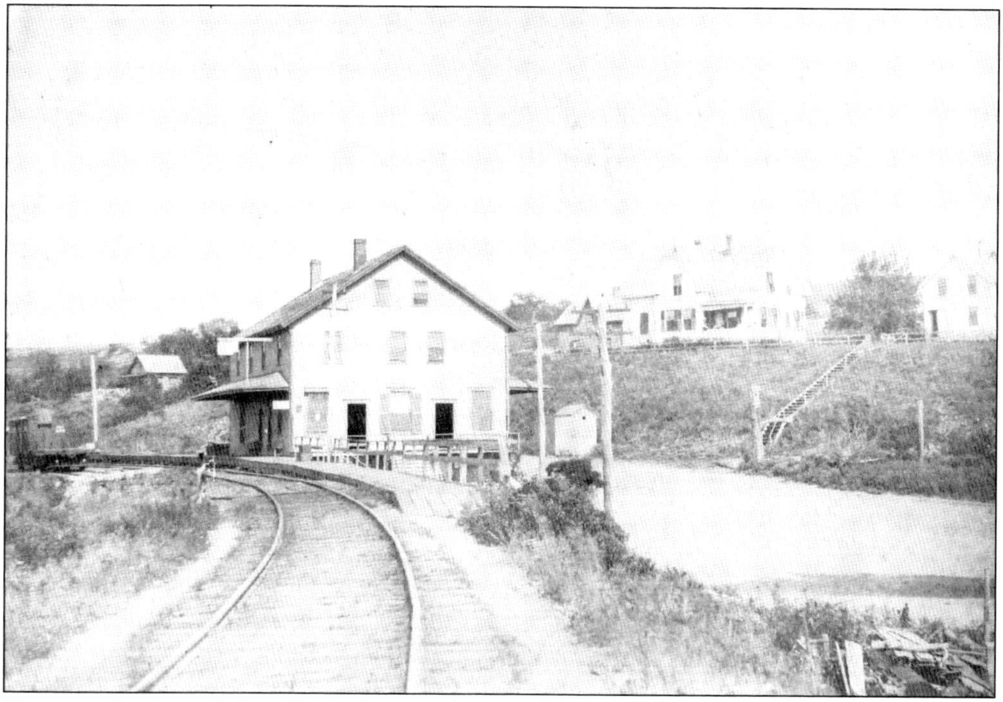

Tiverton Station of the Old Colony and Newport Railroad. The single track crossed the Sakonnet River, ran west to Bristol Ferry and then south and very close to the shoreline. The trains carried passengers until about 1937.

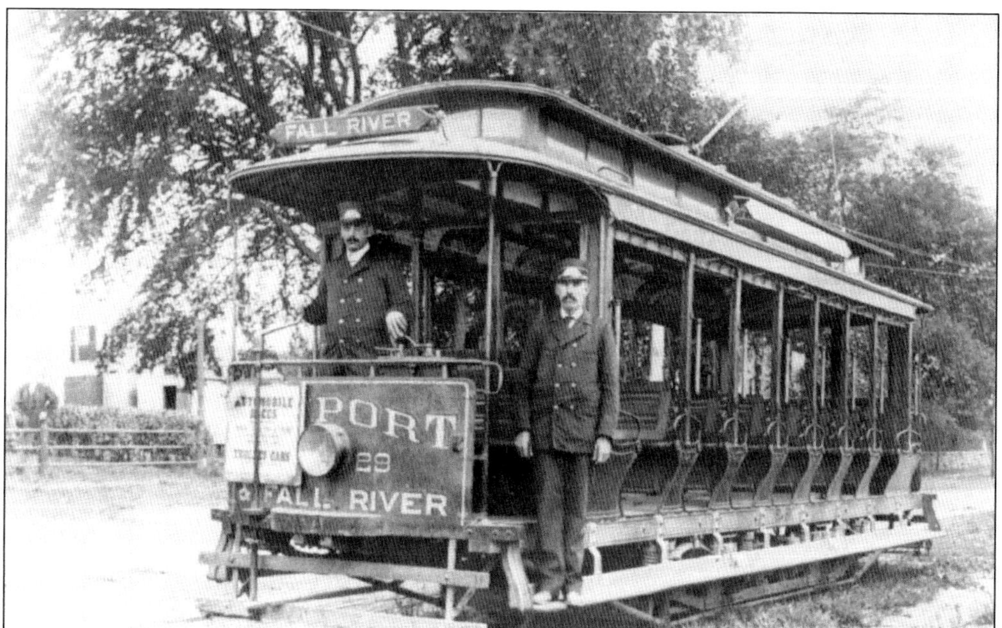

Car 29 of the interurban Newport and Fall River Street Railway at Tallman Switch at the top of Park Avenue, *c.* 1900. The trolley car has stopped to oblige the photographer before swinging onto East Main Road for its run to Newtown and beyond.

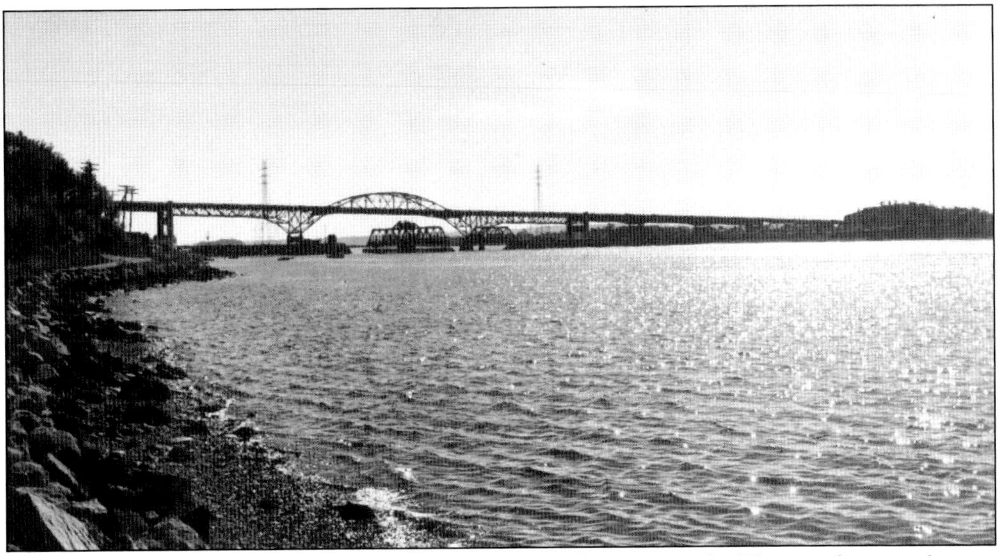

Sakonnet River Bridge connecting Tiverton (left) and Portsmouth. This modern steel truss, arch-type bridge is more than a half mile long, and opened to traffic on September 25, 1956. The old Railroad Bridge is still used.

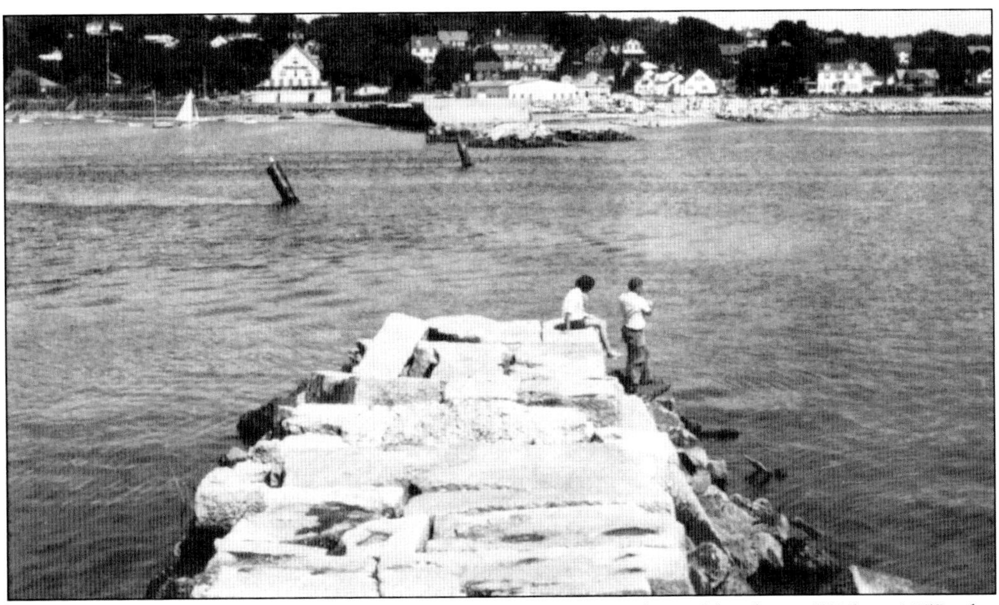

Remnants of the old Stone Bridge causeway. After serving the public from 1795 to 1957, the remains of the causeway on both sides of the Sakonnet River are used as fishing piers.

Four

Harvesting the Land and Sea

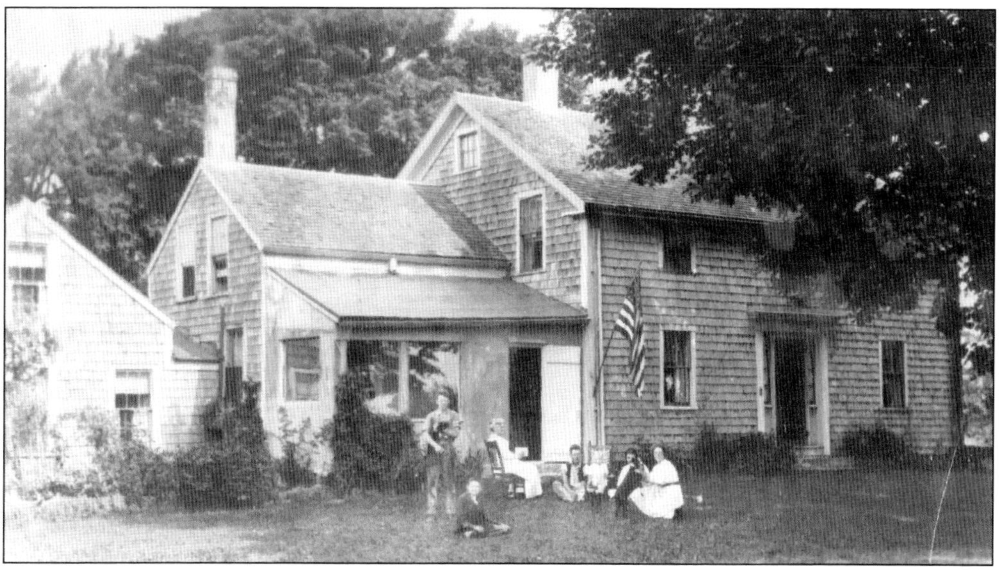

Family-owned and operated farm. Pictured here, *c.* 1920, at the 1850 Chase Farmhouse are Milton Chase, Kennisin Peirce, Miss Potter, Clinton Copeland, Dorothy Copeland Chase, Norma Coggeshall Copeland, and Eva Chase. The house is a one-and-one-half-story Federal/ early Greek Revival structure with one interior and one exterior brick chimney, a central entry with sidelights in a three-bay facade, and a wing and enclosed addition at the south side.

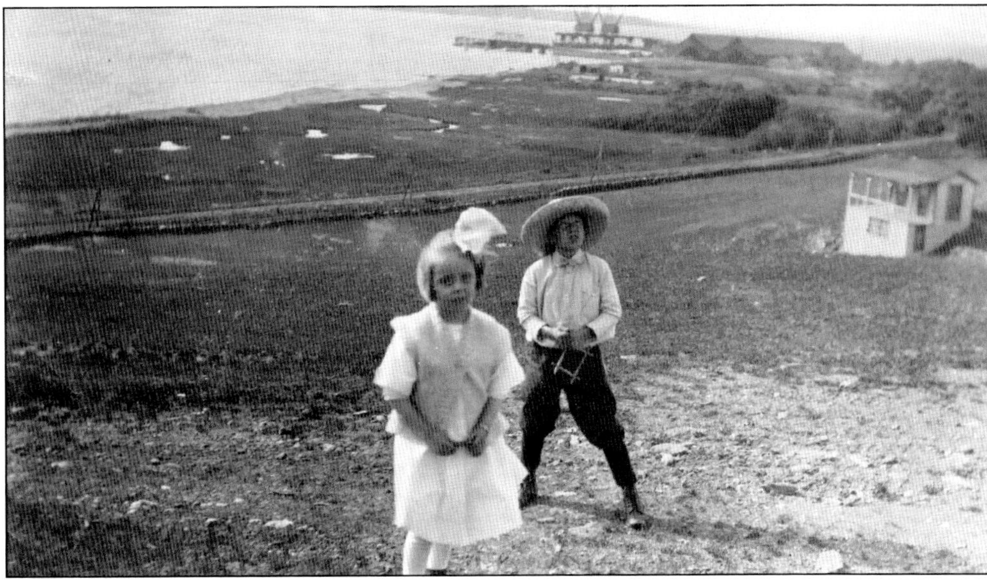

Homestead Farm. Before the federal government condemned much of the Chase land, the farm extended to the shore of Narragansett Bay and included what is now called Melville. Laura and Milton Chase are flying kites down in the pasture of the "Old (George H. Chase) Homestead Farm." Note the railroad tracks and coaling facility at the Melville Fueling Station. A freshwater spring bubbled near the bungalow that served as a changing place for swimmers.

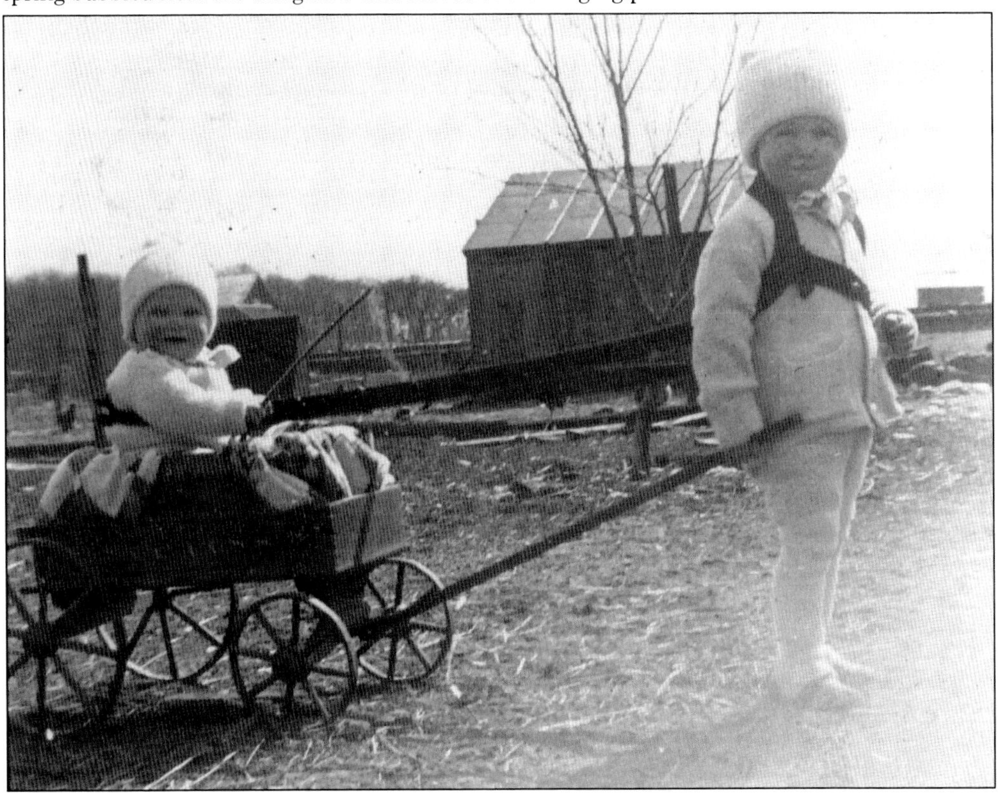

Herbert M. Chase Jr. and his little brother Thayer at the family farm.

Grandma Mary Chase, mother of George H. Chase, at the Homestead Farm, *c*. 1900. Note the front entrance to house as described on p. 49. During these days poultry was allowed to roam at will to forage for grain.

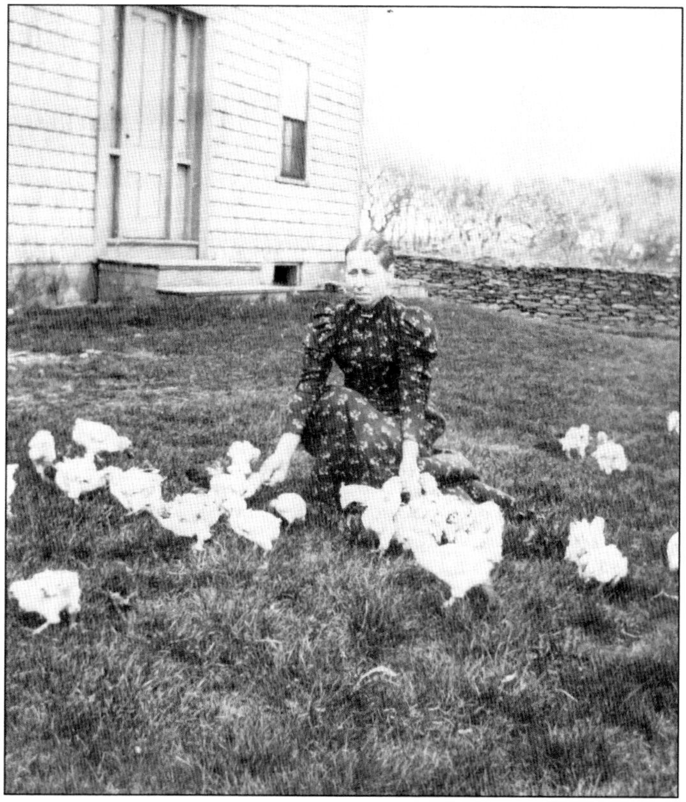

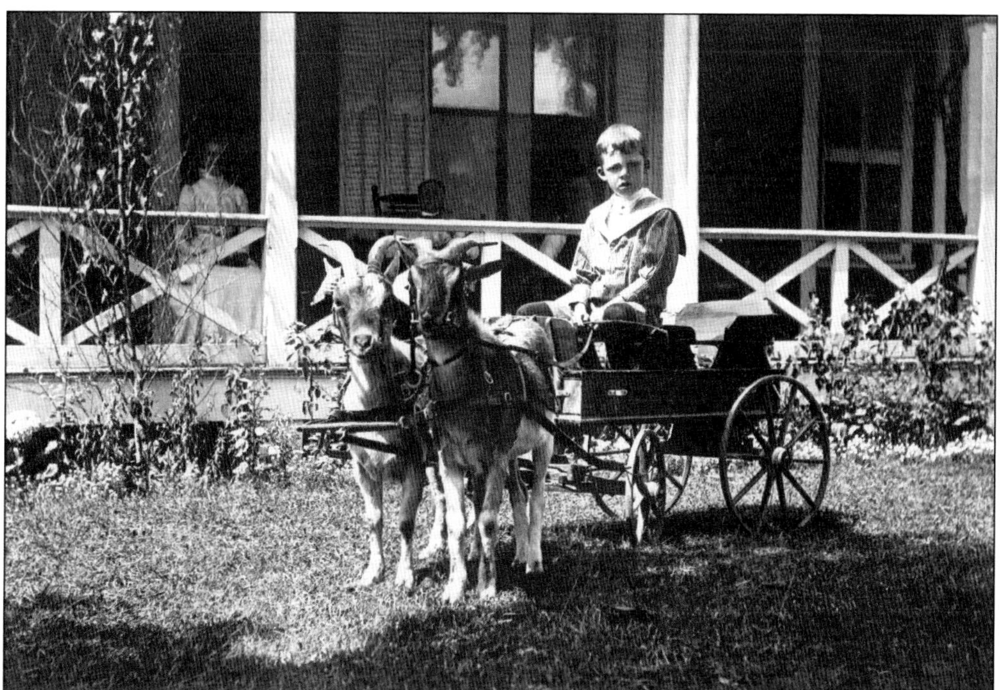

Clinton Babbit Copeland and his two-goat-power coach in a *c*. 1903 photograph.

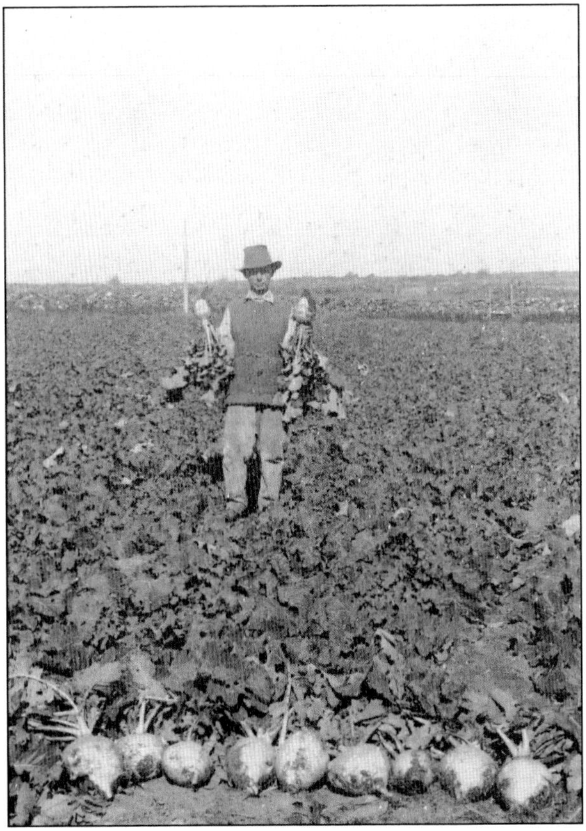

Henry C. Anthony in his west side turnip field with his prize-winning harvest.

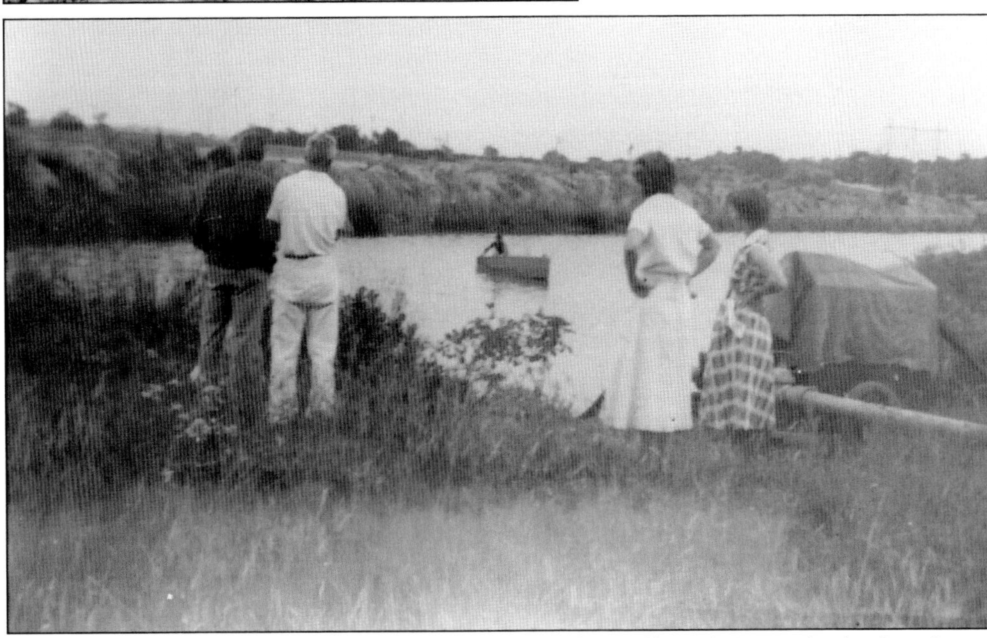

Irrigation ditch on the property of Herbert M. Chase's farm off Boyd's Lane. At this late date—1949—this is all that remains of the Town Pond of colonial days. From left to right are Stan, Herb, Prescott (in boat), Dorothy, and Audrey Chase.

Oakland's main drive from the East Main Road to the Vanderbilt residence.

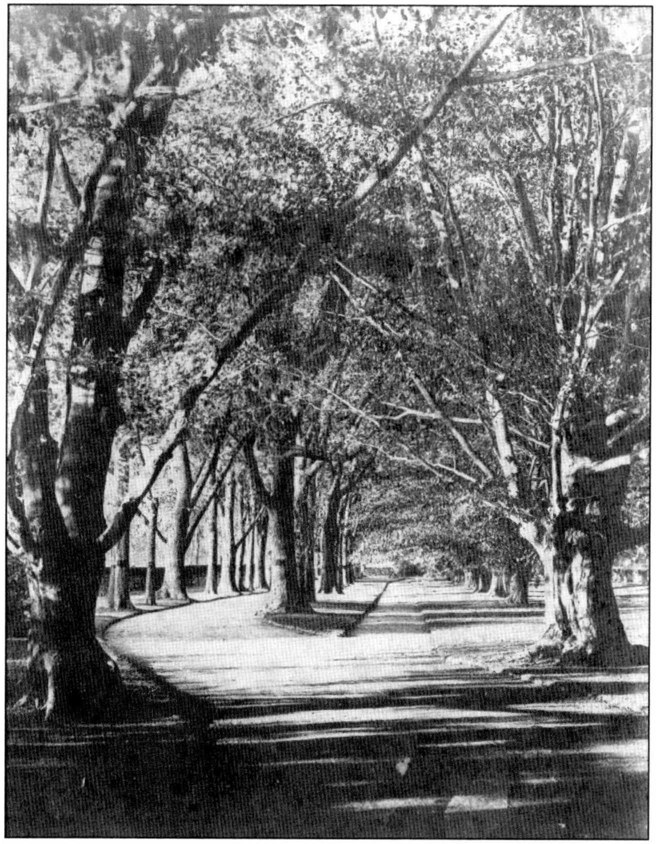

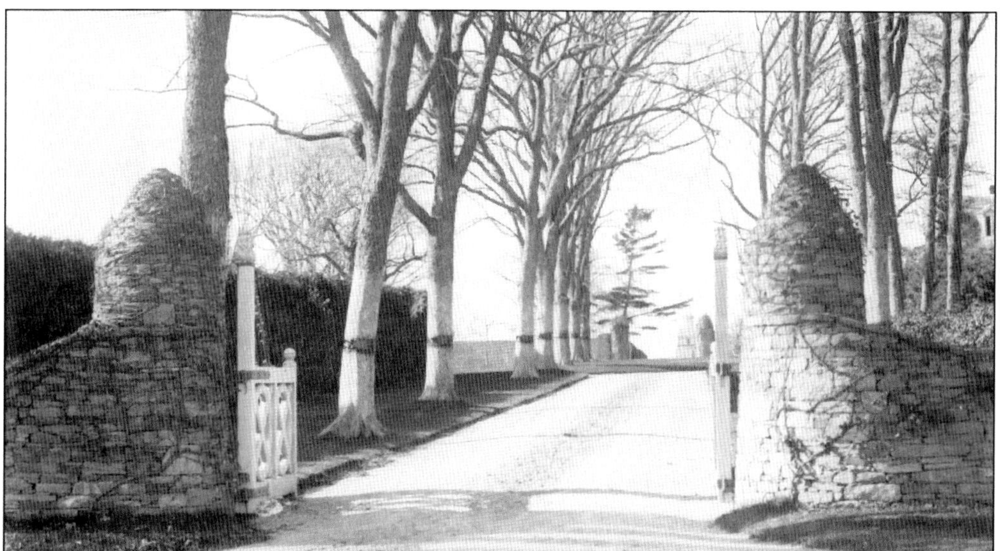

Stone entry posts and wooden gates of Oakland, former estate of Cornelius, Albert G., and William H. Vanderbilt. The grounds, which were mostly along the west side of East Main Road, consisted of about 150 acres.

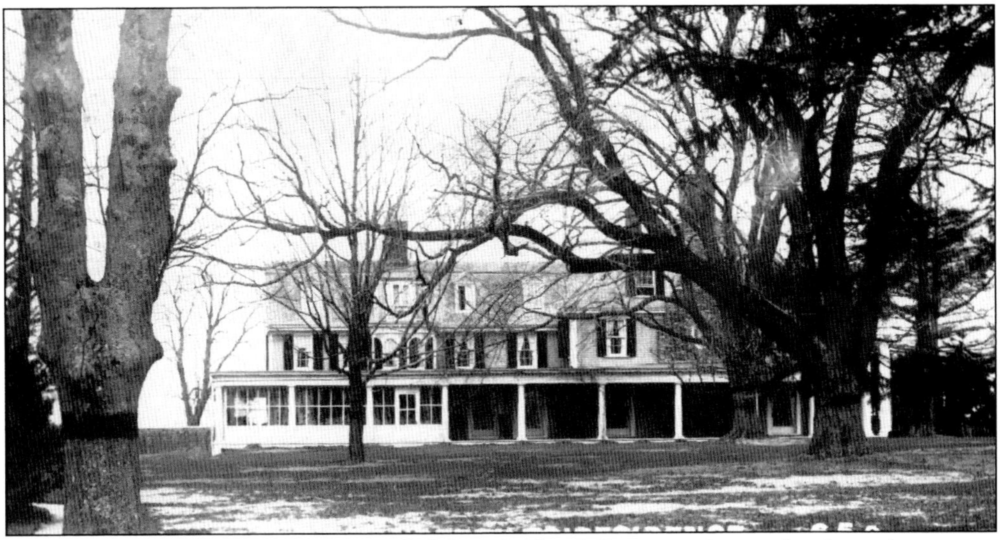

Two perspectives of Alfred G. Vanderbilt's Oakland Farm residence: (top) in the spring, *c.* 1907; (bottom) in the summer, with the awnings drawn to shelter the promenade. Oakland was once suggested as a summer home for President Wilson.

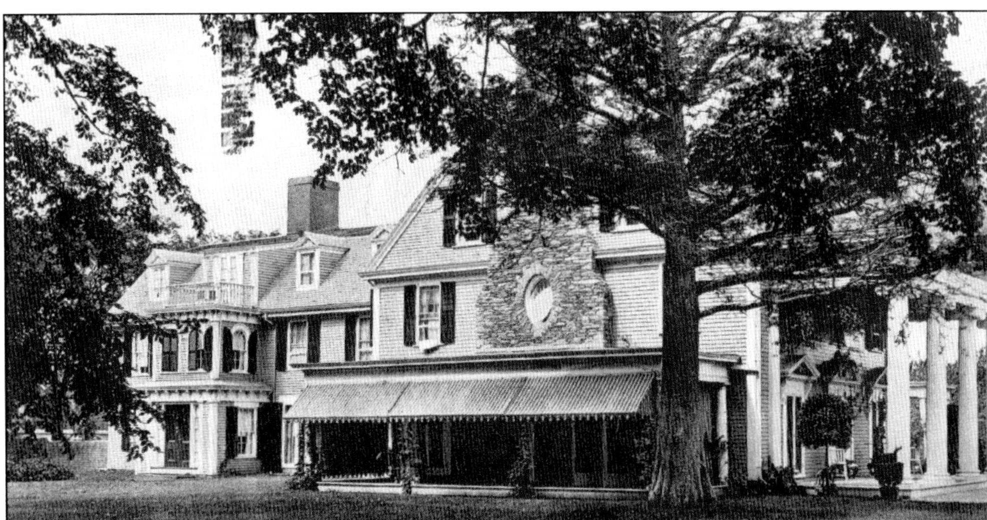

Vanderbilt's residence (*c.* 1895), a large late Victorian villa. Amenities included a powerhouse, a greenhouse, several garages, a polo field, and a large driving ring—an enclosed building constructed when Vanderbilt was the leader in the horse-show world. Sometime between November 1947 and 1950, the buildings were destroyed and little remains of them today.

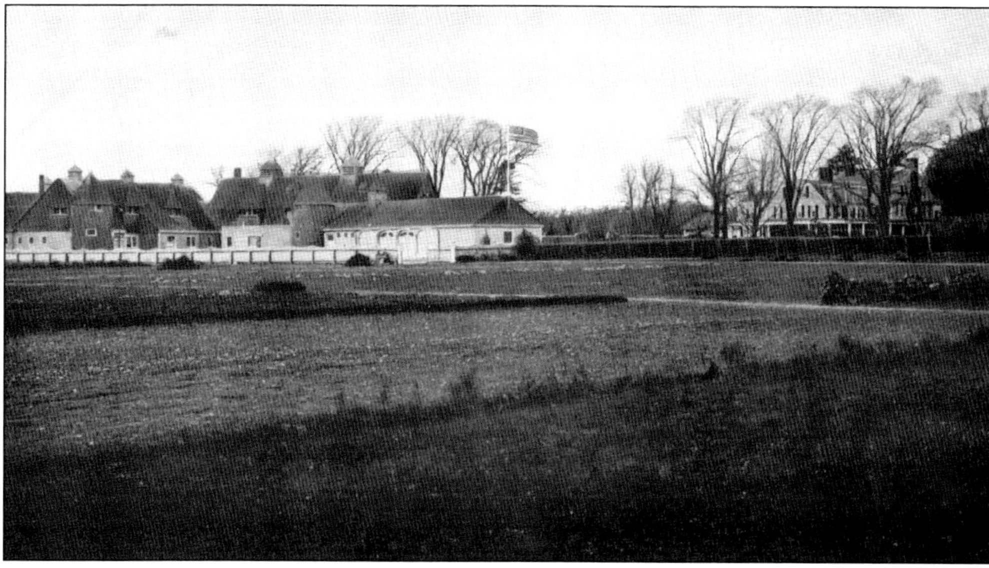

Panorama view of A.G. Vanderbilt's magnificent barns and stables. The residence can be seen at the right.

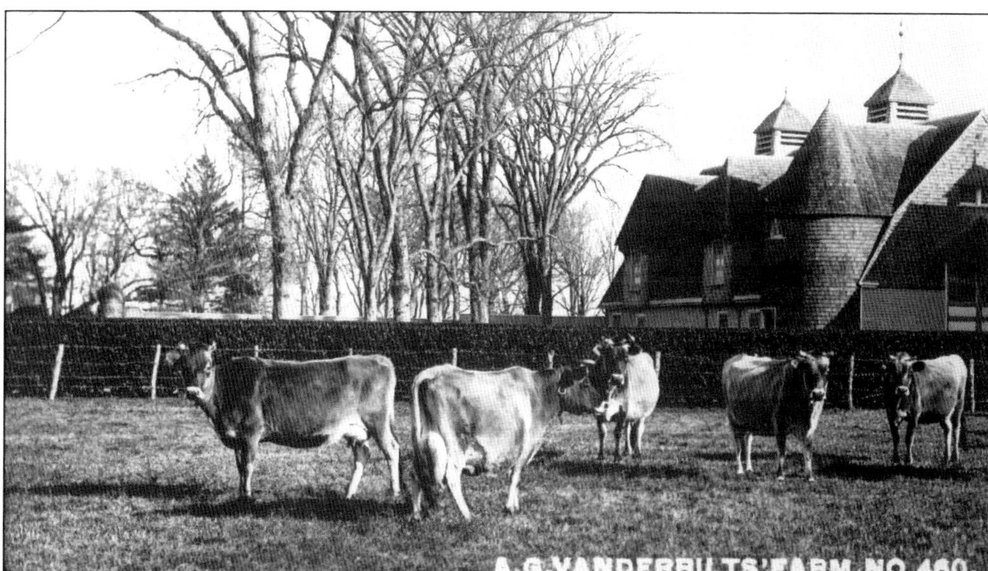

One of Oakland's prize herd of dairy cows in the shadow of a magnificent shingle-style barn.

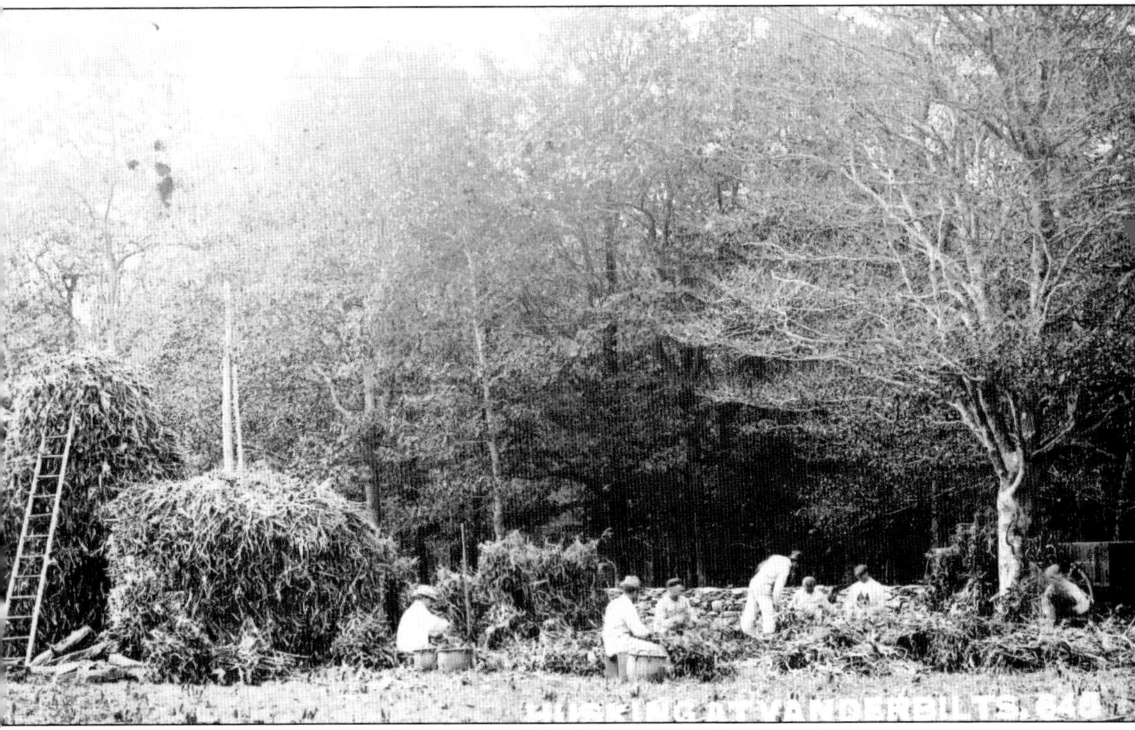

Harvest of 1906. At harvest time, the large farms of Portsmouth hired hundreds of extra hands from the surrounding communities. Itinerant farm workers are shown here husking at a Vanderbilt farm.

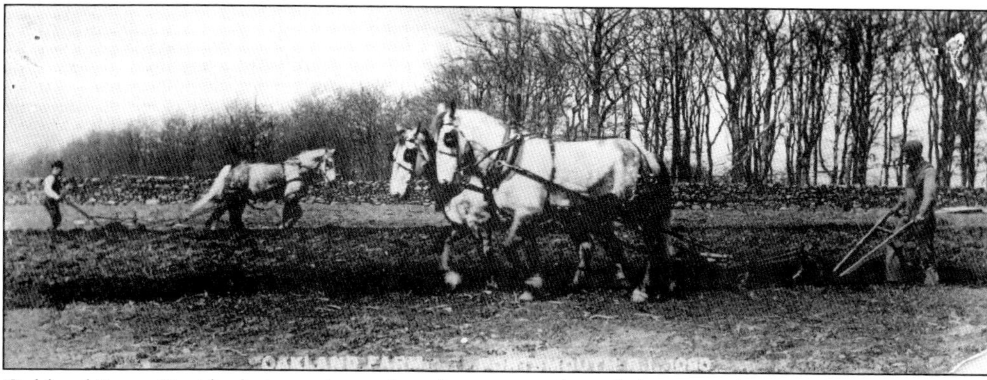

Oakland Farm. Besides being a show place for prize cattle and champion horses, this was a working farm with a large number of acres under cultivation, as can be seen in this *c.* 1900 photograph.

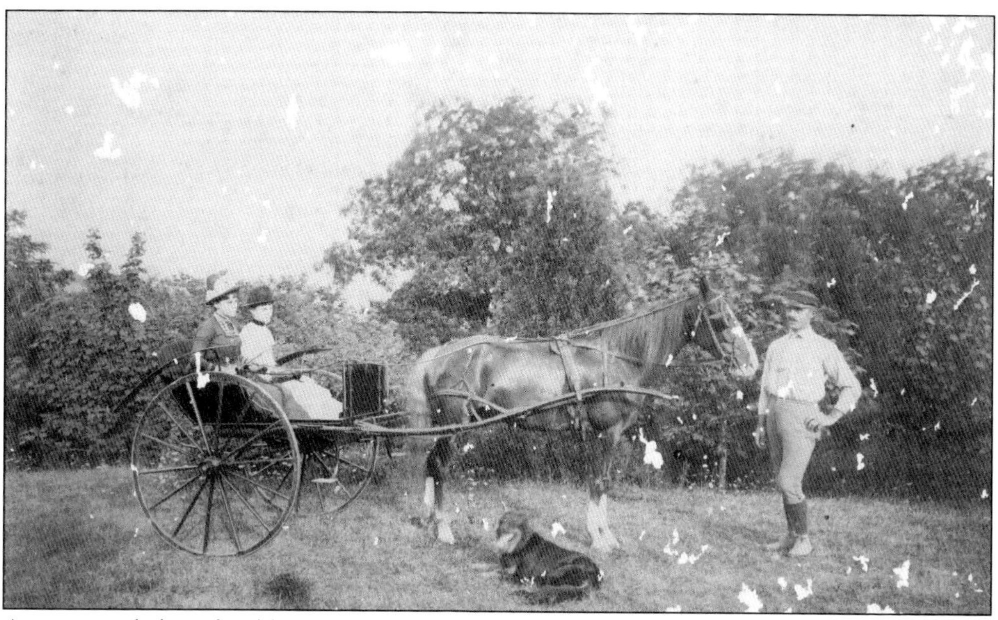

Aristocratic ladies of Oakland Farm and their genteel carriage. For this photograph by Newport landscape photographers Briskham & Davidson, a groom stands ready to steady the horse that is about to be startled by the photographer's flash powder.

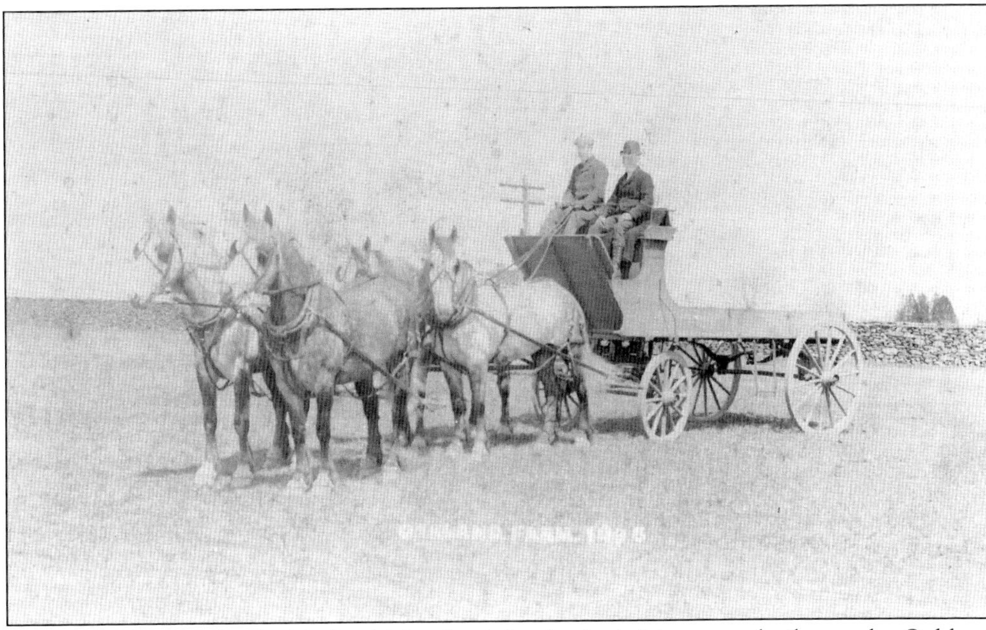

Wagon made to order for Michael Murphy. Murphy had this wagon built to take Oakland farmhands on outings. The body could be removed from the chassis and mounted on runners for winter use. In this photograph Fred Sherman is the driver; he is accompanied by William Gifford.

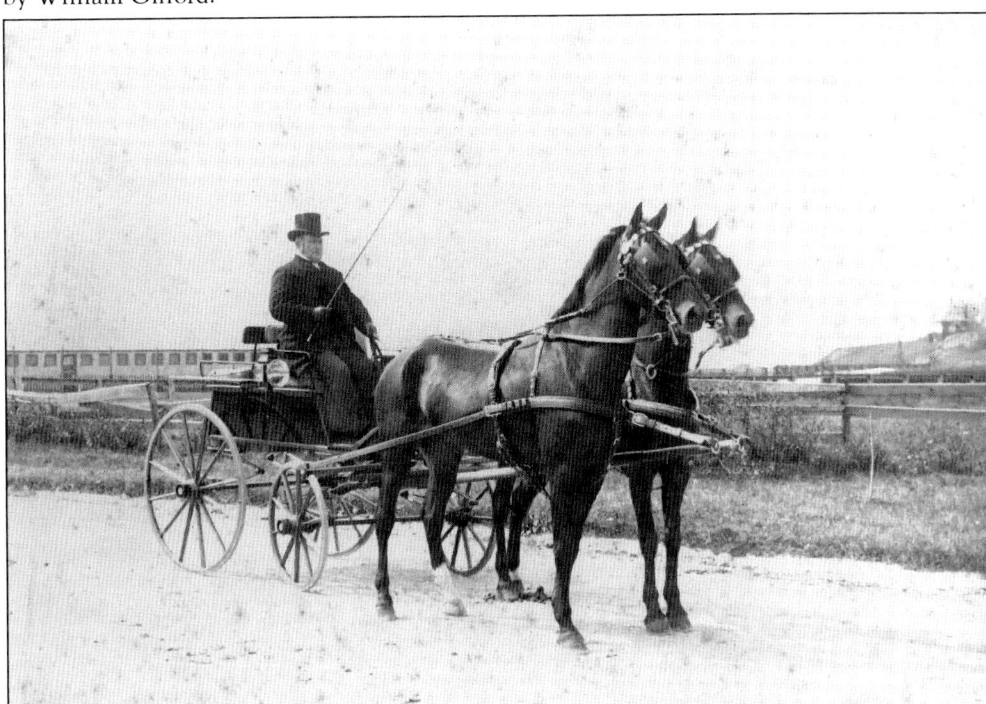

Alfred Vanderbilt's head coach driver Charles Whittaker and a fine pair of street horses. The animals' fine breeding and alertness are evident—Mr. Whittaker, too, is well turned-out in formal driving attire.

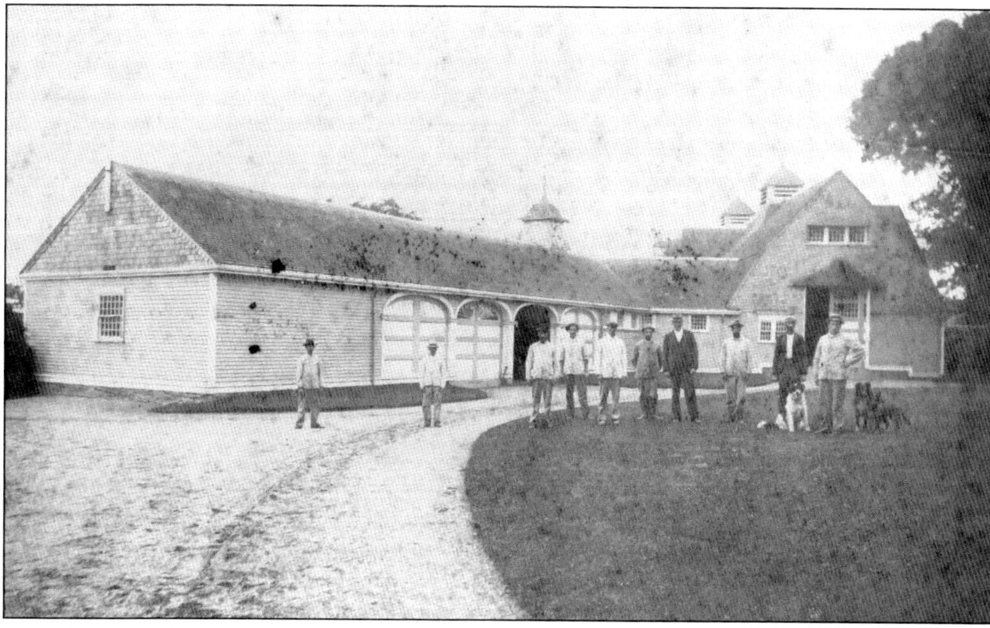

Cornelius Vanderbilt's show horse stables. The horse handlers who showed up for this photograph are, from left to right, G. Peabody, O. Peckham, F. Goncalves, R. Purcell, E. Bishop, A. Walker, superintendent John Allen, J. Fred Sherman, Oliver Wood, and H. Mills.

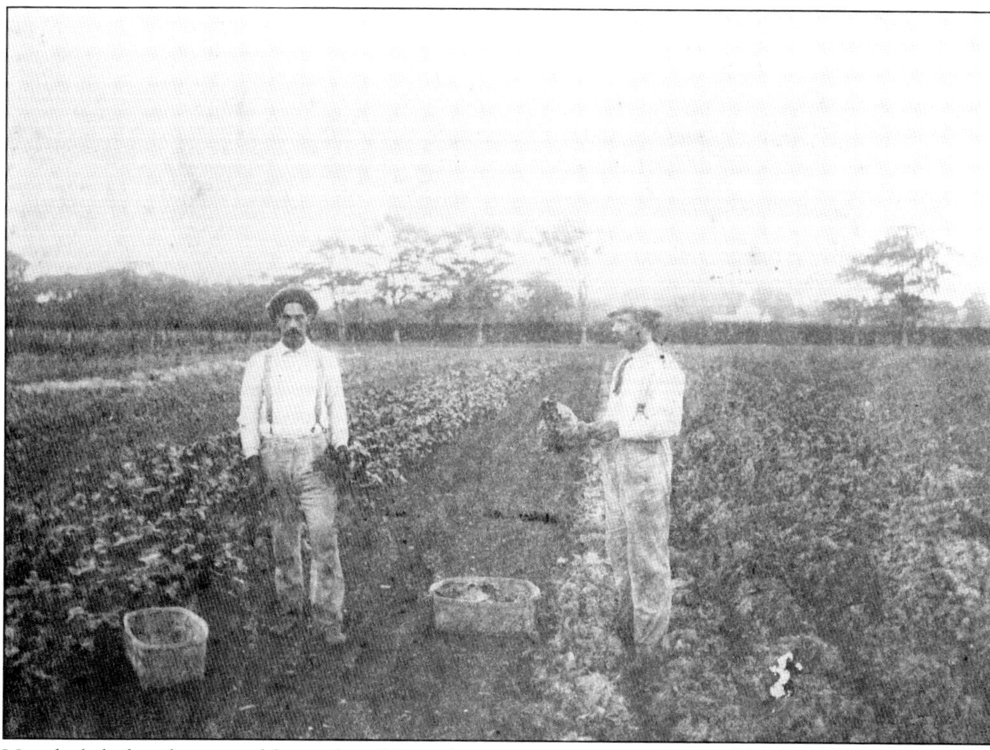

Vanderbilt family vegetable garden. More than just sustenance, vegetables from this garden also fed the farmhands and livestock. J. Fred Sherman (left) and Andrew Walker are shown here finishing the morning's harvest.

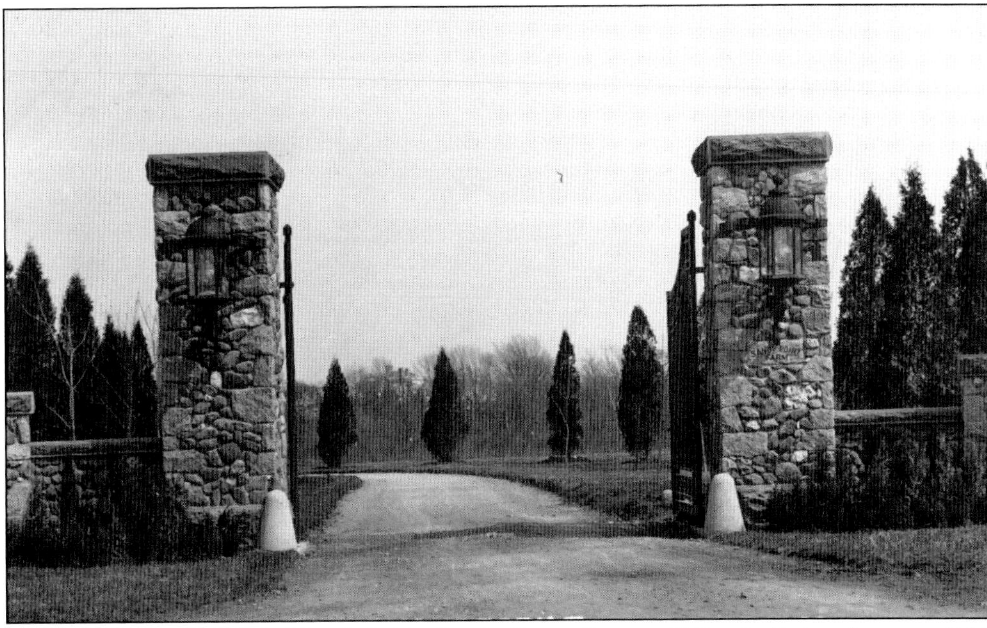

Entrance to Reginald C. Vanderbilt's Sandy Point Farm, off Sandy Point Avenue. P.H. Powell developed the property around 1895; it was bought by Vanderbilt in the early twentieth century.

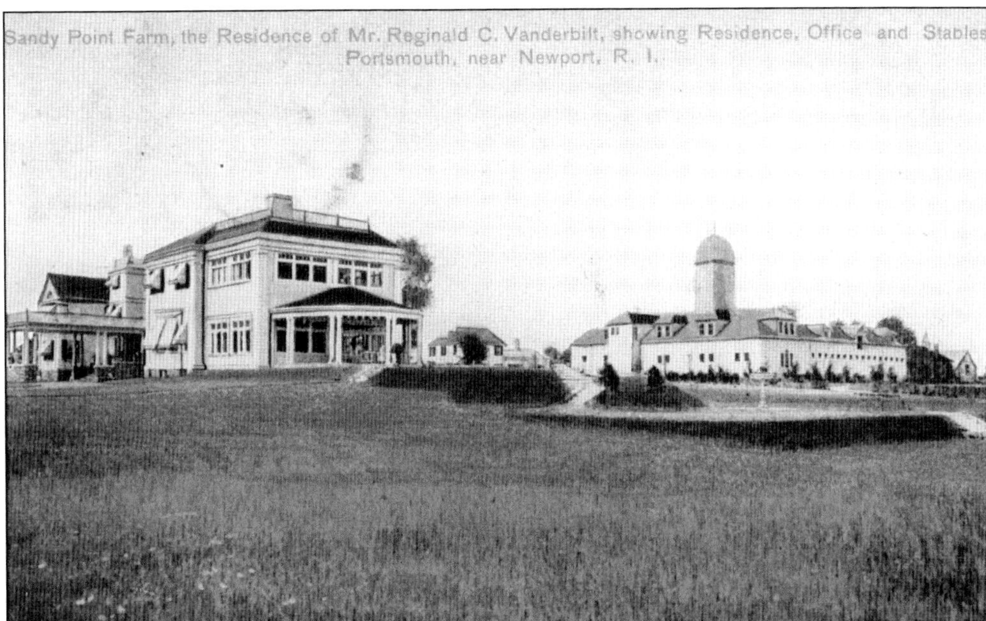

Sandy Point Farm residence, office, and stables, c. 1920. Today, the property retains an outstanding collection of late-Victorian and early-twentieth-century shingle and Colonial Revival farm outbuildings.

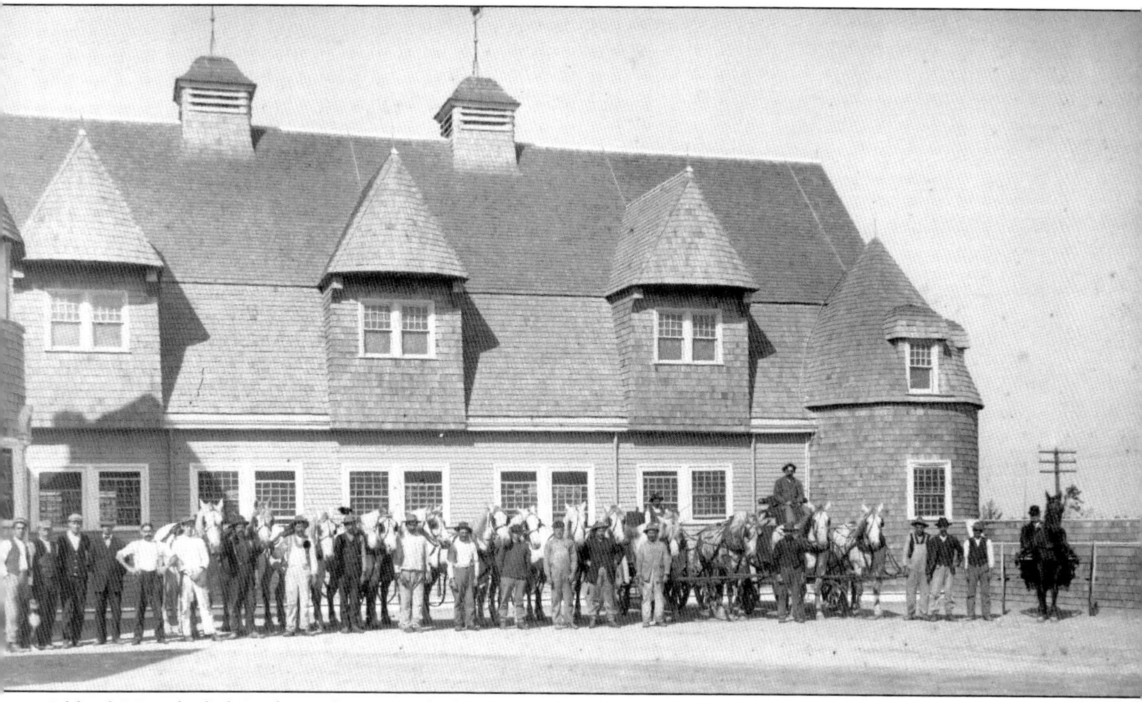

Alfred Vanderbilt's dairy barn with herdsmen, teamsters, and helpers. Oakland's unique dairy barn was bought by railroad financier Robert R. Young. The *Providence Sunday Journal* of November 9, 1947, reported that Young sold all live stock and machinery, and planned to raise sheep.

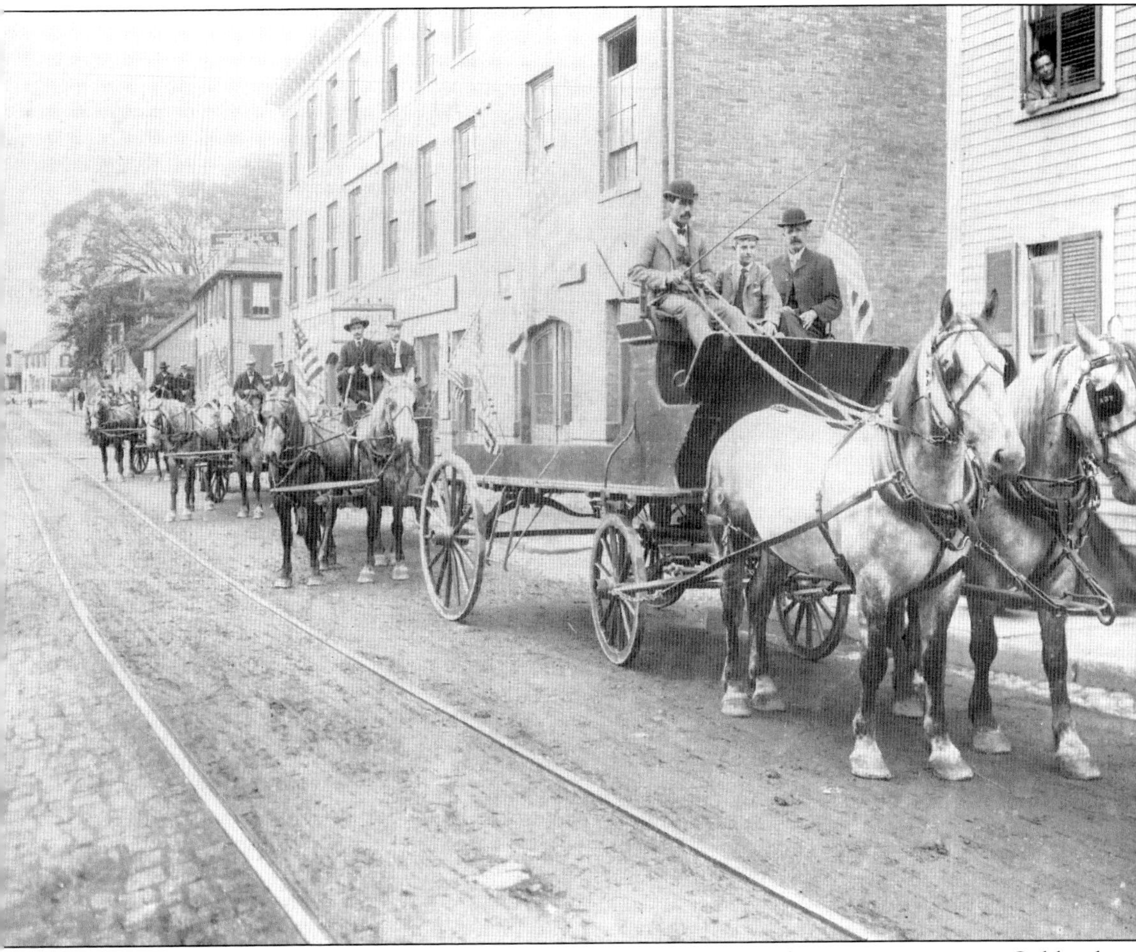

Old Home Week parade in 1900. Vanderbilt sent a contingent of wagons to represent Oakland Farm in the parade. Seen here on Farewell Street are four of Oakland's teams: (first wagon) driver J. Fred Sherman, Billy Adams, and superintendent of Oakland Farm Alee Adams; (second wagon) driver Frank Goncalves and herdsman Henry Mills; (third wagon) driver William Gifford and Harry Groom; (fourth wagon) driver Manuel Freitas and Ed Saddington.

Vaucluse (1784). Gervais Elam built this country estate, spending the princely sum of $80,000 on the house and formal gardens covering 17 acres. Thomas R. Hazard, "Shepherd Tom," retired to Vaucluse in 1840.

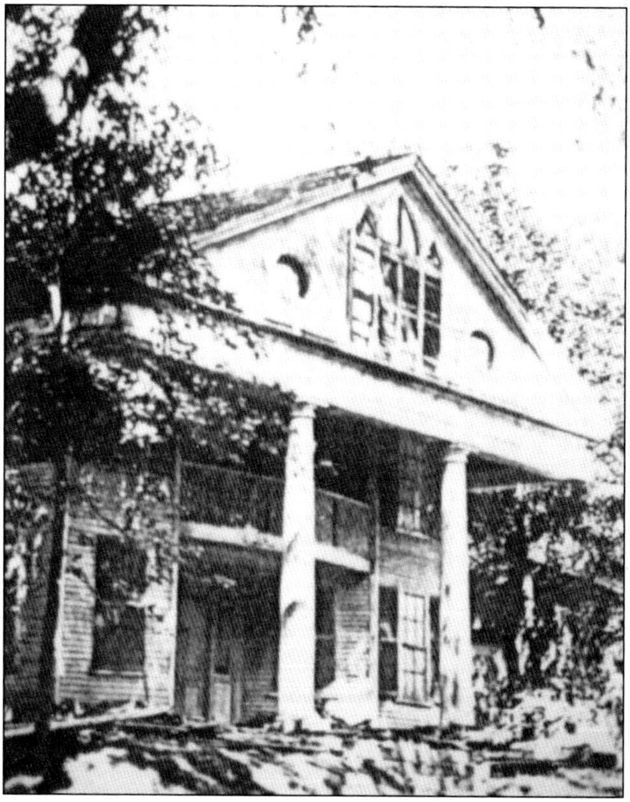

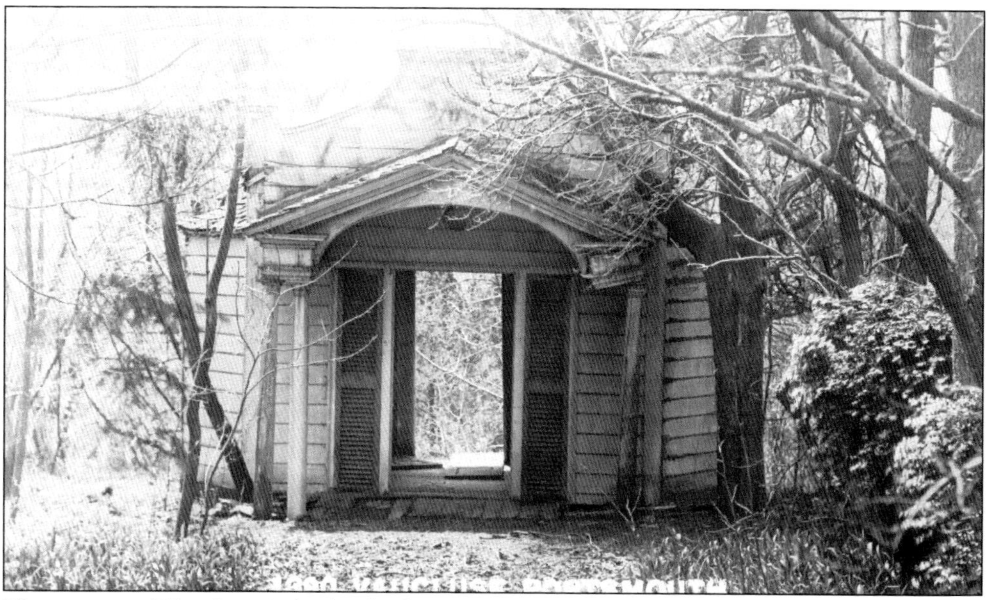

The remains of Vaucluse. In his book *The Jonny-Cake Papers*, T.R. Hazard describes his Vaucluse estate: ". . . the residence of 'Shepherd Tom,' there lies the old Isaac Chase farm, which in the olden time was owned and occupied, in the summer season, by Mr. Bowler, a rich East India merchant of Newport." The early mansion was later abandoned and deteriorated; it was destroyed in the early twentieth century.

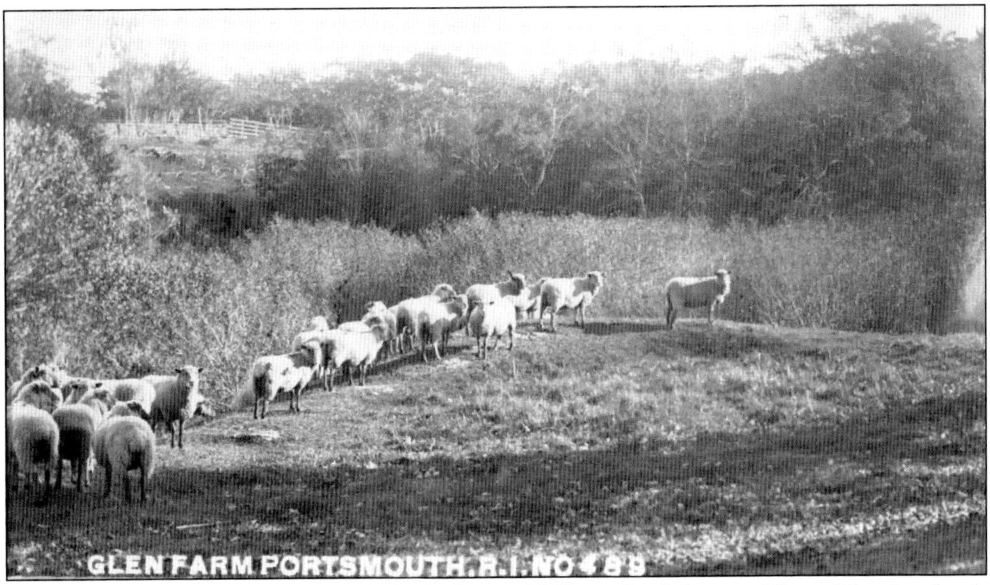

Glen Farm, established by Henry A.C. Taylor in 1885 on the Sakonnet River. The farmlands lie in the Southeast Rural Estate Historic District. This large district along the Sakonnet River, bounded by Glen Road to the north and East Main Road and Wapping Road to the west, is an area of open fields, stone walls, and at least six late 1800s–early-1900s rural estates.

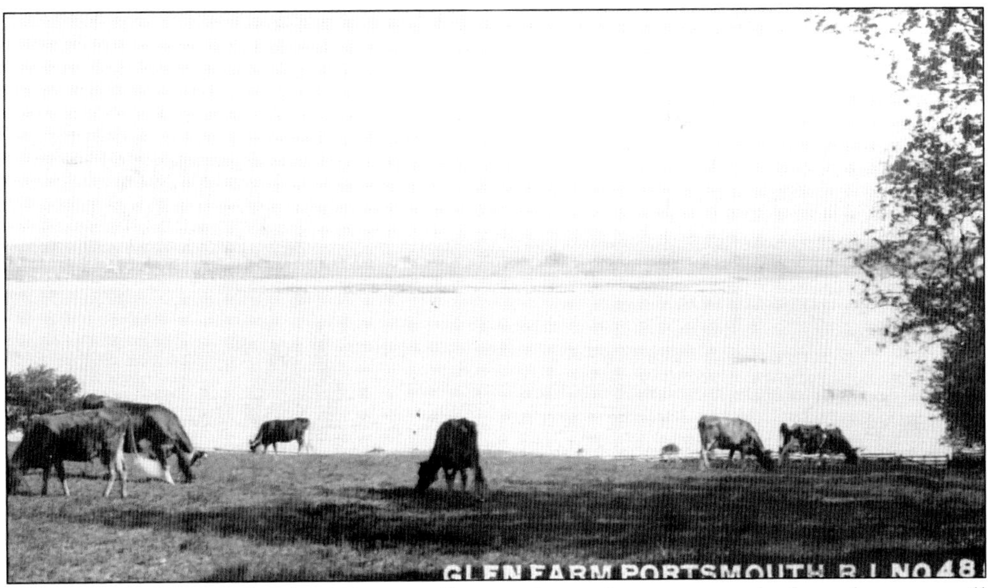
Glen Farm dairy cows by the Sakonnet. Farming began here at an early date; there are still several farmsteads surviving from the eighteenth century, and the remains of an eighteenth-century gristmill at the Glen. A small stream, flowing through a steep valley into the Sakonnet, powered the gristmill; a stone dam across the stream and a raceway survive.

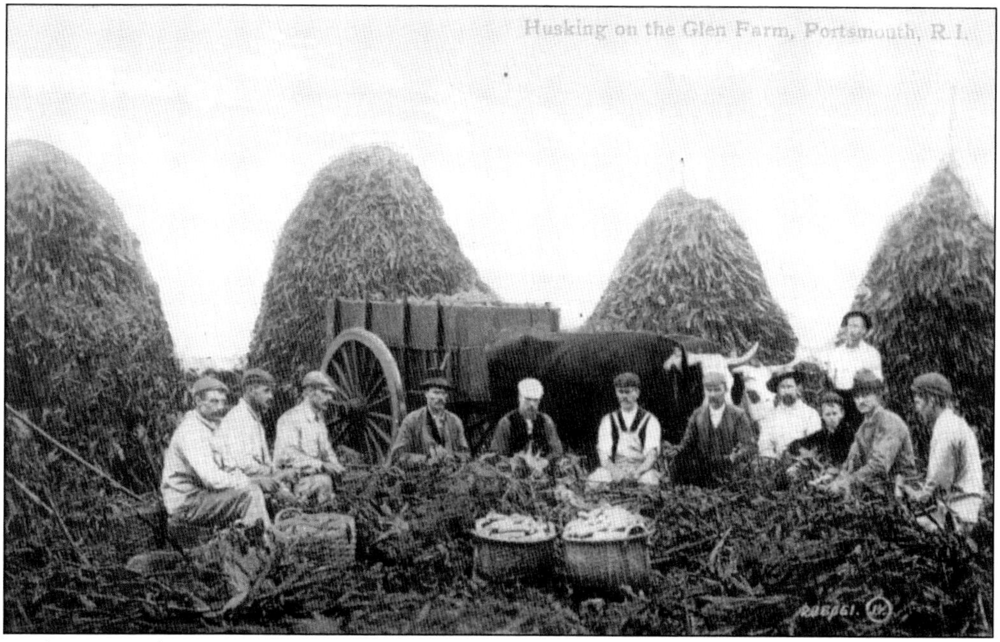

Husking on Glen Farm. Off Glen Road, on a hill above the Sakonnet, is a complex of early twentieth-century outbuildings, including a 1926 field-stone barn and a silo. From approximately St. Mary's Episcopal Church in the south to Glen Road in the north, East Main Road is lined with fine dry-laid stone walls and mature trees.

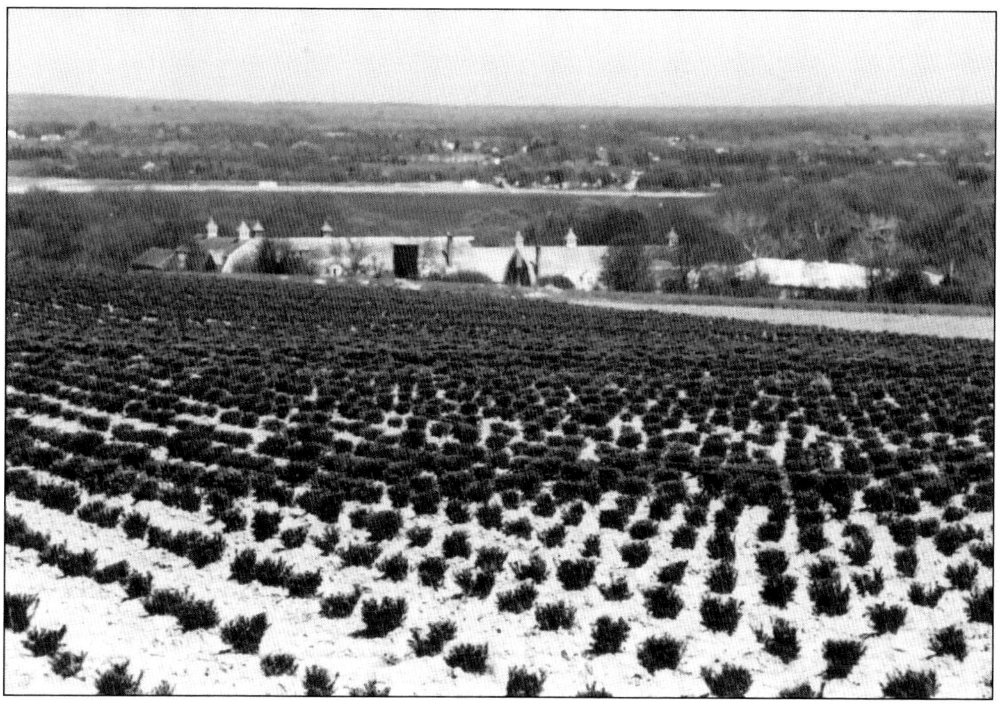

Contemporary view from East Main Road overlooking the cultivated fields of the former Glen Farm and beyond to the Sakonnet River and Tiverton. This field and the farm buildings are now publicly owned and leased to local nursery farmers.

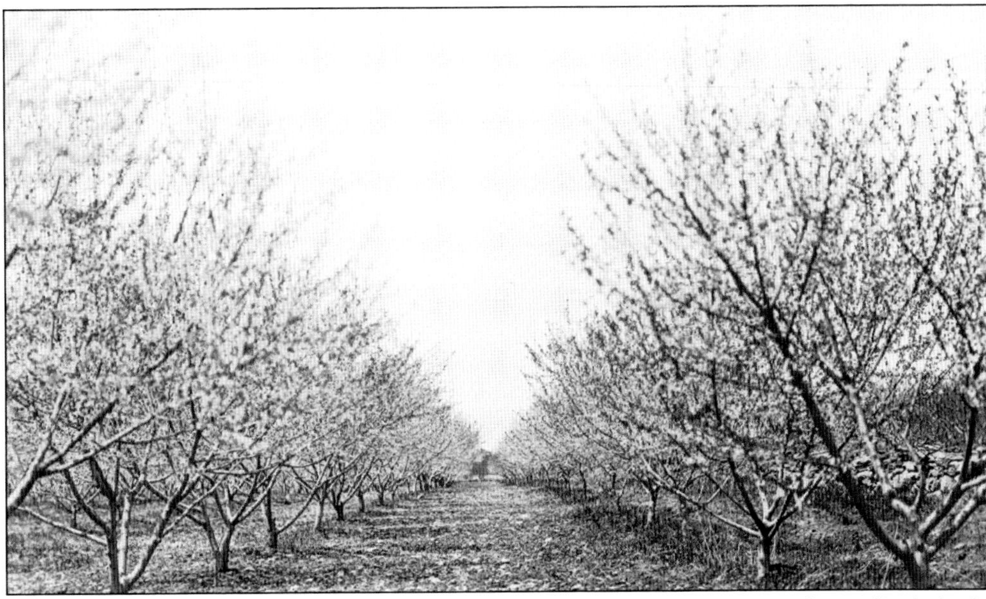

Brookside Orchard of Luther P. Chace. The orchard extended from near the traffic light by the Getty station and the embroidery shop, down the road to the construction company, and around the corner to the property of Founder's Brook Motel. The house in front of the motel was the home of Luther P. Chace.

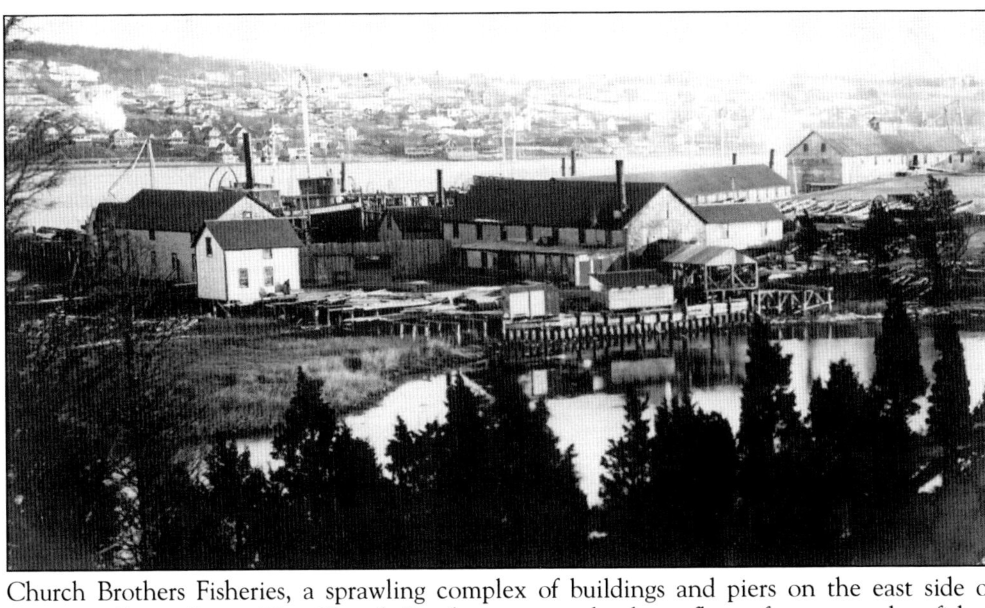

Church Brothers Fisheries, a sprawling complex of buildings and piers on the east side of Common Fence Point. The Church Brothers operated a large fleet of steamers that fished for menhaden (pogy), a fish valuable for its oil and for use as fertilizer. The *Seven Brothers*, the first steam-powered fisherman of its type, was built for the Churches by the Herreshoff Manufacturing Co. of Bristol.

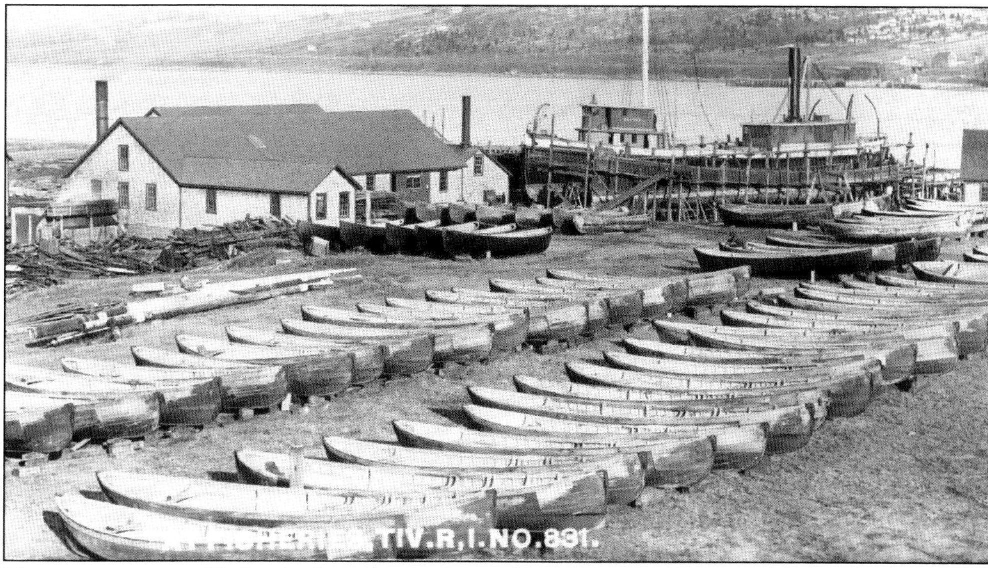

The pogy steamer *Alaska*, high in the water at the fisheries after unloading her catch. Fishing boats such as the *Alaska* varied in size from 100 to 175 feet. Seen in this 1907 postcard view are dozens of double-ender seine boats. Five oil and fertilizer factories worked at one time—three at Common Fence Point and two on Prudence.

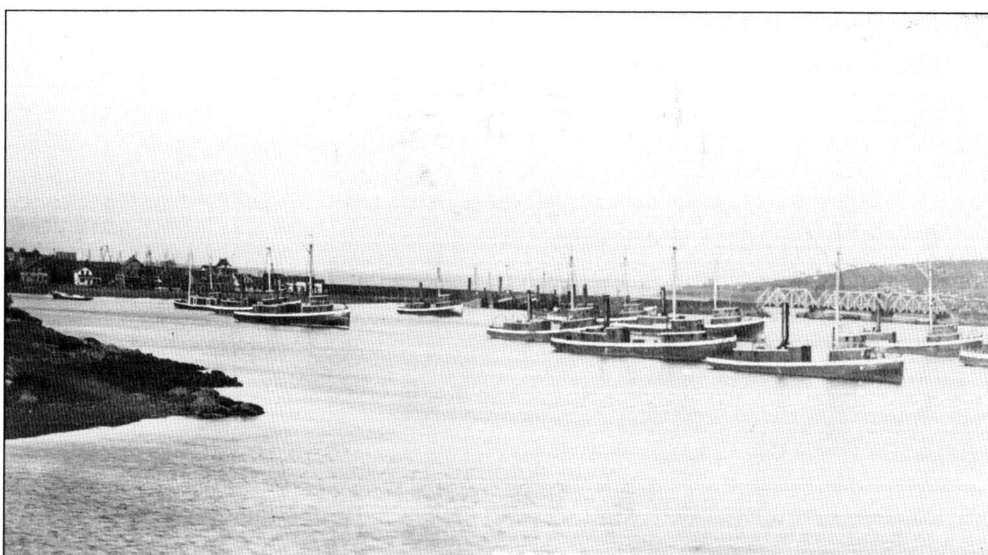

Several pogys in the cove formed by the causeway of the Railroad Bridge (right), from a 1911 postcard. The Church fleet, and boats owned by independent fishermen, used the Portsmouth facility for the sale and processing of their catch. Occasionally, as many as 75–80 steamers wintered in the narrows between Portsmouth and Tiverton.

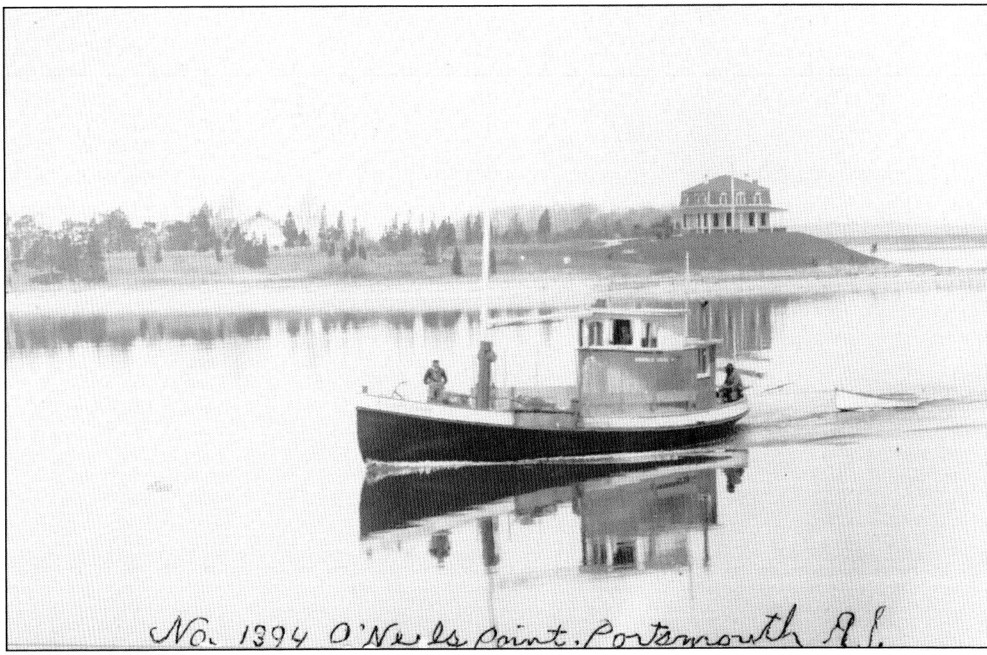

The *Faith E. Clark*, a small independent fisherman, near O'Neil's Point and Hen Island.

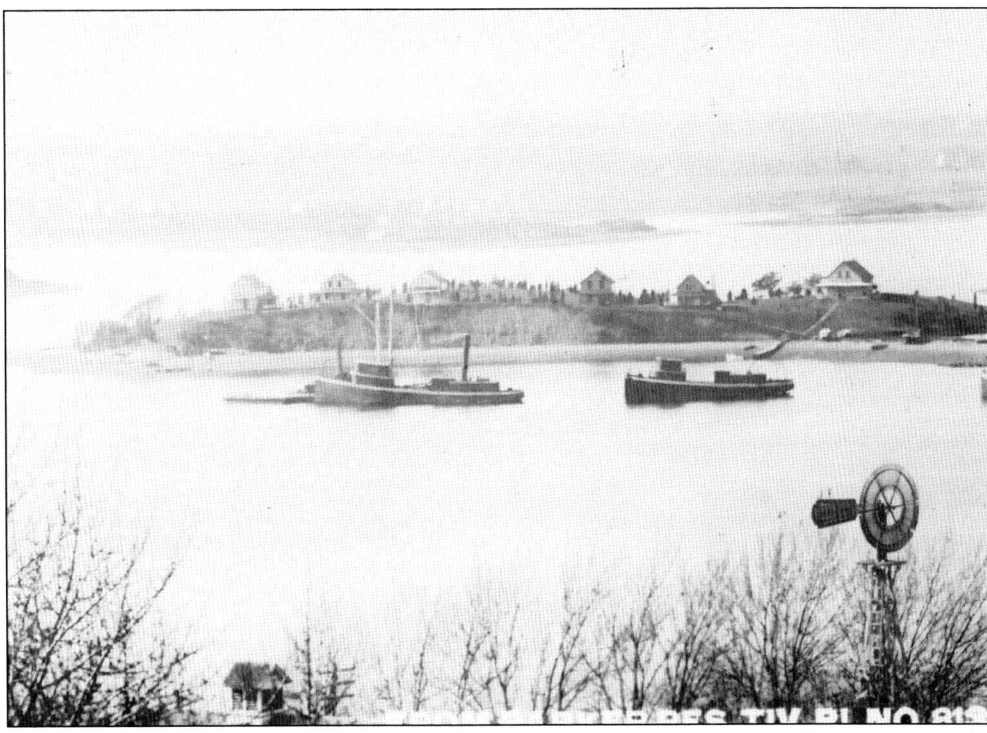

Anchored pogy steamers, seen from the Barker residence on the Tiverton shore in 1906. The thriving Church Brothers' fisheries business had its best days before 1914. After the war, the paint and varnish industry, which had previously relied on fish oil, found new sources for its needs, and the pogy fishing fleets and a great Portsmouth industry gradually disappeared.

Five

Mills and Mines

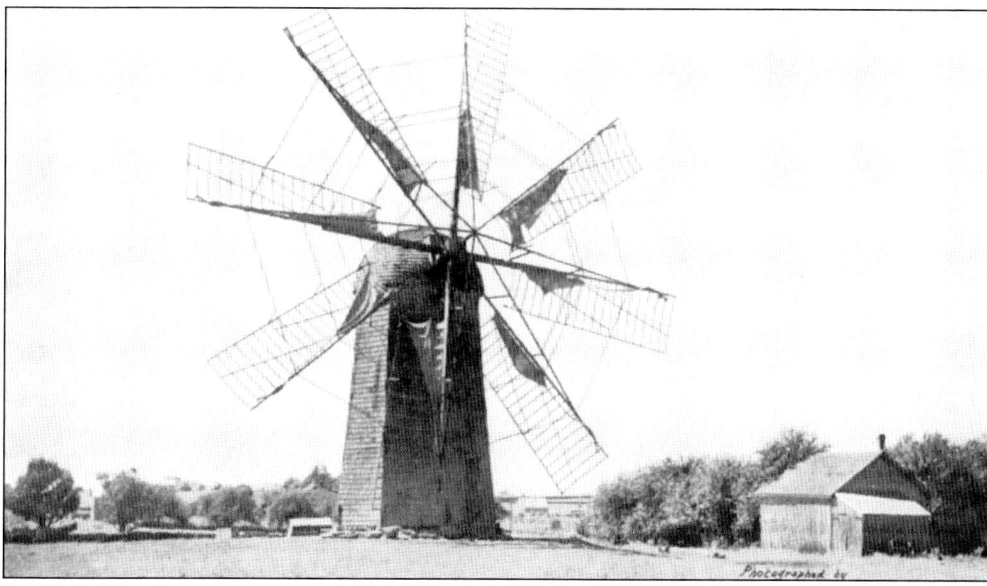

Boyd's Mill, a historic treasure fully restored to its original working condition. The milling of corn for local domestic use became an important adjunct to farming, and several water mills and windmills were constructed. Boyd's Mill, built in the first decade of the 1800s on Mill Lane near West Main Road, is unique for its eight vanes. Originally constructed with the usual four vanes, four additional vanes were added later, when production of greater energy was required. After the mill's vanes were destroyed in the Hurricane of 1938, grain continued to be milled here under diesel power until the early 1950s. Boyd's Mill, now fully restored, may again grind "jonny-cake" meal for afficianadoes of the original Rhode Island pancake.

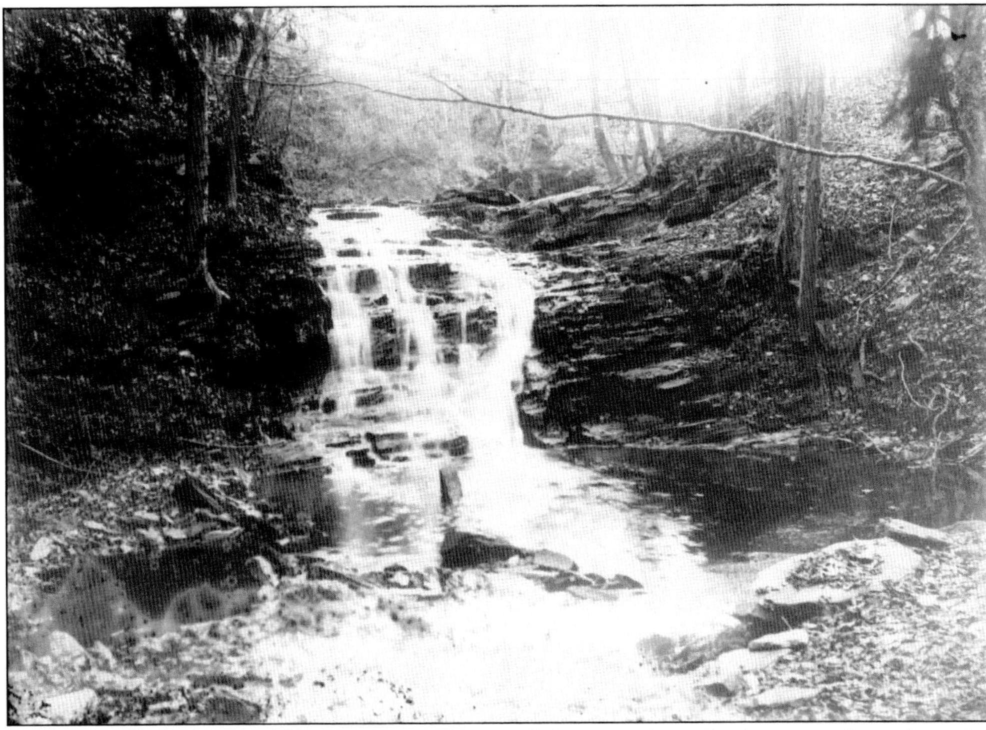

Waterfall at Lawton('s) Valley, c. 1890. The round object in the right foreground is a discarded mill stone. Early water-powered gristmills were established in Lawton Valley and at the Glen.

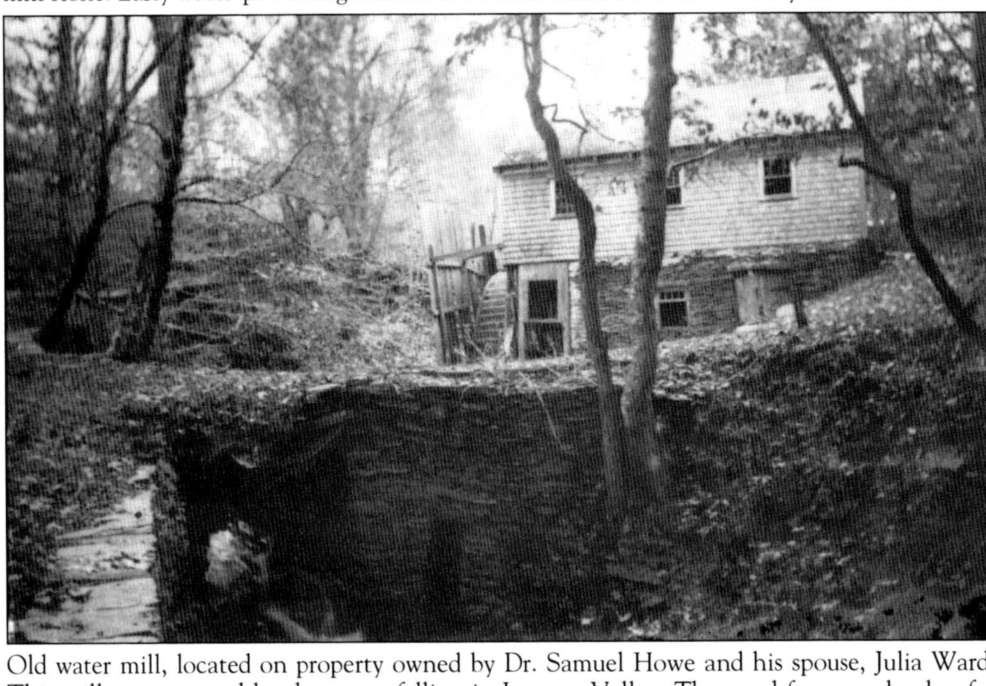

Old water mill, located on property owned by Dr. Samuel Howe and his spouse, Julia Ward. This mill was powered by the water falling in Lawton Valley. The need for sawn lumber for houses and fences made a sawmill a necessity; in 1642, land was given to James Sands for a sawmill on Mill River (known later as Barker Brook).

Portsmouth windmill. Numerous postcard images of Portsmouth windmills exist; however, except for the general location of Portsmouth, few owners are specifically named.

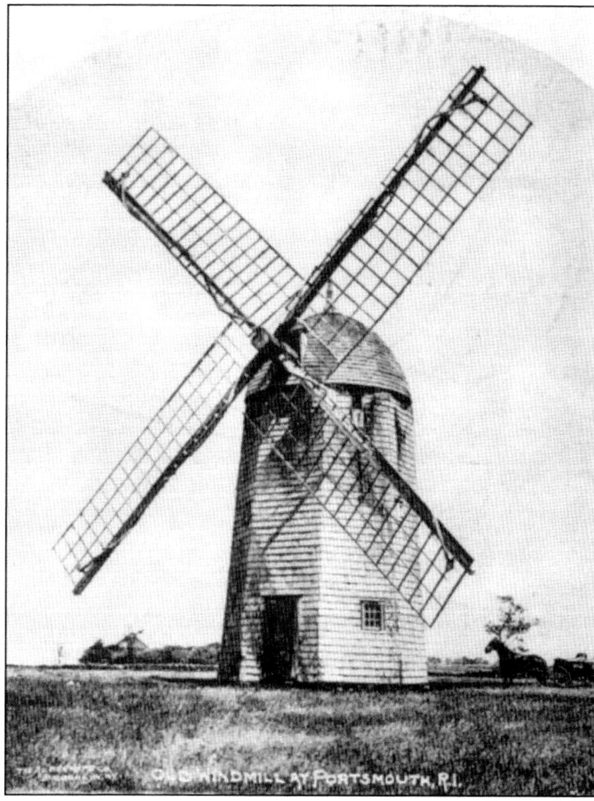

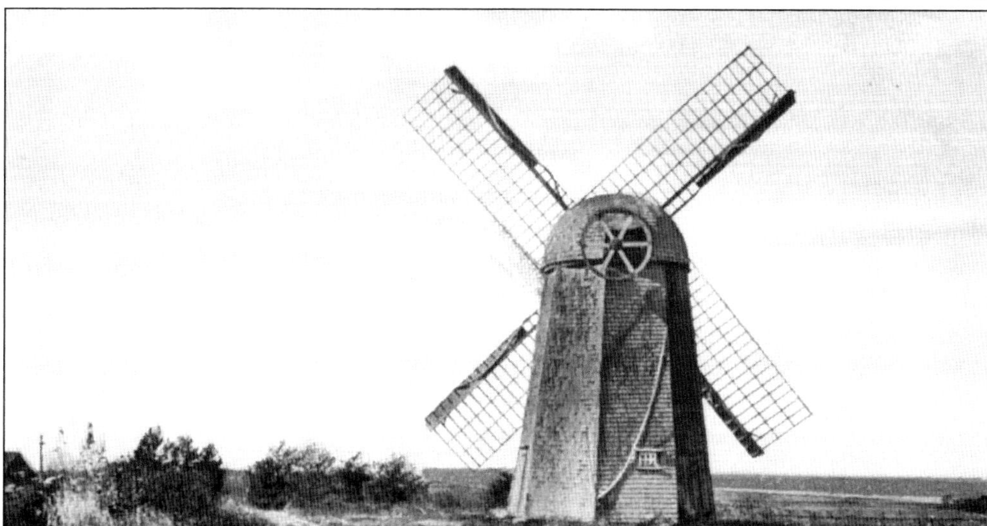

Windmill (1668) at Briggs Hill, later called Windmill Hill. From the description of the windmill pictured on this 1908 postcard, we discover that the old Briggs Hill Windmill ". . . On Windmill Hill at Portsmouth, R.I., is an old-fashioned Dutch windmill built over 100 years ago. It is about 8 miles from Fall River, and on a hill rising to an elevation of 206 feet."

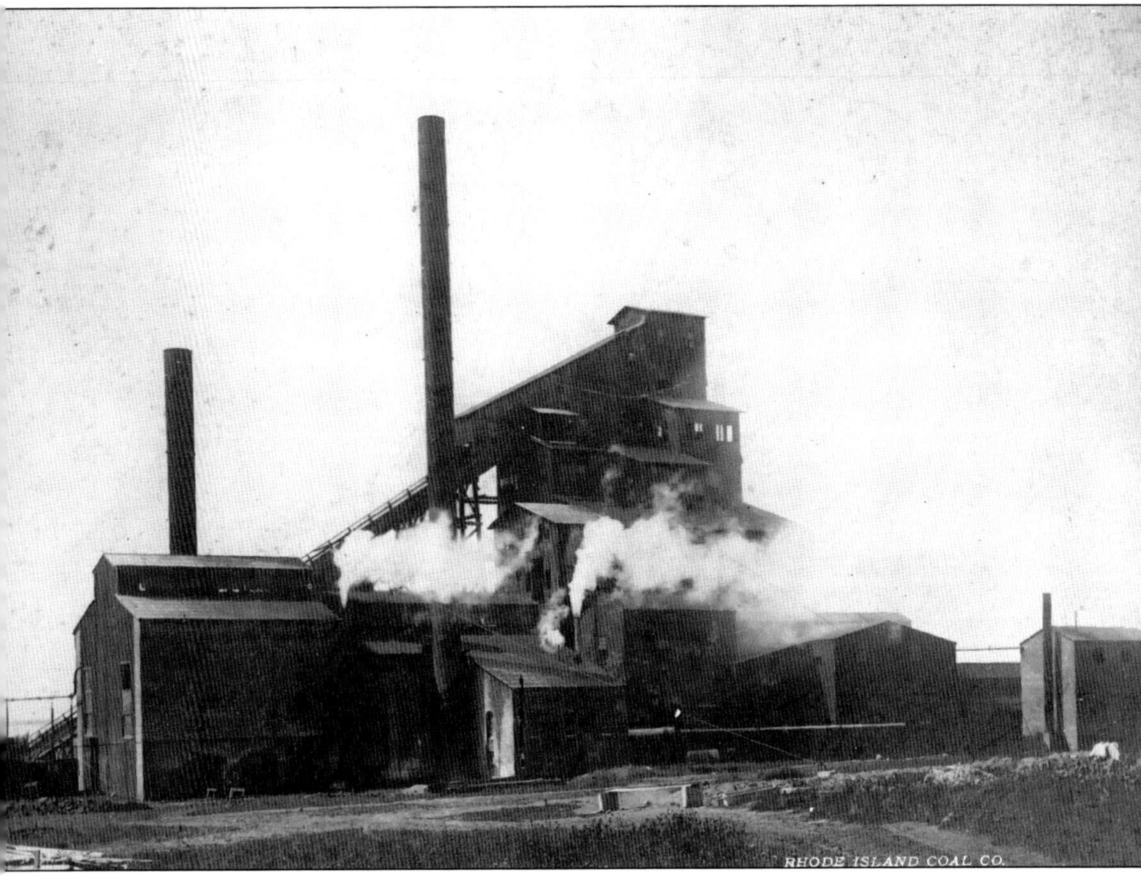

Old south breaker building, built before 1900. Coal deposits were discovered near Bristol Ferry in 1809; the Rhode Island Coal Company and the Aquidneck Coal Company were soon incorporated and mining began. The coal deposits had been used previous to this, however: British soldiers, in 1760, tried to use the coal for heat, and in 1887 Rhode Island Governor Lippett said that his grandfather had mined Portsmouth coal before 1787. The Portsmouth coal mines were many; there was a mine called the Case Mine (also known as the Aquidneck Mine) at the end of Willow Lane, and one called the New England Mine at the intersection of East Main and Sprague Streets.

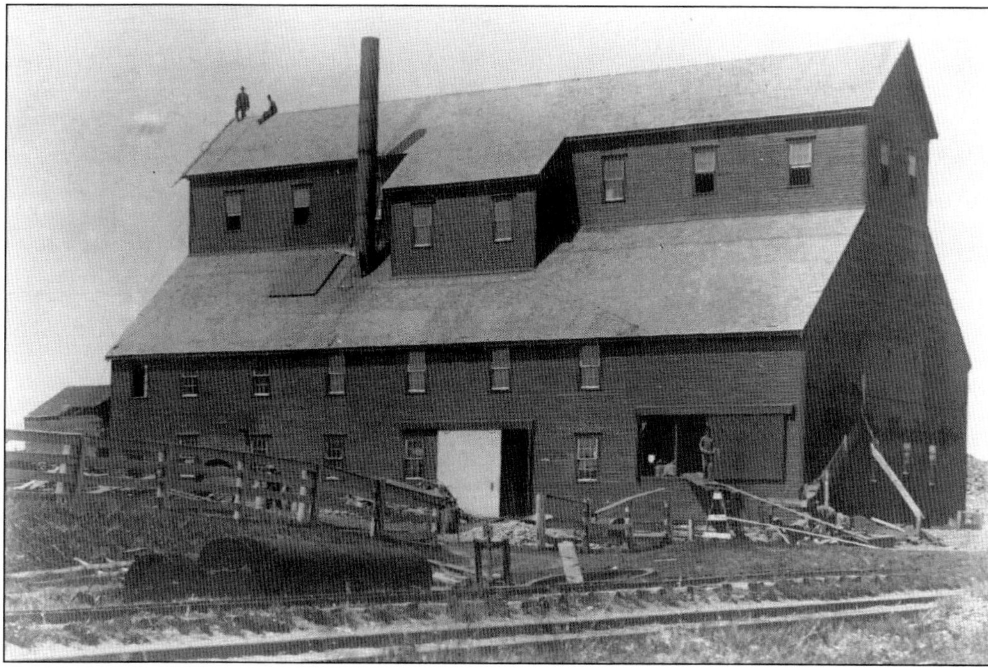

New breaker building, part of the 1909–11 construction. Early in 1909, the Rhode Island Coal Company incorporated in the state of Maine. The new company bought 400 acres off Willow Lane and reopened the mine in the Bristol Ferry area with modern equipment for the mining operation and safety of the miners.

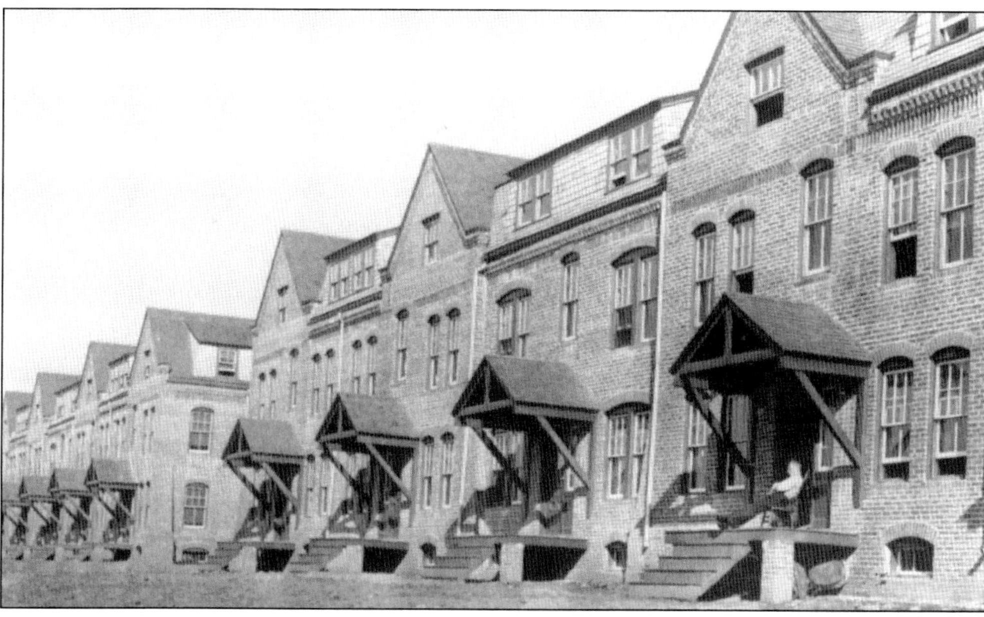

Brick apartment houses on West Main Road just west of Lehigh Hill, built for Portsmouth coal miners in 1910 by the Rhode Island Coal Company. A whole community sprang up around the area, including the Crocker Brothers & Cobb general store, a tavern, a Roman Catholic church, and other sundry commercial establishments including—we may assume—the ever-present company store.

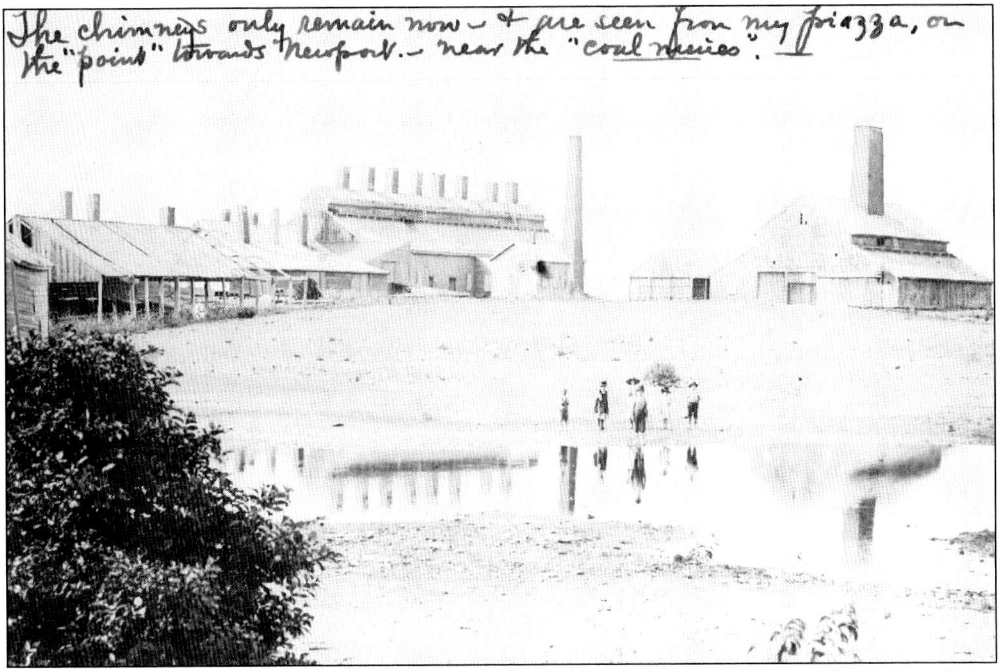

Abandoned smelting works in 1906. In 1866, the Taunton Copper Company built a smelting works near the coal mines at Arnold's Point. It consisted of eight blast furnaces, twenty-two kilns, engine houses, tenements, a store, a school, a powder magazine, workshops, a barn, an office, and a depot on the Old Colony and Newport Railroad. After the last ore was smelted in 1883, the operation was abandoned.

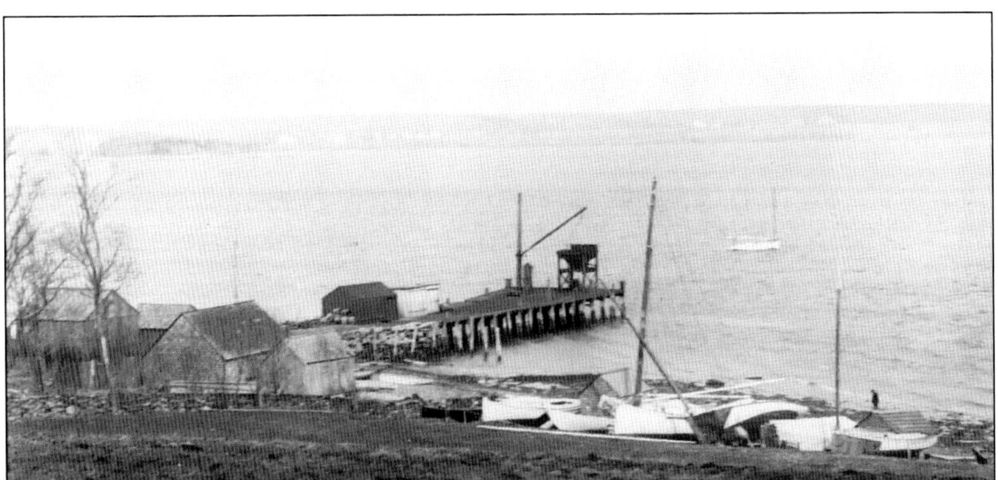

Power Street Wharf (also known as Brownell's Wharf), so named because coal was received here for the adjacent electric power station. The power station, built in 1898, generated electricity for the street railroad that traversed the island.

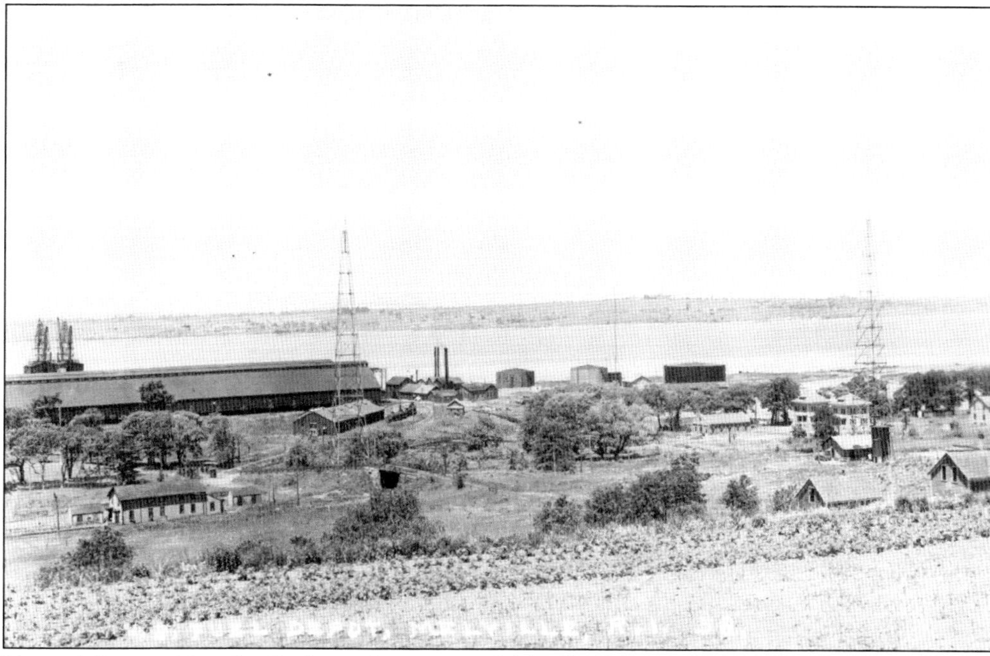

United States Navy's Coaling Station at Melville (an area sometimes referred to as Bradford). Fuel for warships based in Newport was received here from large colliers. This is some of the Chase Farm land condemned and taken by the federal government. Prudence Island is in the background.

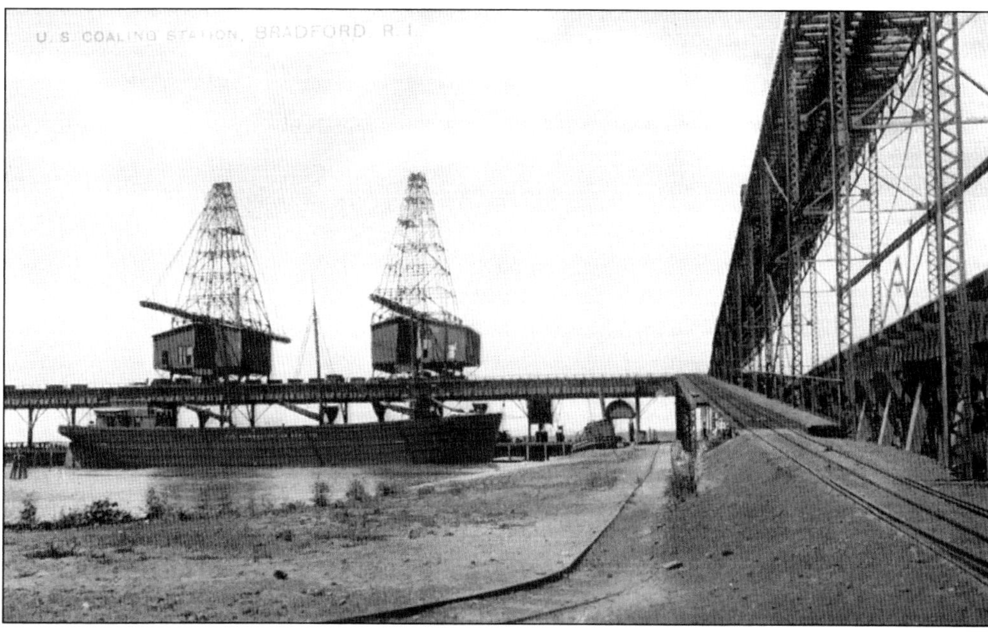

Coaling station's rolling cranes, used to transport coal from colliers to storage and from storage to ship's bunkers. The use of the Melville Basin as a coaling station began in the 1890s. During World War II, Melville became an important petroleum depot and center for patrol-torpedo boat training.

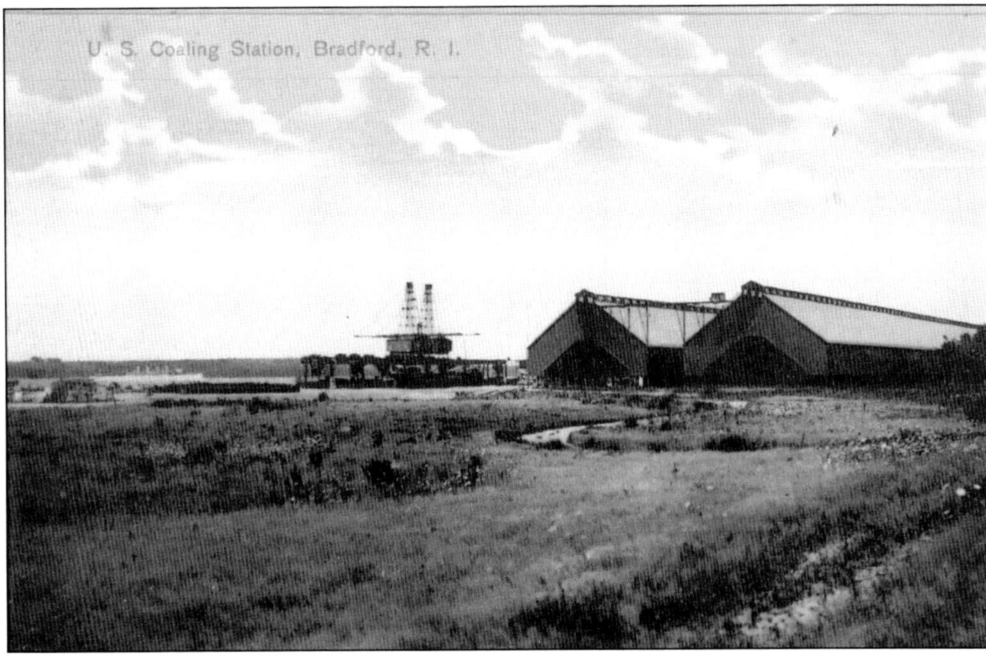

Coaling station. Before World War II, the Navy occupied less than 500 acres on Aquidneck Island. By 1973, the Navy controlled 30.7 miles of shoreline and more than 6,000 acres of shorefront property, much of which was obtained during World War II.

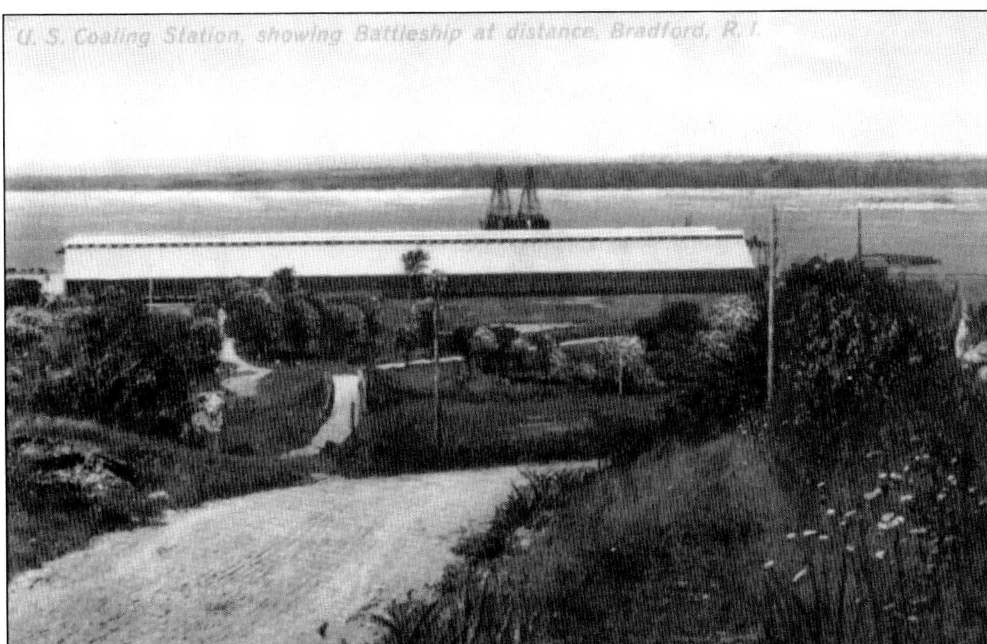

Part of the Burma Road, also known as Defense Highway, leading to the coaling station. The message on this c. 1910s postcard reads, "had a big fire at this place about 2 months ago—and lost lots of Bldgs, right on the water, but could not put the fire out. Oh my, it's funny ain't it?"

Six

Education and Faith of Their Fathers

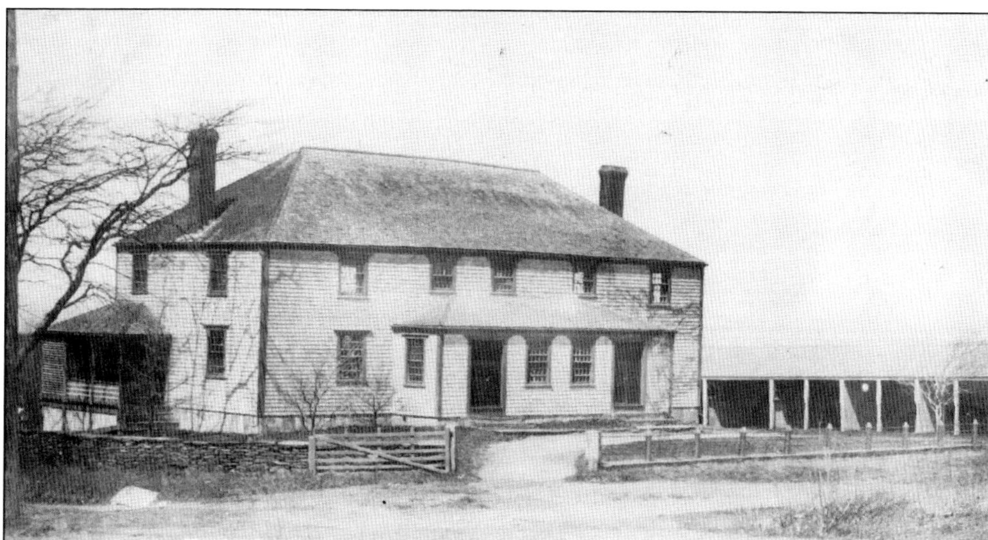

Plain wooden meetinghouse (*c.* 1700) on Quaker Hill. Religion had an important presence in Portsmouth life from the very beginning; religious meetings were held as early as 1641. The first Friends, or Quakers, seeking refuge from persecution, settled on Aquidneck in 1657. When George Fox, founder of the Society of Friends, visited the island in 1672, he attended several meetings in Portsmouth.

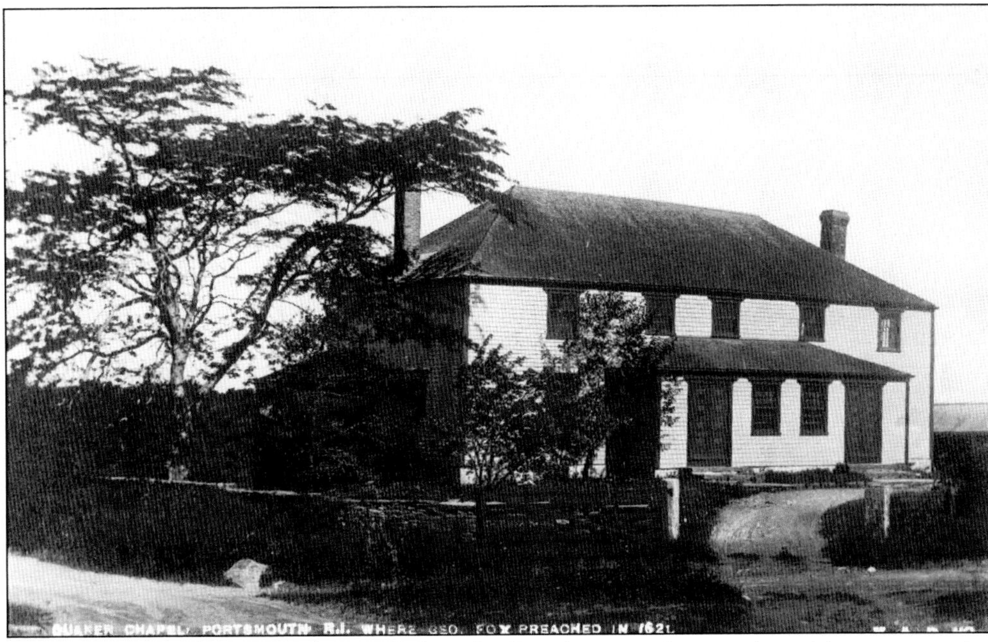

Postcard view of the meetinghouse. Before the Revolution, a large and wealthy congregation supported the society, but many left for other places during the war and never returned. The meetinghouse was used during the war as a barracks by both American and British troops. The date (1621) on the face of this postcard is erroneous.

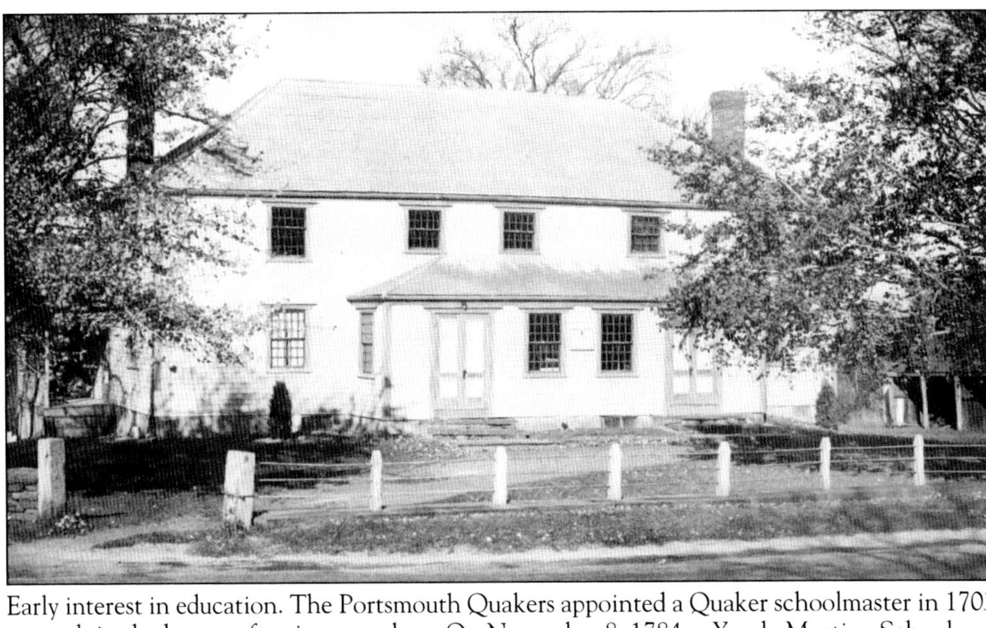

Early interest in education. The Portsmouth Quakers appointed a Quaker schoolmaster in 1703 to teach in the homes of society members. On November 8, 1784, a Yearly Meeting School was established at the meetinghouse; but for lack of financial support, the school closed four years later. The school reopened in Providence in 1819 as the Moses Brown School.

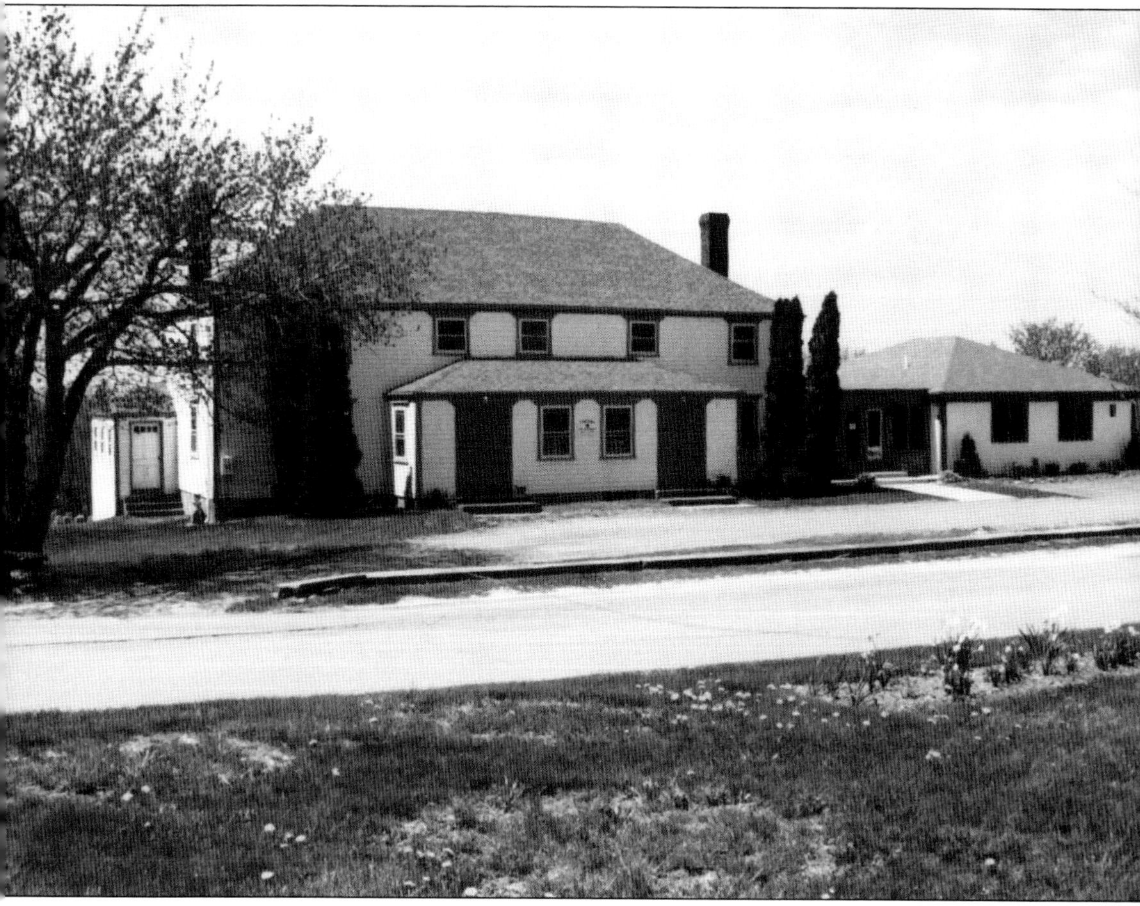

Contemporary (May 1996) view of the Friends Meeting House. As the oldest remaining religious structure in Portsmouth, it is a historic architectural treasure.

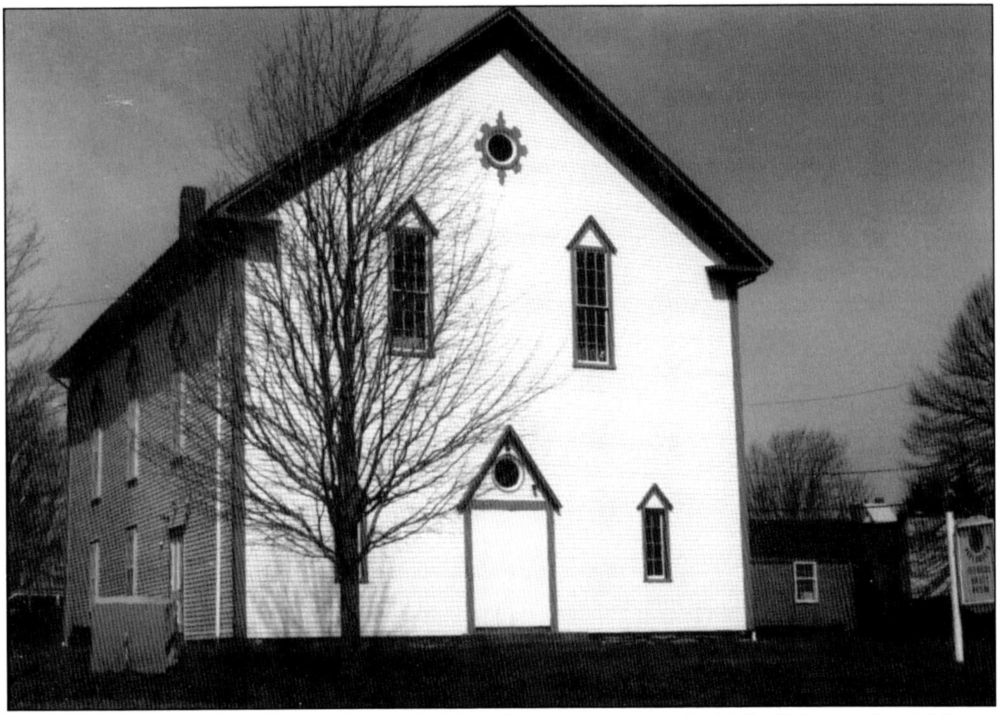

Christian Union Church building. In 1821 a religious society called The Rhode Island Union Society incorporated; in 1824, the society built its meetinghouse at the corner of Union Street and East Main Road. In 1865–66 the church shown here was erected on the same site by the Christian Church in the Town of Portsmouth.

Detail of restored mid-nineteenth-century stenciled border in the meeting room of the Christian Union Church/Portsmouth Historical Society building.

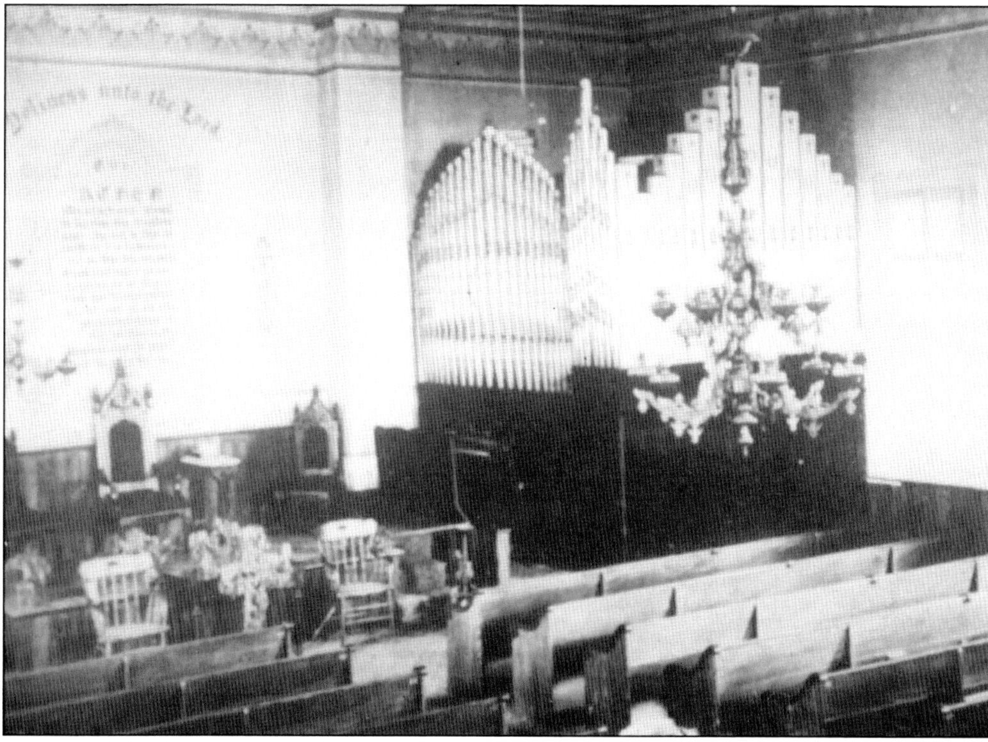

Interior of the Union Church/Historical Society building. Between the Civil War and World War I, the church had an active and flourishing congregation; it enjoyed growth for about a half-century. It then went into decline, and the last service was held in the summer of 1937. In 1940, the fourteen remaining members of the Christian Union Church voted to give the property to the Portsmouth Historical Society.

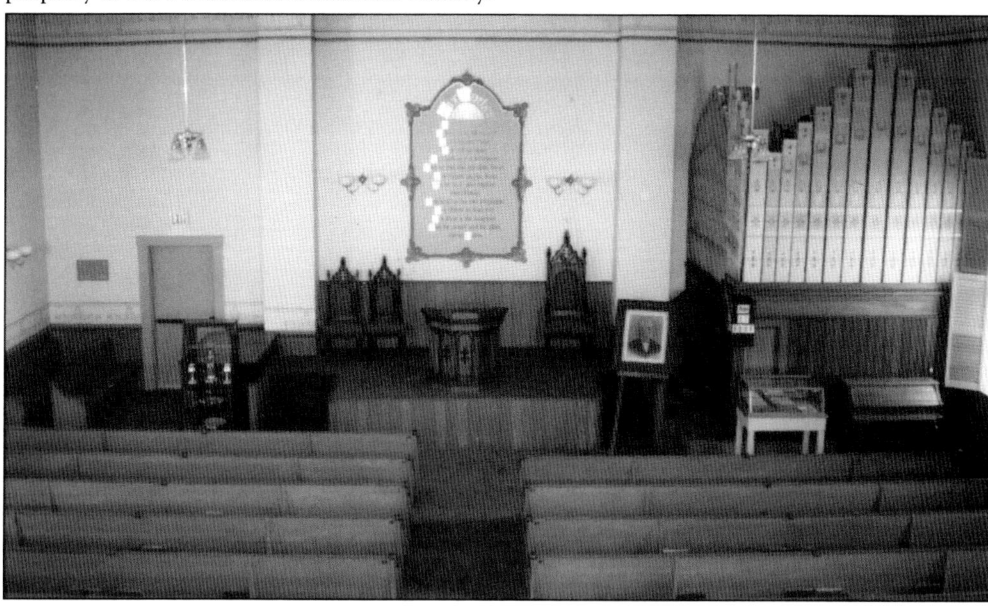

Contemporary (June 1996) view of the restored interior. Restoration was accomplished through three grants totaling $150,000 by the Champlin Foundation between the years 1992 and 1996.

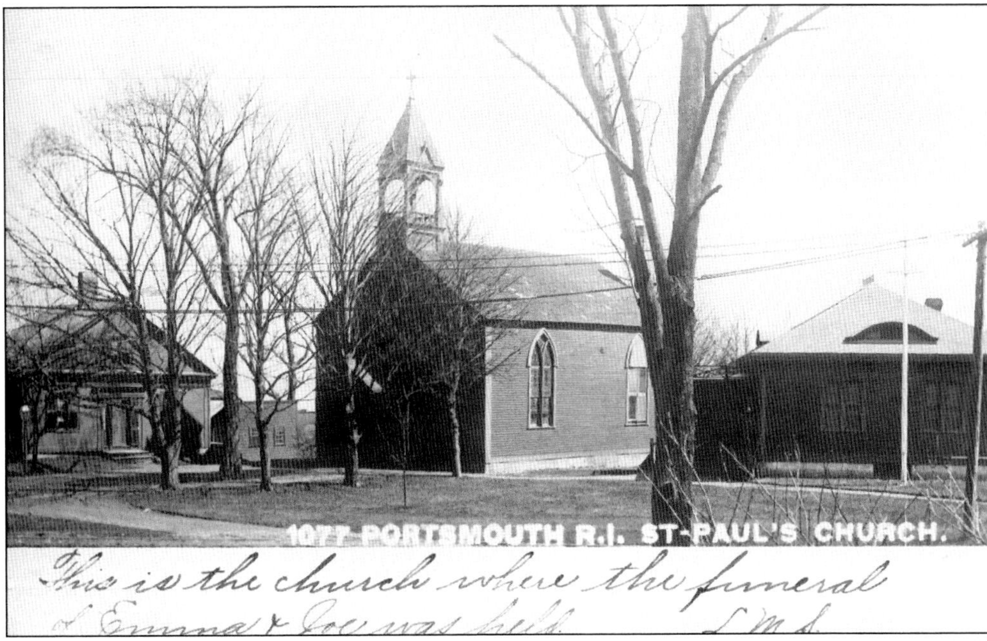

St. Paul's Episcopal Church complex. On the left is the Parsonage (1840), a one-and-one-half-story, Greek Revival building, end-to-end, with a central entry in the gable end. In the center is the church building (1833) designed by Bristol architect Russell Warren, a one-and-one-half-story, early Victorian/Gothic structure, end-to-end, with an open belfry and an enclosed entry in the gable end. To the right is the Parish Hall (1886), a one-story, hip-roof, late Victorian building, with eyelid dormers and some late Victorian details.

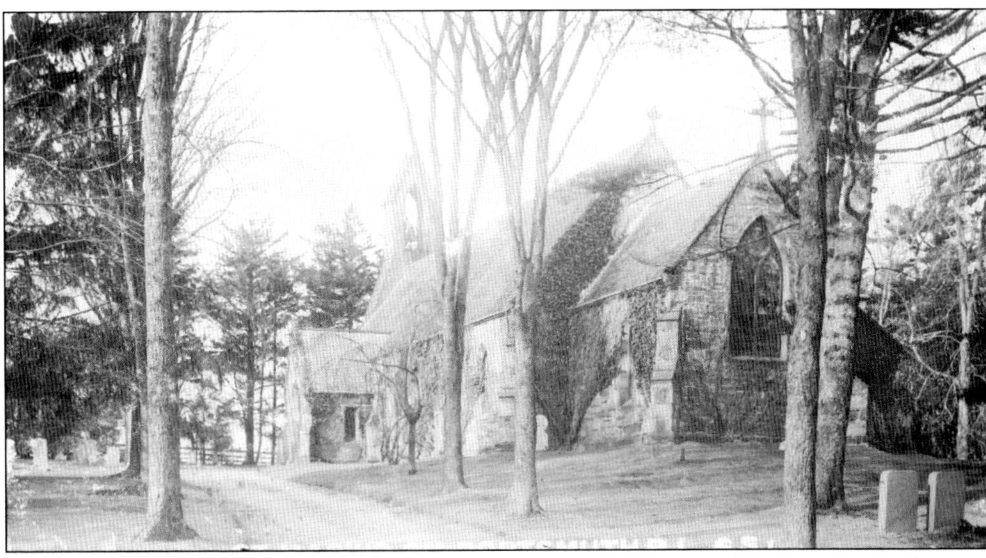

St. Mary's Episcopal Church (1850). A brown-stone, early Victorian/Gothic church designed by Richard Upjohn, the commanding features of this building are the projecting bell tower, stone chimney, and stained-glass window. The church and cemetery are on land donated to St. Mary's in 1844 by Sarah Gibbs.

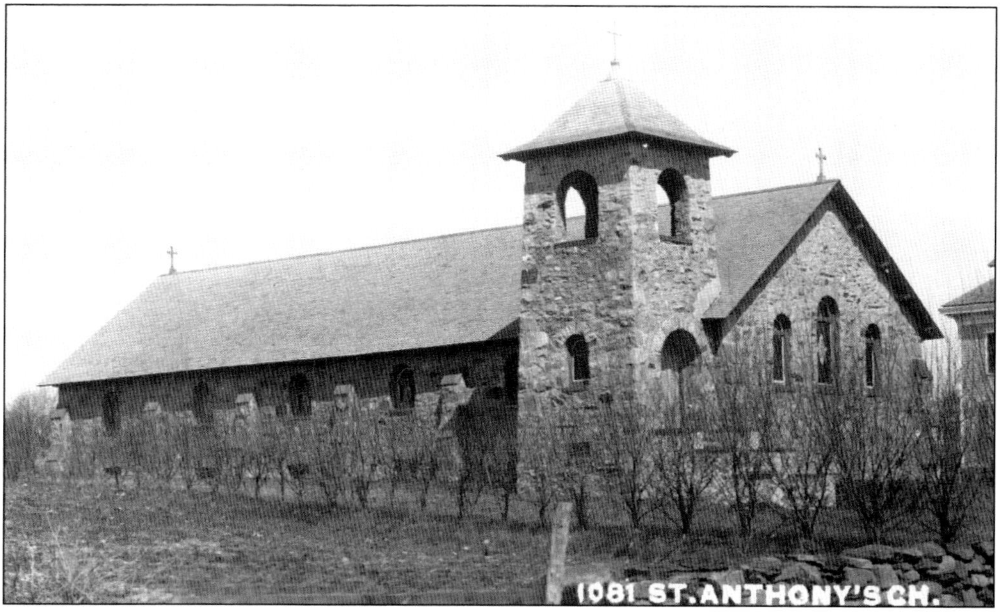

St. Anthony's Roman Catholic Church (1907). This is a one-story, early-twentieth-century, Mission-style field-stone structure, end-to-end, featuring a two-story square corner tower with a round-head door and belfry. The first pastor came here in 1908 when the parish also included Tiverton and Little Compton.

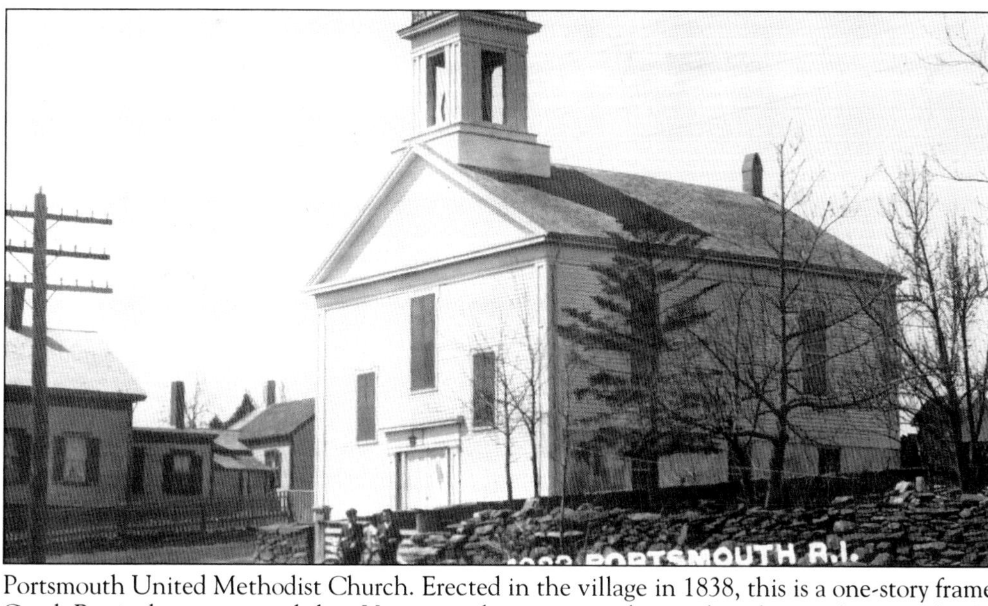

Portsmouth United Methodist Church. Erected in the village in 1838, this is a one-story frame Greek Revival structure with late Victorian alterations, end-to-end, and a simple square belfry in front. Unseen in this 1907 photograph is the large projecting pavilion with a central double-door entry, added in the late 1960s.

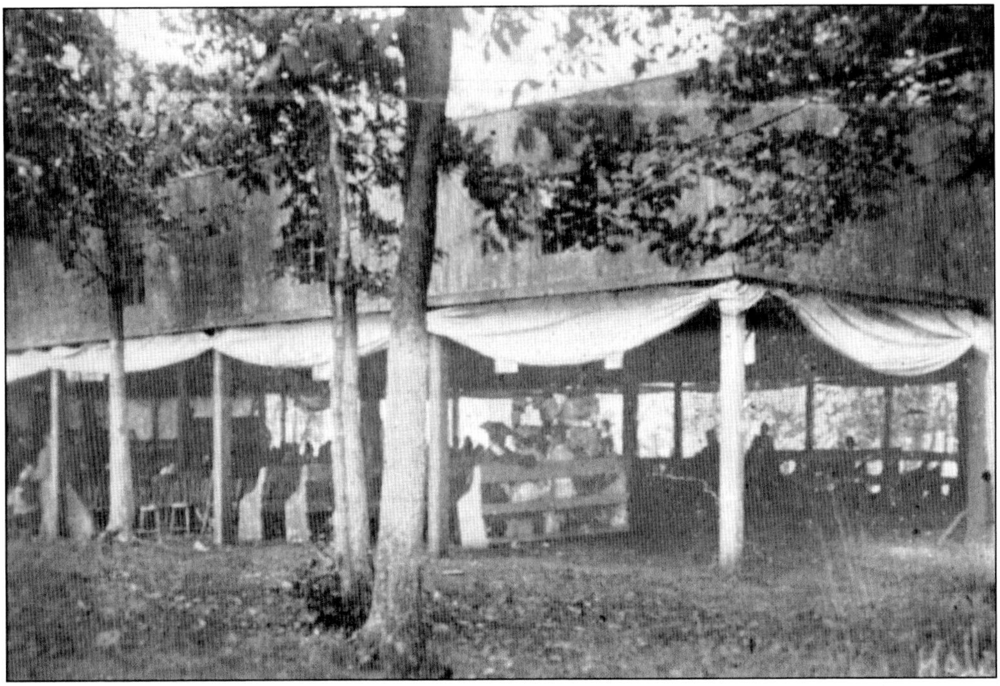

Tabernacle at the Portsmouth Camp Grounds. The Portsmouth Camp Meeting Association began meeting at the Hedly Street Grove possibly as early as 1891. This postcard's message reads, "Went to Portsmouth, R.I. Camp last Saturday and came home Sunday eve., had a good time in the Holy Ghost. Bless God for me."

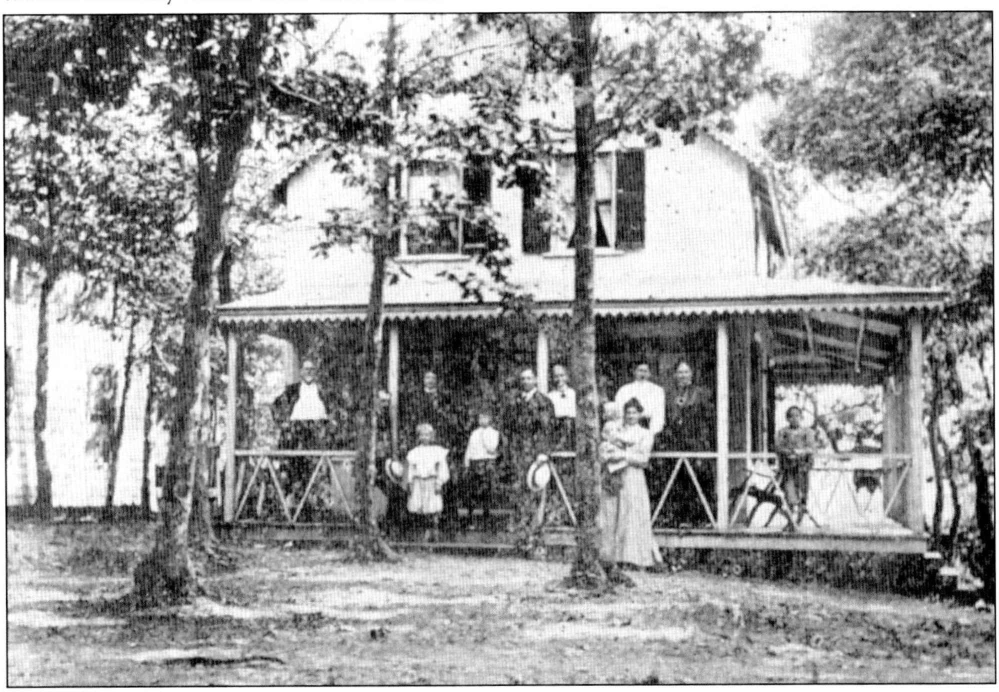

Gospel worker's cottage at the Portsmouth Camp Meeting. The grove is a complex of small and large wood-frame structures used for Gospel readings and other social and religious functions.

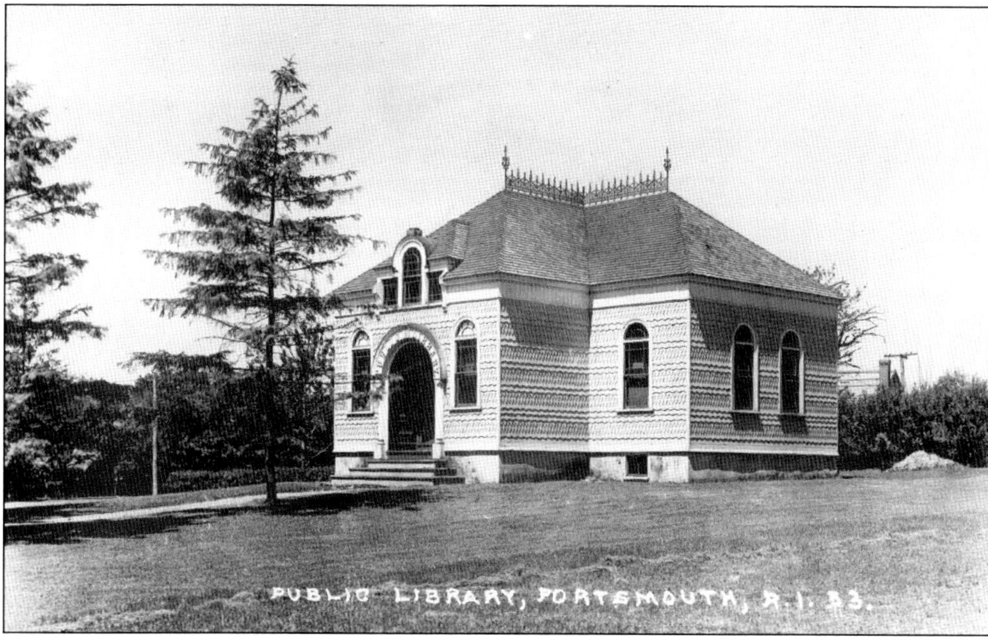

Portsmouth Free Library (1898), erected on land donated by the Borden family. This is a one-story wood-framed early Victorian, hip-roofed, with patterned shingles of unusual design. Note restrained symmetry of the building's overall design in this *c.* 1910s photograph.

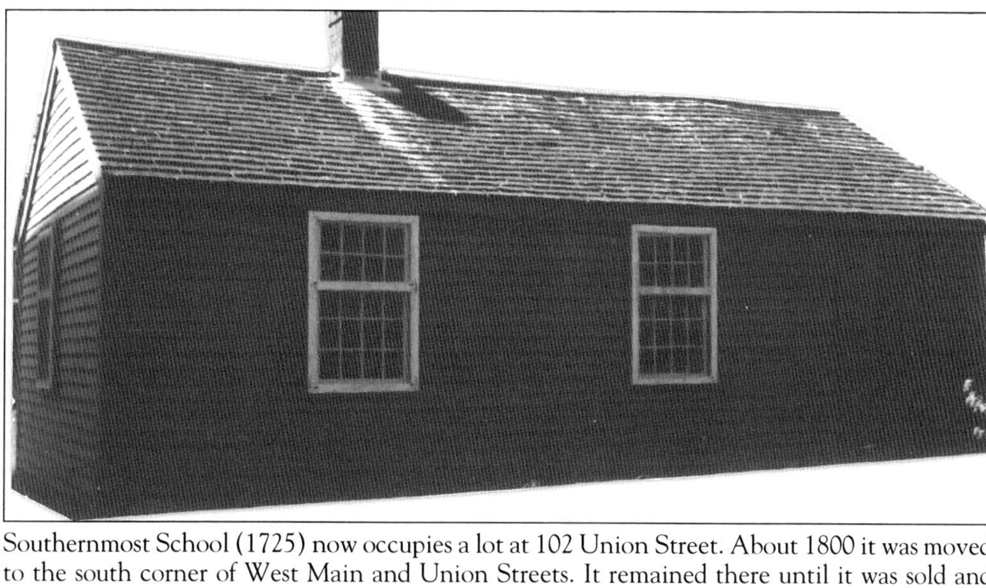

Southernmost School (1725) now occupies a lot at 102 Union Street. About 1800 it was moved to the south corner of West Main and Union Streets. It remained there until it was sold and moved to Lakeside Farm (559 Union Street), where it was used as a harness shed until 1952, when it was given to the Portsmouth Historical Society.

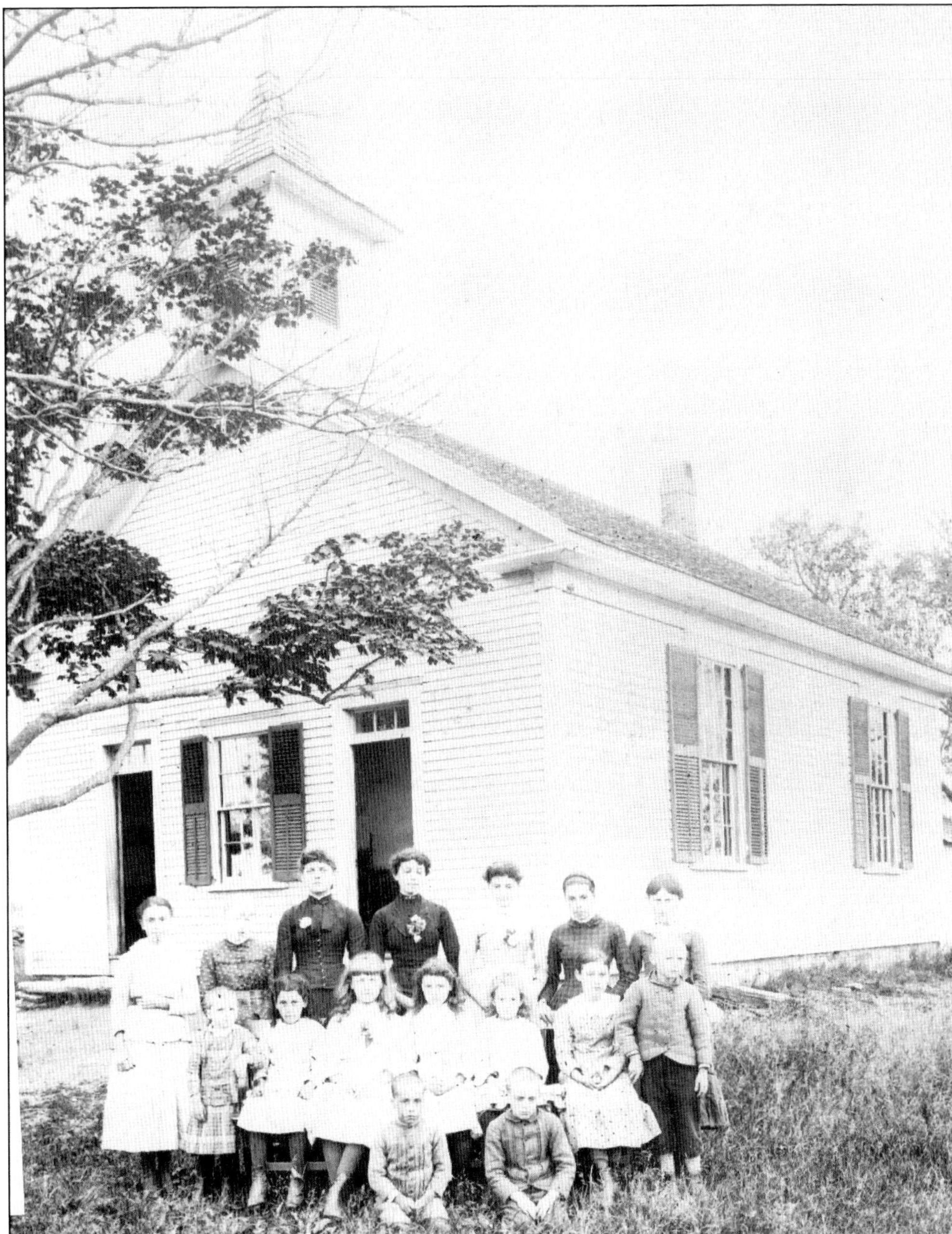

McCorrie School teachers and scholars, c. 1884. From left to right are as follows: (front row) J. Fred Sherman and Abner Anthony; (middle row) Eugene Coggeshall (visitor), Anna G. Sherman (Mrs. William M. Chace), Fannie Sherman (Mrs. Lewis Darling), Ruth Anthony (Mrs. John Spooner), Bertha Main (Mrs. Elmer Coggeshall), Jessie Allen, and William H. Coggeshall; (back row) Etta M. Sherman (Mrs. Donald P. Hurlburt), Annie Sherman, Sarah Almy (Mrs. Harry Sherman), Lilian Collins (Mrs. Alonzo E. Borden), Lois Anthony (Mrs. Frank A. White), Sarah B. Sherman (Mrs. A. Howard Bailey), and Gertrude Sisson (Mrs. [?] Cory).

Seven

Welcome to Prudence and Hog

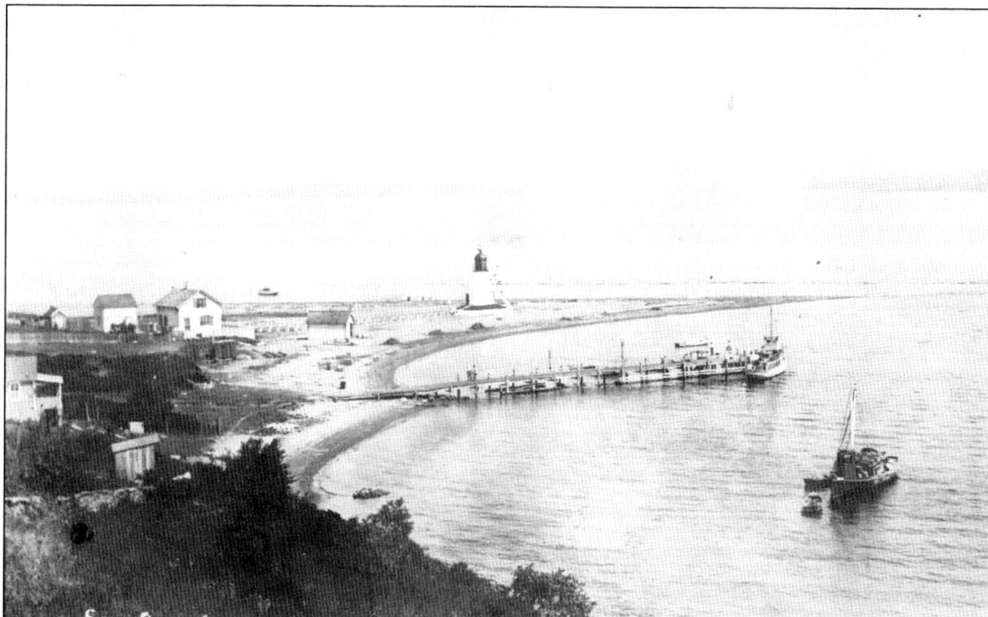

A 1919 view of the ferry landing at Sand Point Light, Prudence Island. The Sandy Point Lighthouse, established on Prudence in 1852, is recommended for the National Register. The pyramidal, cut-granite, octagonal structure has battered walls painted white, an iron-frame dome and cowl, a wrought-iron balustrade, and an outside gallery with a lantern 30 feet above mean sea level. Originally built in 1823 on the breakwater on Goat Island, it was moved to its one-acre Sandy Point reservation in 1852. The unmanned lighthouse was rebuilt, repaired, and renovated in 1855–56; it was electrified in 1939, and is still active.

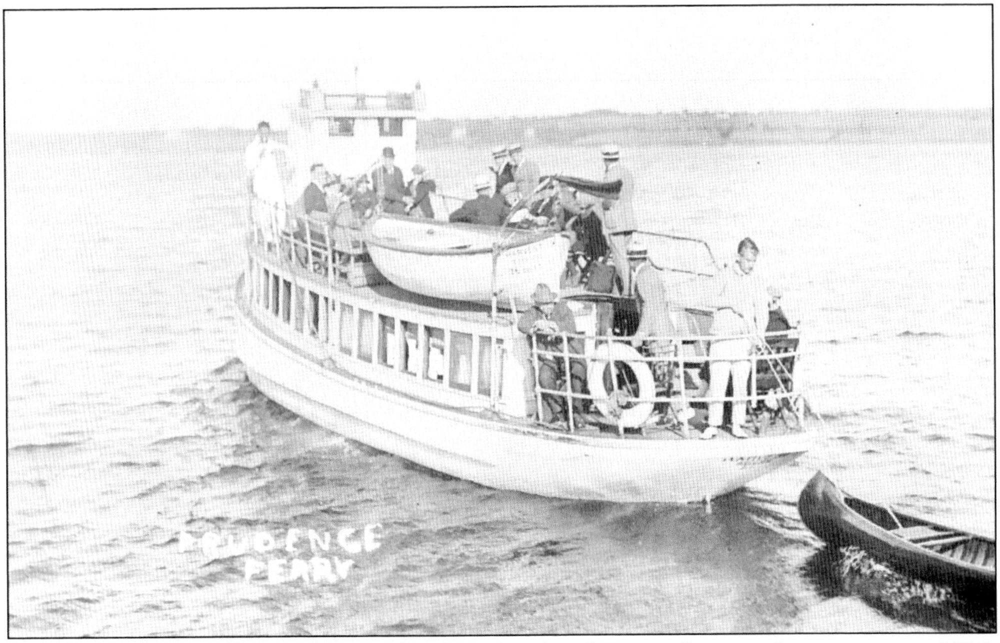

The *Mv Harvest* leaving Sandy Point for Bristol with a full compliment of commuters, *c.* 1918. In 1904, the present ferry service from Bristol was started by Captain Halsey Chase, who also ran Homestead Hotel on the island. Young Roswell S. Bosworth, future publisher of the *Bristol Phoenix*, is the lad starboard, by the pilot house.

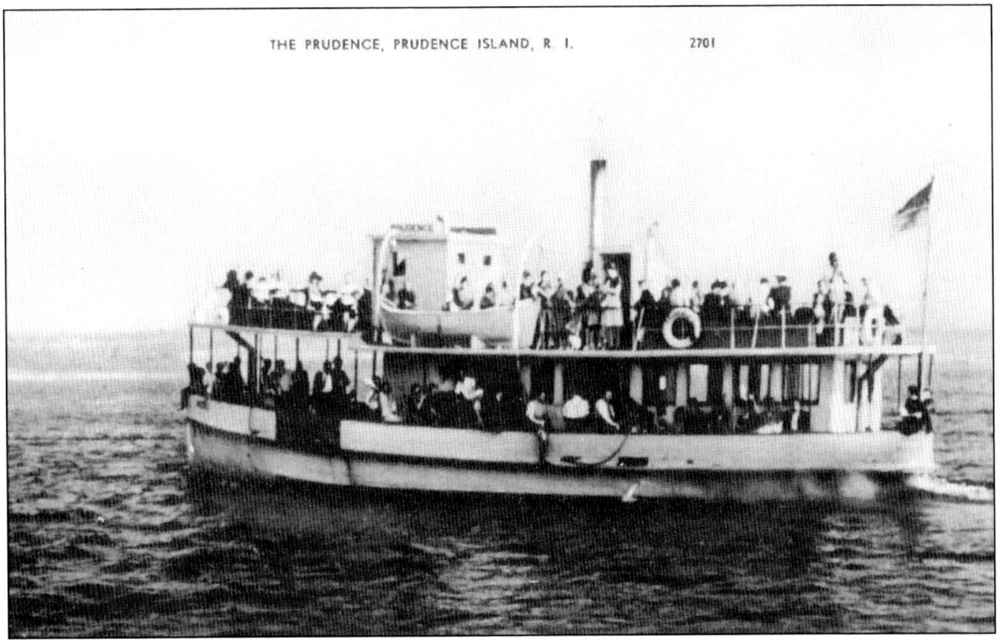

The *Mv Prudence, c.* 1912. In 1921, the Prudence Island Navigation Company received its charter to begin regular trips to the island. The *Mv Prudence*, skippered by Halsey Chase, made daily summer round trips, 1910–29.

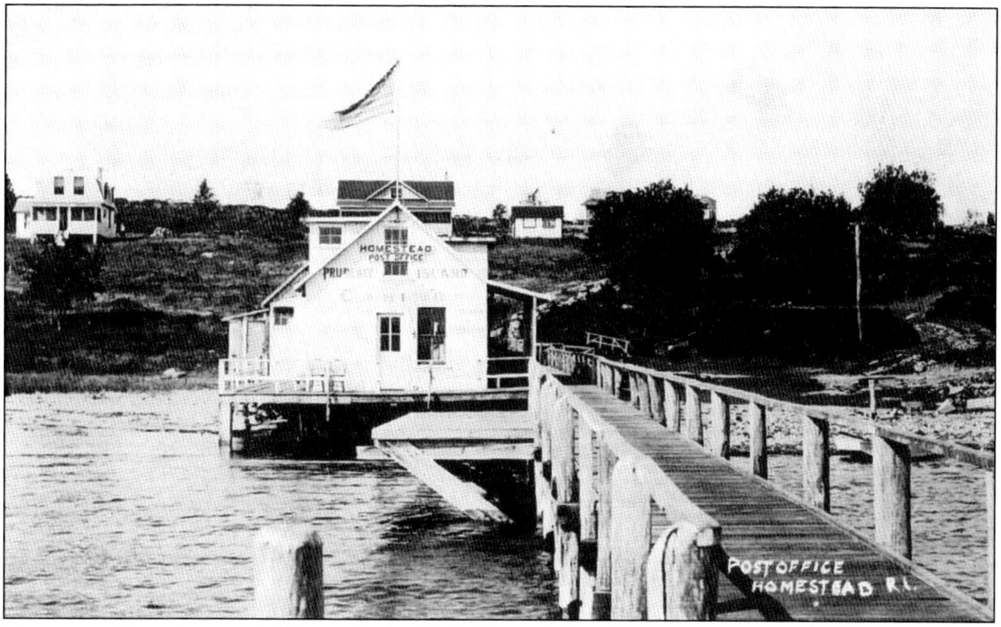

Homestead Landing, c. 1910, with the U.S. Post Office and the Homestead Casino building. In 1634, John Oldham received the island Chibachuwesa as a gift from the Narragansetts. After Oldham's death in 1636, the tribe reclaimed the island, and in 1637 granted it to Roger Williams and Boston Governor John Winthrop. Williams renamed the island Prudence; in 1647, it became part of Portsmouth.

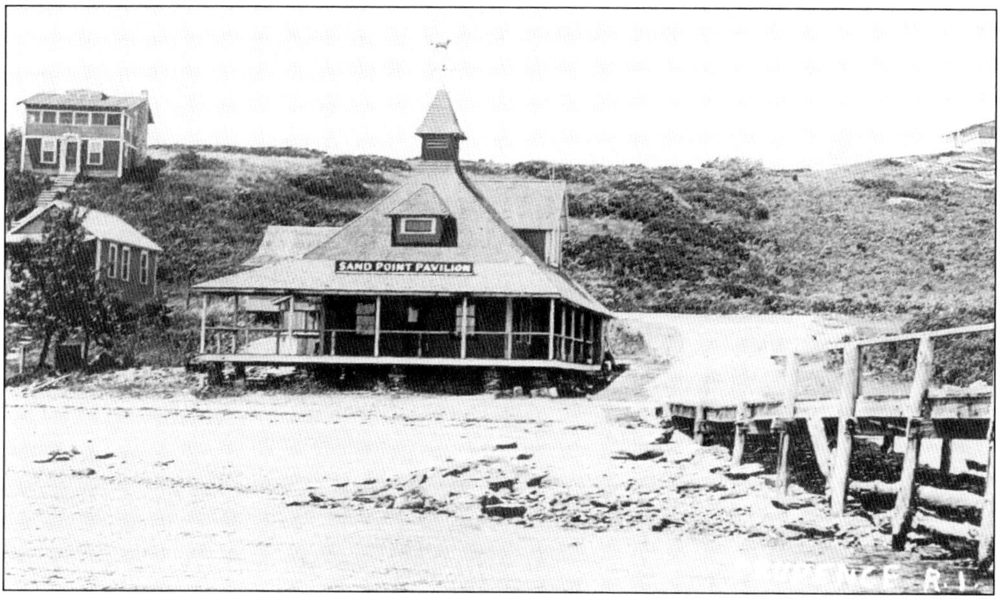

Wharf built in 1909 on the island's east side. At the end of the eighteenth century, Prudence, as other areas around the Narragansett Bay shore, began attracting summer residents. Around 1876, two cottages were built on the west shore of the island, and by the end of the century, Prudence Park was developed and seasonal steamboat service began. The wharf shown here, built on the island's east side in 1909 by the Herreshoffs of Bristol, helped engender a summer settlement. Later, a wharf was built at Sandy Point.

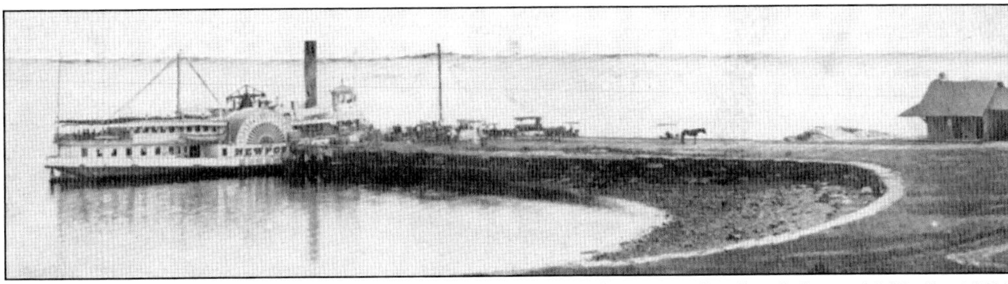

The excursion steamer *The City Of Newport* at the Prudence Park wharf about 1909. In 1874, the Sweet Farm, a 380-acre tract, was bought by the Prudence Island Land Company, and a small community developed, with streets named for streets on Providence's west side. About 1876, W.E. Barrett and G.W. Williams built "imposing cottages" in close proximity to each other; *c.* 1889, after more cottages were built, a casino complete with bowling alley, pool tables, and a dance hall was built.

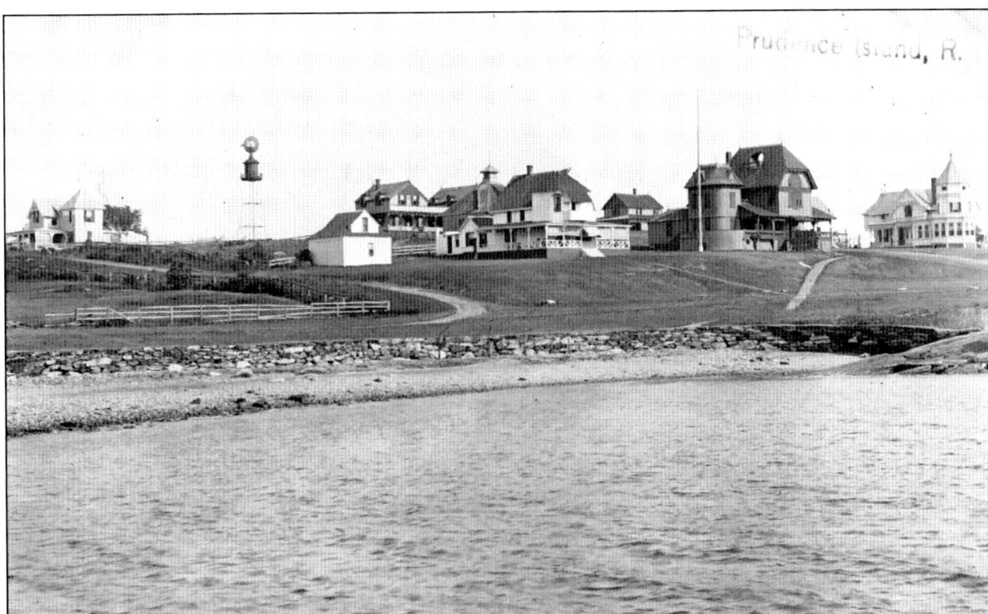

Prudence Park cottages, 1908. In the 1940s, the island's west side was abandoned by the steam boat service, as the east side began extensive development. Today, Prudence Park is a quiet and charming spot in an otherwise busy world.

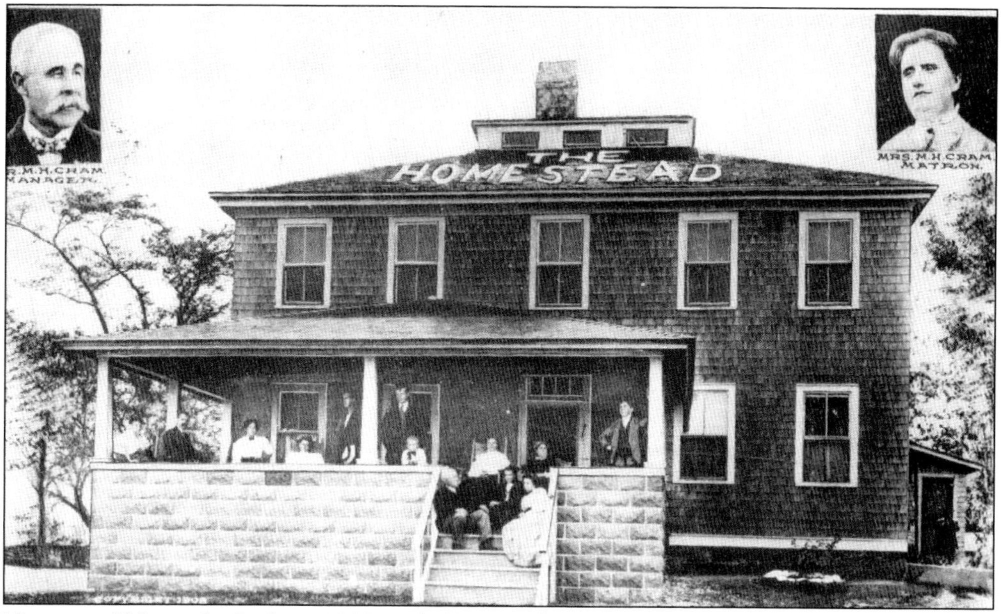

Homestead House, built about 1820–22 by Darius Chase, a great uncle of Captain Halsey Chase. Homestead is a two-story, wood-shingle, hip-roof building with a stucco brick chimney off-set from the roof's center. The central entry features a four-light transom in a five-bay facade. Homestead is one of the few early houses that survives. In this 1908 photograph the resort's managers, Mr. and Mrs. Madison H. Cram, are pictured.

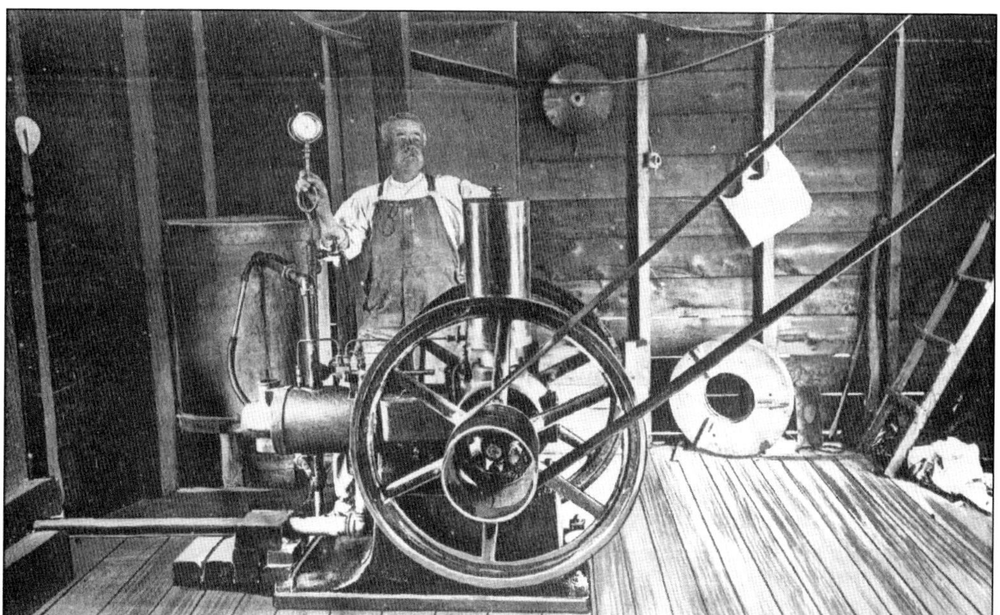

Interior of the Homestead House pumping plant. This coal-fired engine supplied enough energy for all the needs of the main house and its outbuildings.

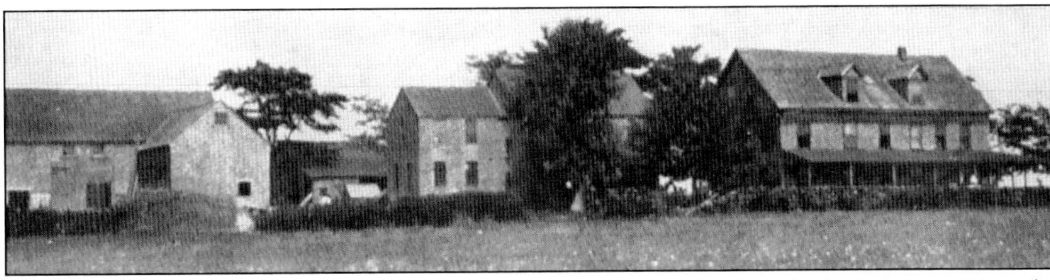

Prudence Inn (1894). Shown here in 1910, the inn was managed by Paul Chase from 1902 to the 1920s. The original structure, built on the highest point of the island by Lewis Herreshoff, was a two-story building with two interior brick chimneys, a recessed central entry, and two separate single-door entrances on the left side. It is near Sandy Point with a grassy front lawn that slopes gently to the water's edge. The house, built as a summer residence, underwent considerable extensions about 1940, when it was converted for use as a boarding house and hotel.

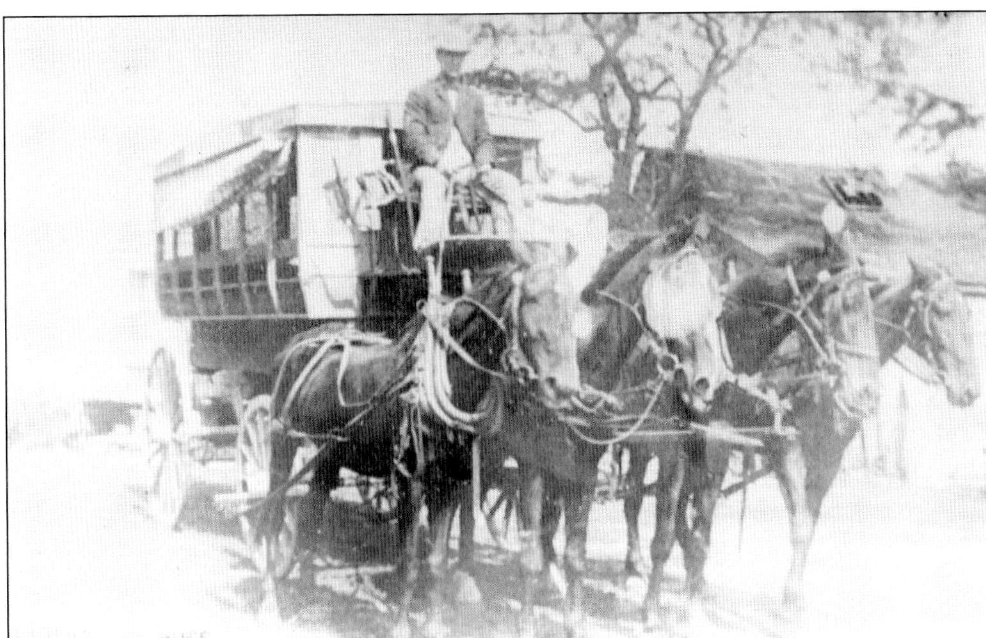

Prudence Inn bus, *c.* 1906, an important vehicle when Prudence first became an island resort. This four-horse-powered wagon brought passengers from the west side landing to Prudence Inn. Paul Chase is the driver.

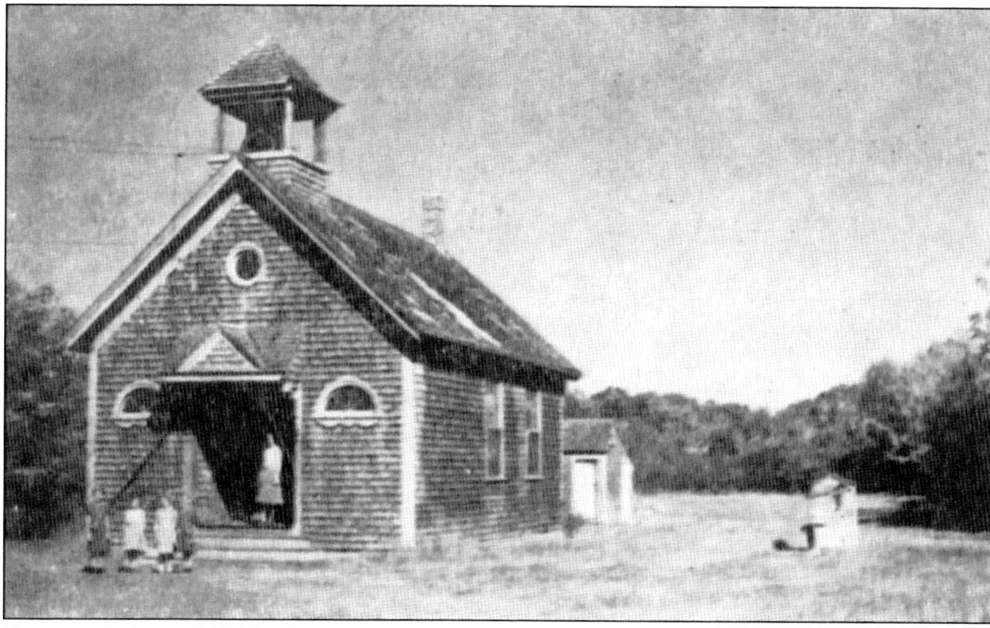

Prudence School (1896). A one-story frame structure, end-to-end, with a belfry at the ridge, it has a double-door entry in the front. A one-story addition at the right side was built in 1954. This was the fourth schoolhouse built on the island, the first in 1763. It is one of the smallest one-room schools in America.

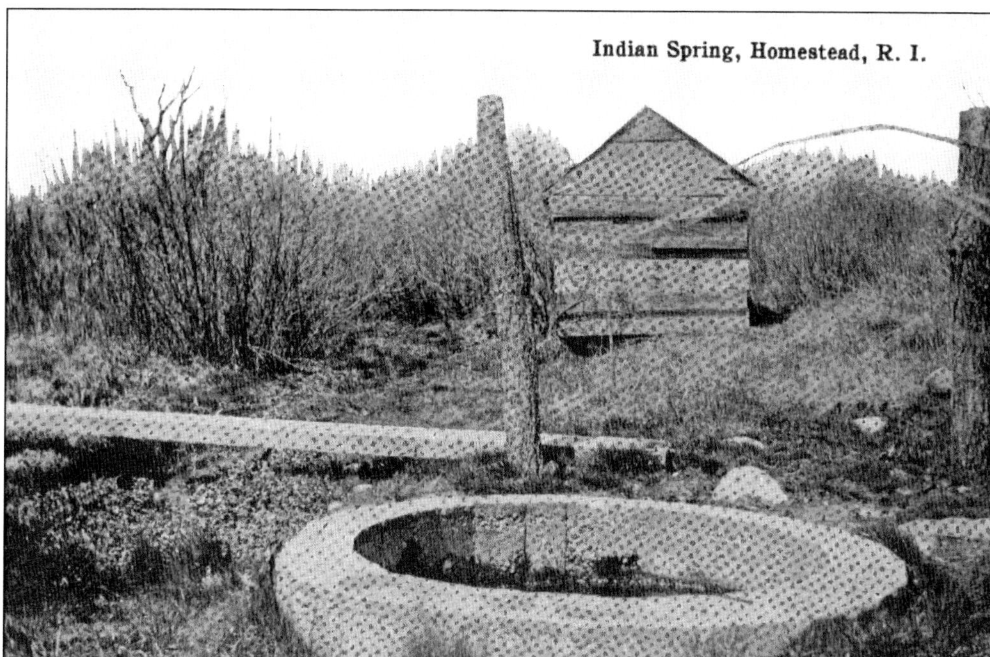

Old Indian Spring in 1915. Water has been drawn from this natural spring since the Narragansetts occupied the island. To this day, the spring yields a bountiful supply of crystal pure water.

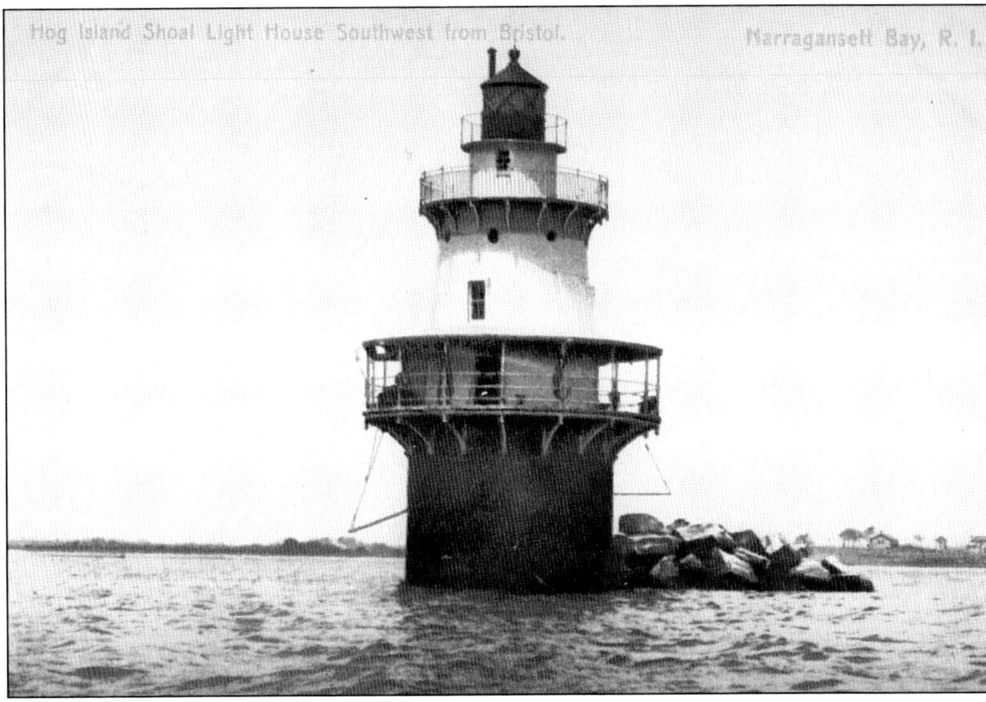

Hog Island Shoal Lighthouse southwest of Bristol. First lit in 1901, the Hog Island Light is a white conical tower on a black cylindrical pier with a white light 54 feet above sea level. This light is still active.

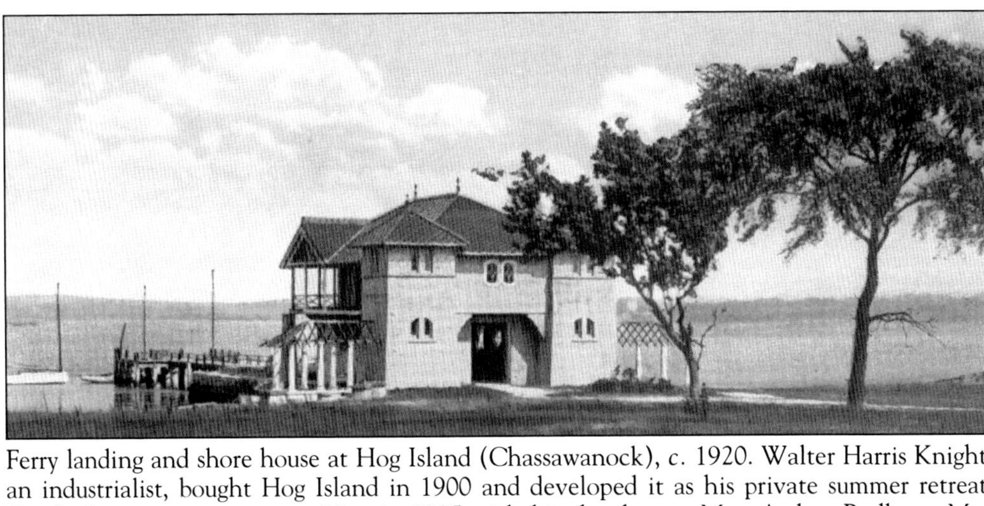

Ferry landing and shore house at Hog Island (Chassawanock), c. 1920. Walter Harris Knight, an industrialist, bought Hog Island in 1900 and developed it as his private summer retreat. Knight began summering on Hog in 1925 with his daughters—Mrs. Arthur Budlong, Mrs. Daniel Fairchild, Mrs. Harry Brice, Mrs. Arleene Wray—and their husbands, children, and extended families.

Manuel Sousa, a deck hand aboard the ferry boat *Ann M*, photographed September 1939. Sousa, as captain of the *Mv Prudence*, would later become an important link in the tri-angle service between Hog, Prudence, and Bristol. As his last important career move, Sousa later became Bristol Harbor Master.

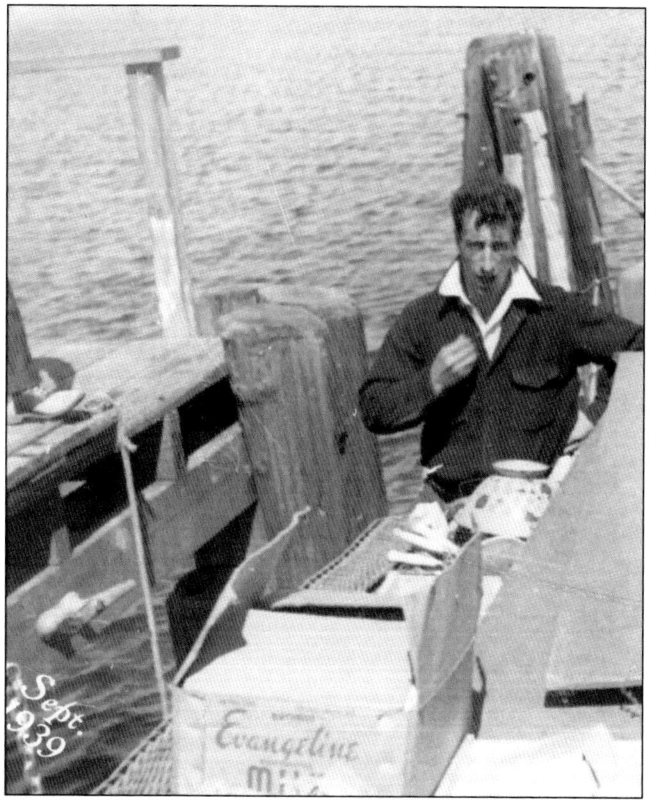

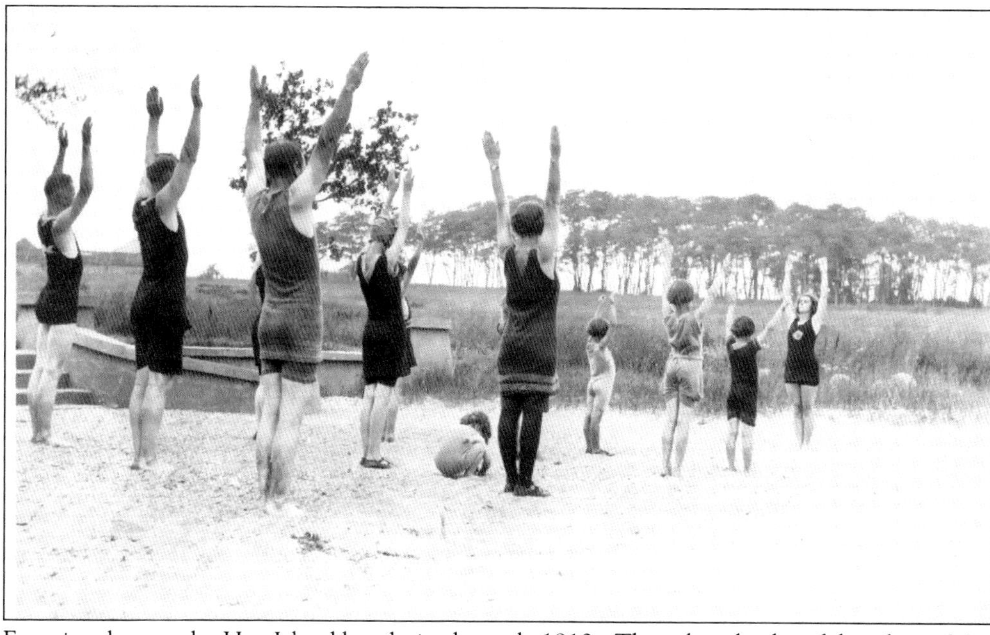

Exercise class on the Hog Island beach, in the early 1910s. The robust leader of this class is Miss Becky Chase, who became the first woman to be U.S. Coast Guard certified, and the first and only woman to captain the Hog Island ferry. Becky Chase eventually married and became the mother of Bristol's Halsey C. Herreshoff.

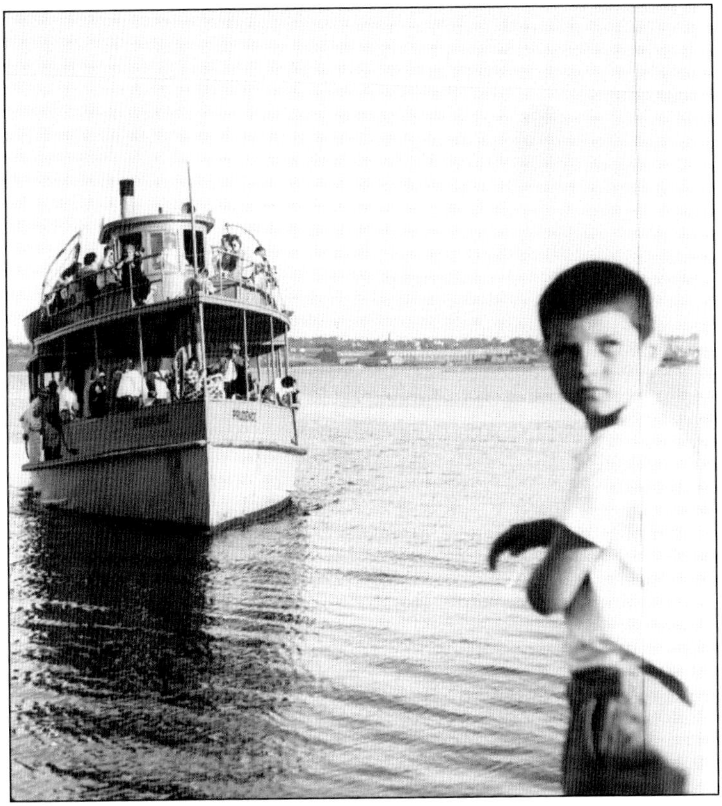

The *Mv Prudence*, *c.* 1940s. This is a seldom photographed head-on view of the ferry as she approaches the Hog Island landing. The lad at right is Gordon Fairchild, the great-grandson of W.H. Knight.

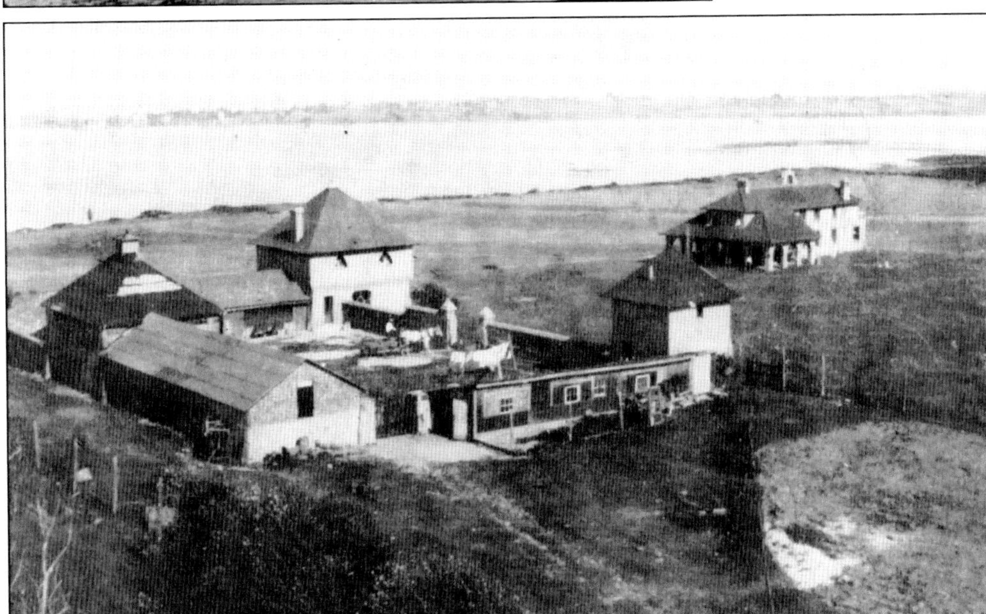

Bird's-eye view of the Knight compound on Hog Island, *c.* 1905, from the light tower. The building on the right is Knight's residence, called "the Big House" by the family; also visible in the enclosed complex is the farmhouse, the milk house, and the barn. The Bristol shore is in silhouette in the far background.

Eight

Retreat to Island Park

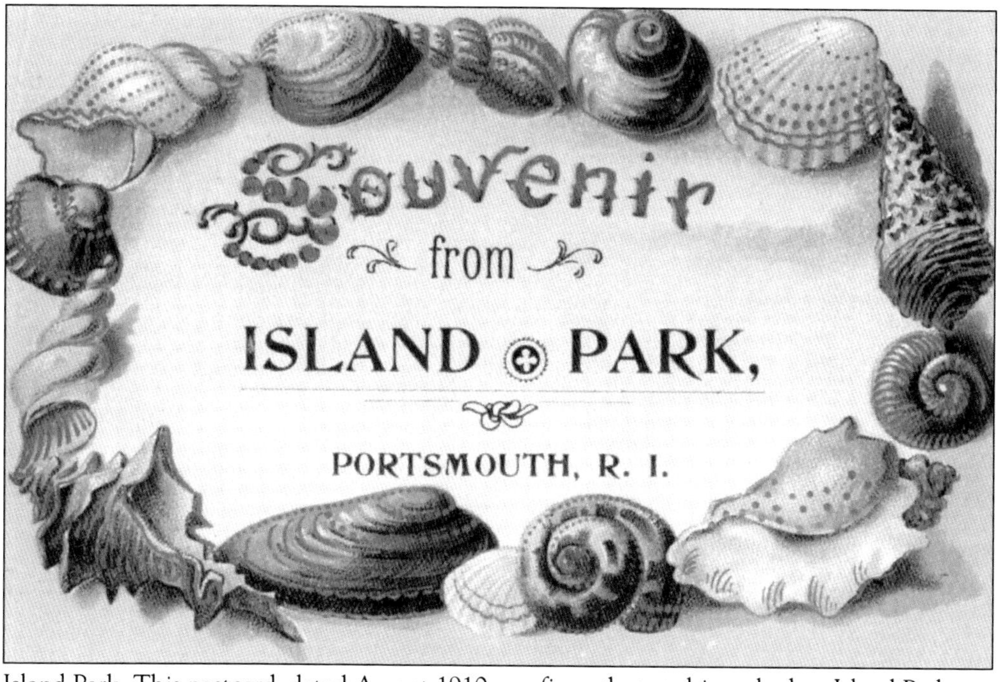

Island Park. This postcard, dated August 1910, confirms that at this early date Island Park was already a well-established resort. This general area was first officially known as Ferry Neck, then Greene Farm, and finally Island Park. Though the section has a long and diverse history, from pre-colonial days to present, permanent development of the section came about because the principal dirt road through the area was the main highway to the ferry. The road was generally called Ferry Neck Road, but it was called Buffum's Lane by local area residents. To end confusion, on February 13, 1899, the thoroughfare's name officially became Park Avenue.

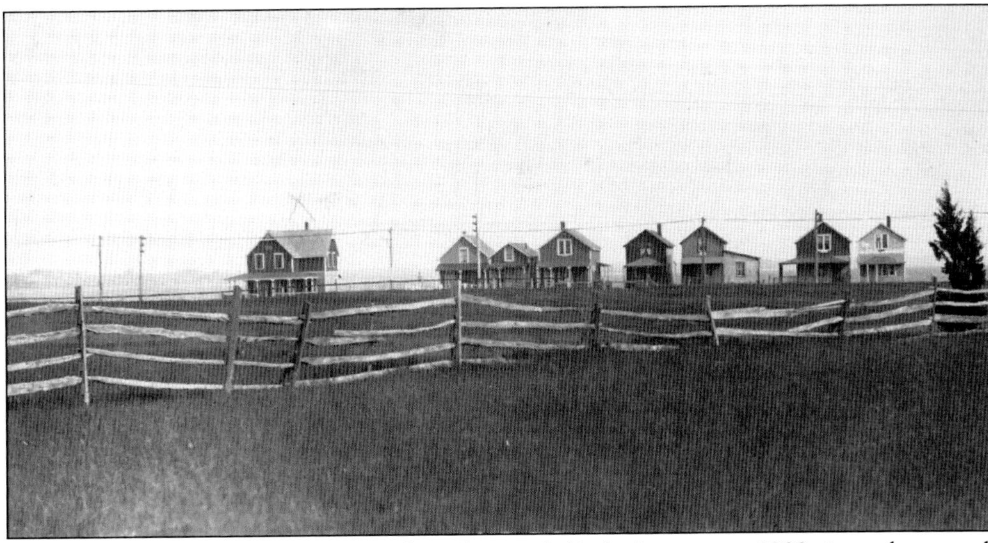

Several of the cottages beginning to line shore-side Park Avenue, *c.* 1908, in a photograph taken from a grazing pasture. In 1901, the Portsmouth Town Council granted a license to Joseph Lunan and Son to establish a shooting gallery on the Greene Estate. It is on this license that the name Island Park first appears in town records.

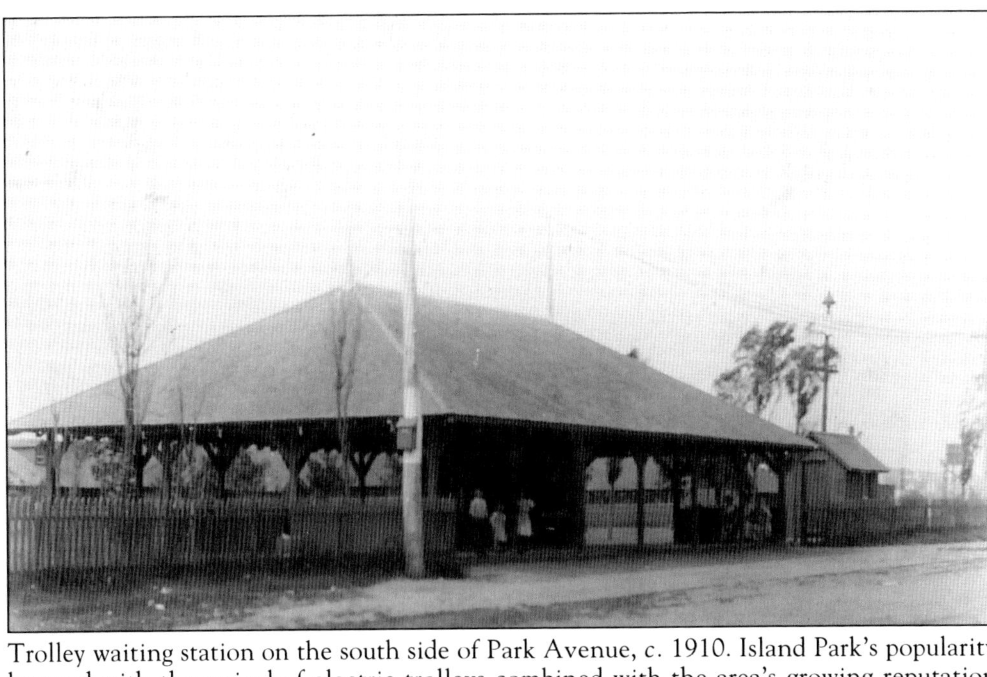

Trolley waiting station on the south side of Park Avenue, *c.* 1910. Island Park's popularity boomed with the arrival of electric trolleys combined with the area's growing reputation as place for amusements to suit all tastes. This postcard's message proclaims, ". . . Bill of Fare: BEER 25 cents, ICE-CREAM SODA 10 cents, POST CARDS 5 cents each, and clamfritters galore."

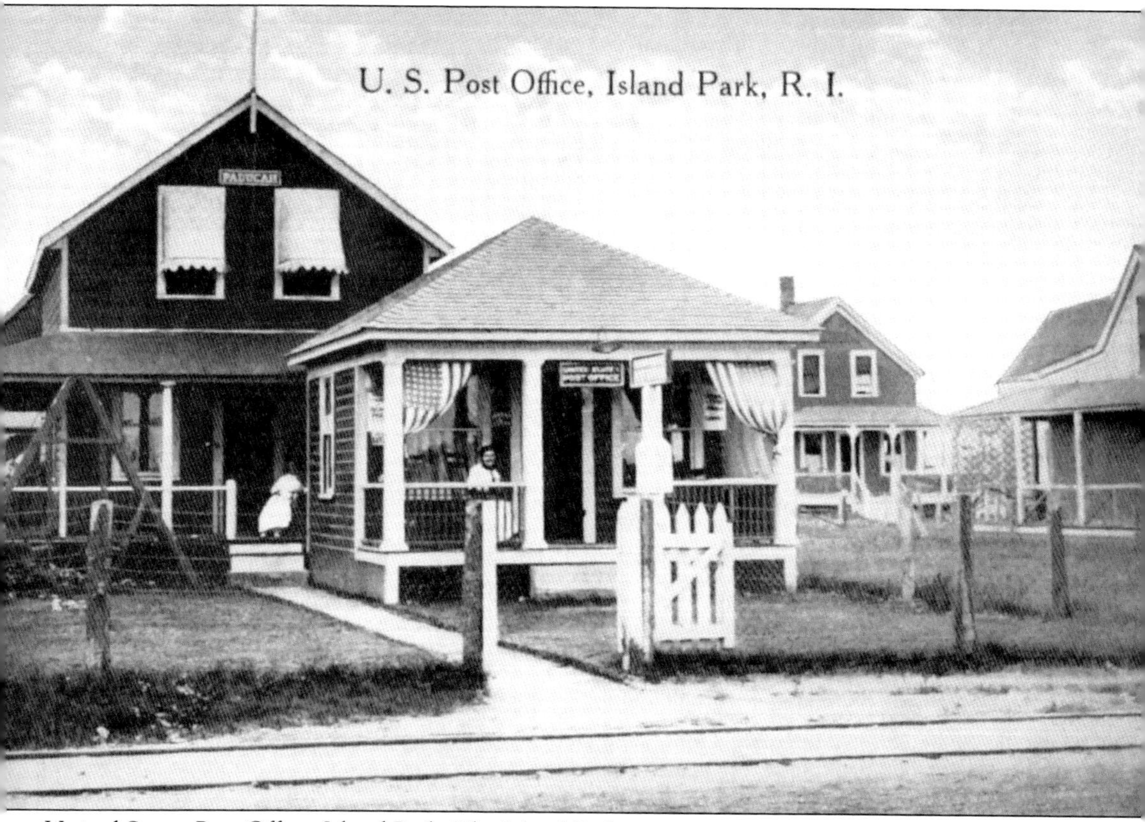

United States Post Office, Island Park. The Island Park community grew as increasing numbers of people arrived, lured by the amusements and concessions established by owners of the electric trolley company. Even the United States Post Office set up a small office to serve the growing numbers of permanent and summer residents.

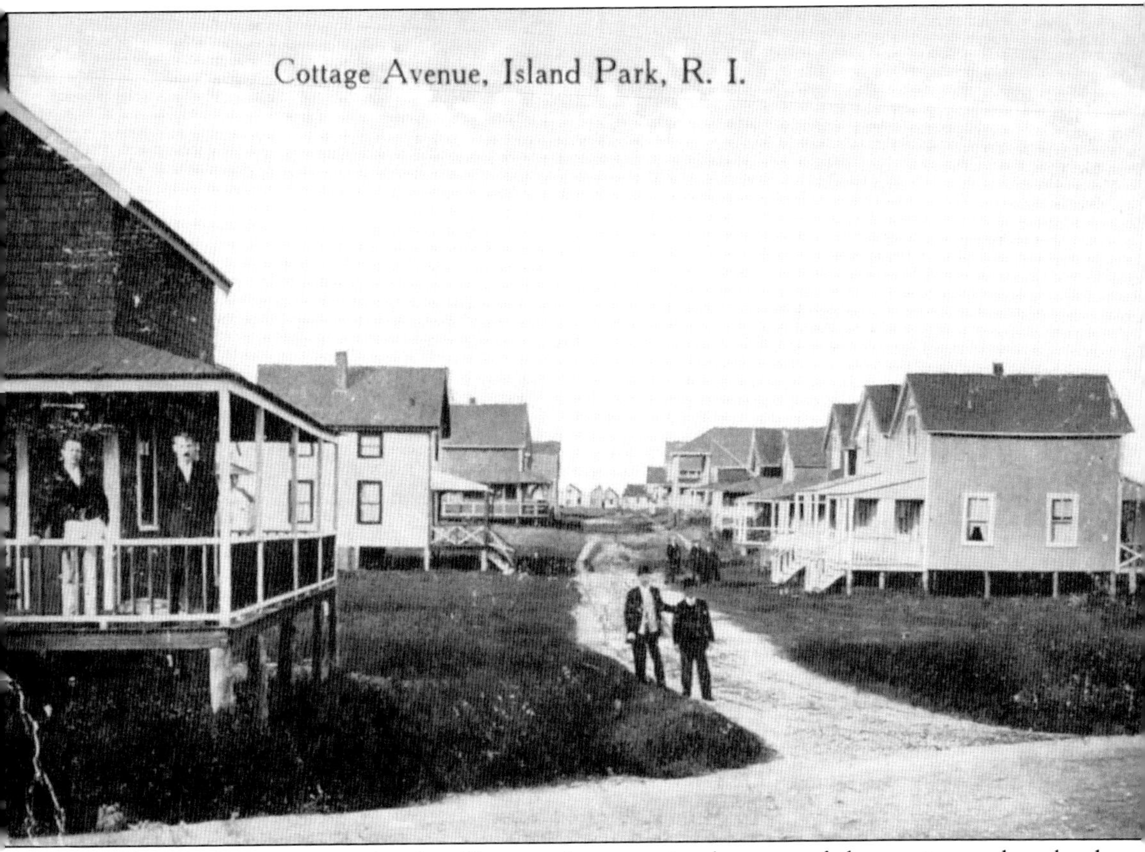

Cluster of cottages on the dirt Cottage Avenue. At the turn of the century, when land was comparatively cheap and zoning and sanitary regulations hardly existed, the area experienced a building boom. This cluster of cottages on Cottage Avenue seems to disappear into deep perspective.

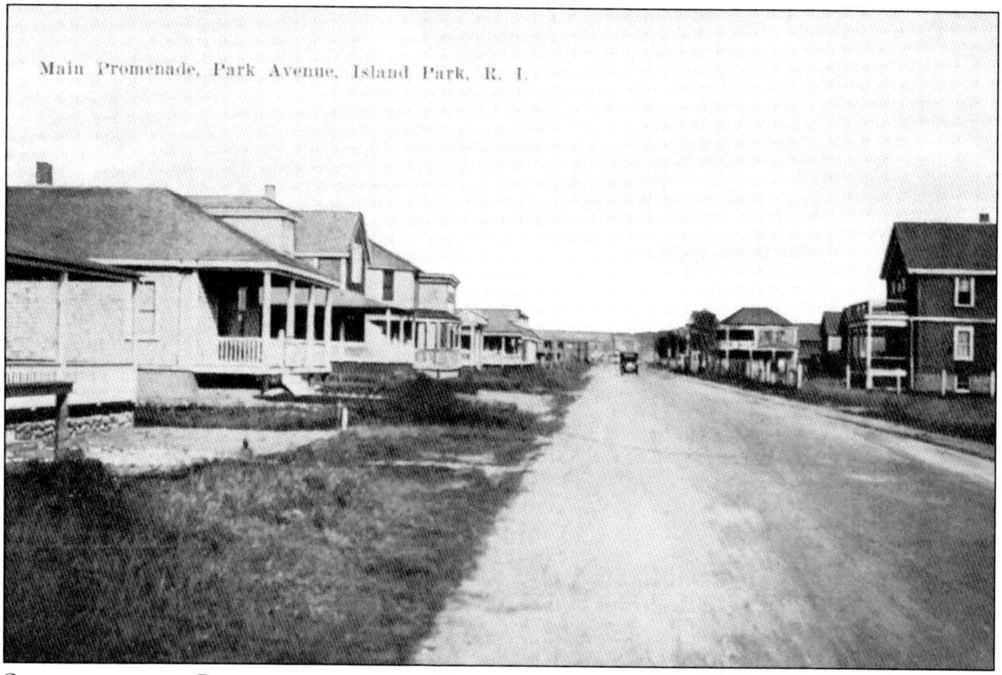

Summer cottages. Permanent, year-round homes were soon outnumbered by summer cottages, many of which were built precariously close to the water and by questionable building practices. This would eventually be the undoing of the community and bring an end to its flamboyant speak-easy and rum-running days.

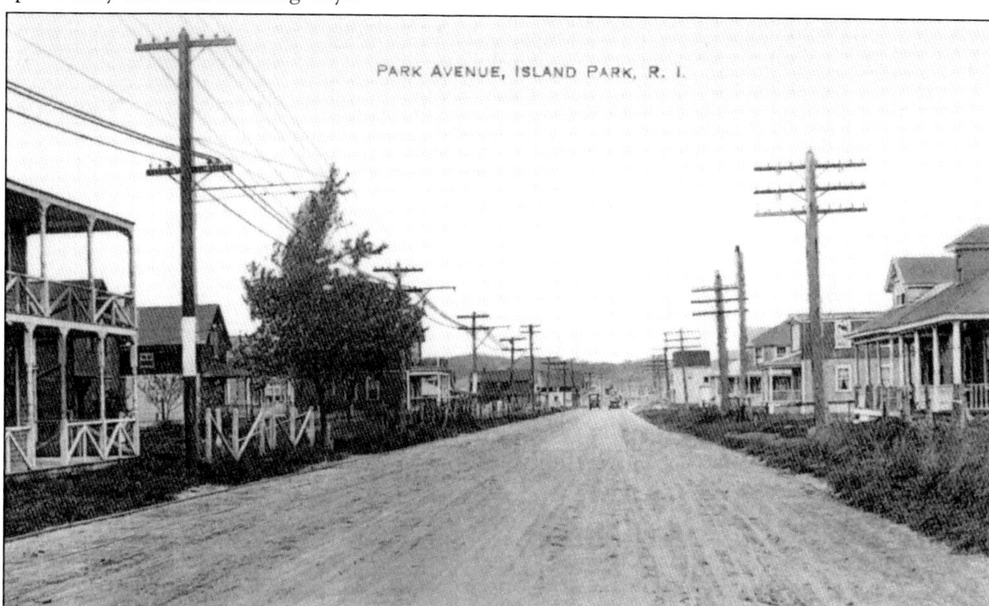

Park Avenue? It is difficult to date or place the exact location of the two views on this page. Both postcards are by the same Taunton, MA publisher, and both identify the street as Park Avenue; trolley tracks are not shown in either photo, and one photo has utilities poles, while the other does not. However, the construction style of the buildings and their closeness to each other are indicative of the turn-of-the-century Island Park community.

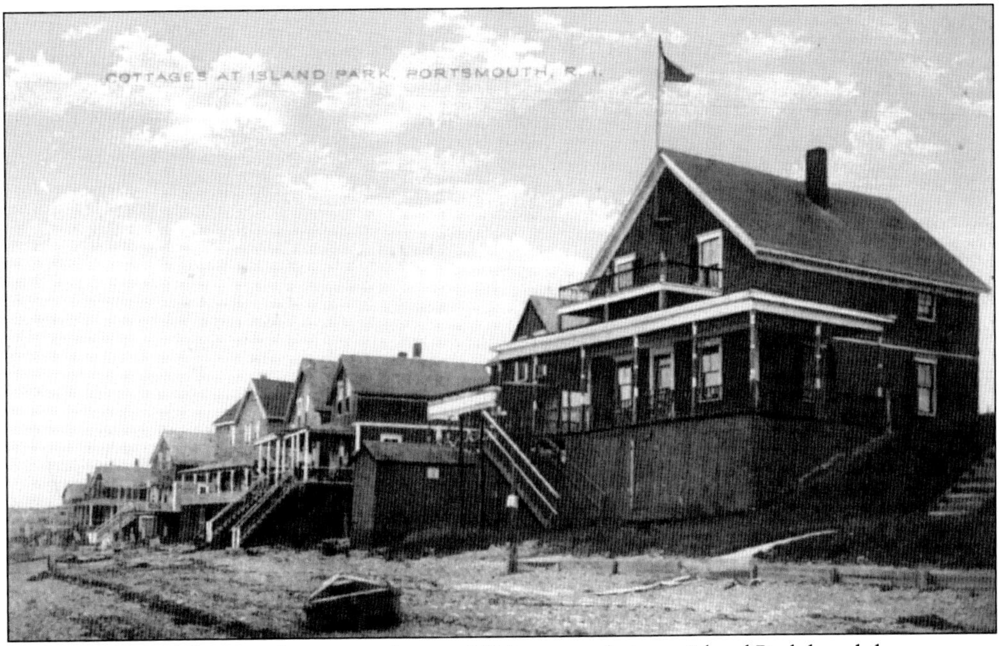

Island Park beach houses. As seen in these c. 1910 postcard views, Island Park beach houses were generally large frame, shingled affairs, with verandahs facing the ocean. Using today's building standards as a guide, it is difficult to understand how the obviously astute owners allowed their cottages to be constructed at the water's edge, directly on unstable sandy soil.

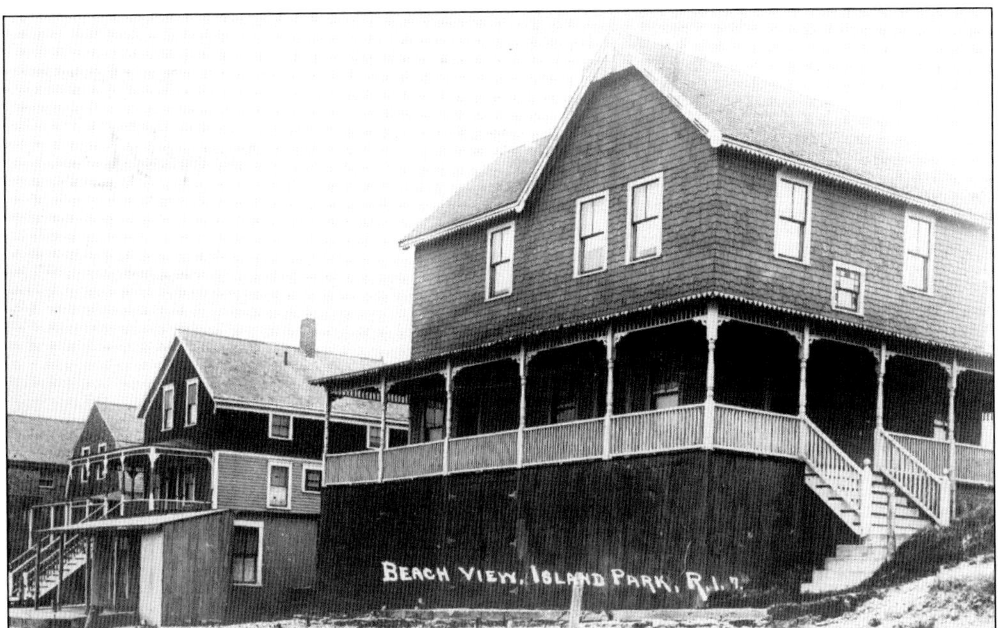

Cottages on the shores of the Sakonnet River. Enterprising cottage owners rented single rooms, suites of rooms, and sometimes the entire cottage to city folks desiring a weekend getaway by the seashore; the sea in this case being the Sakonnet River.

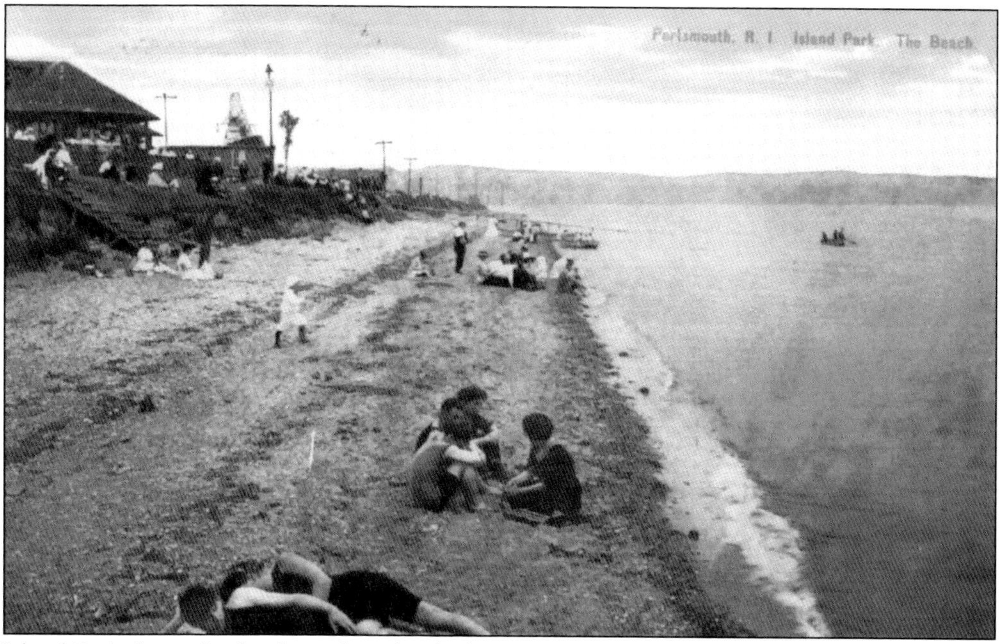

Island Park shore. In the days when few bathers actually practiced the sport of swimming, the Island Park shore, with its gentle surf, was ideal for strolling, picnicking, and lolling in the sun; its usually flat sea welcomed small-boat rowing.

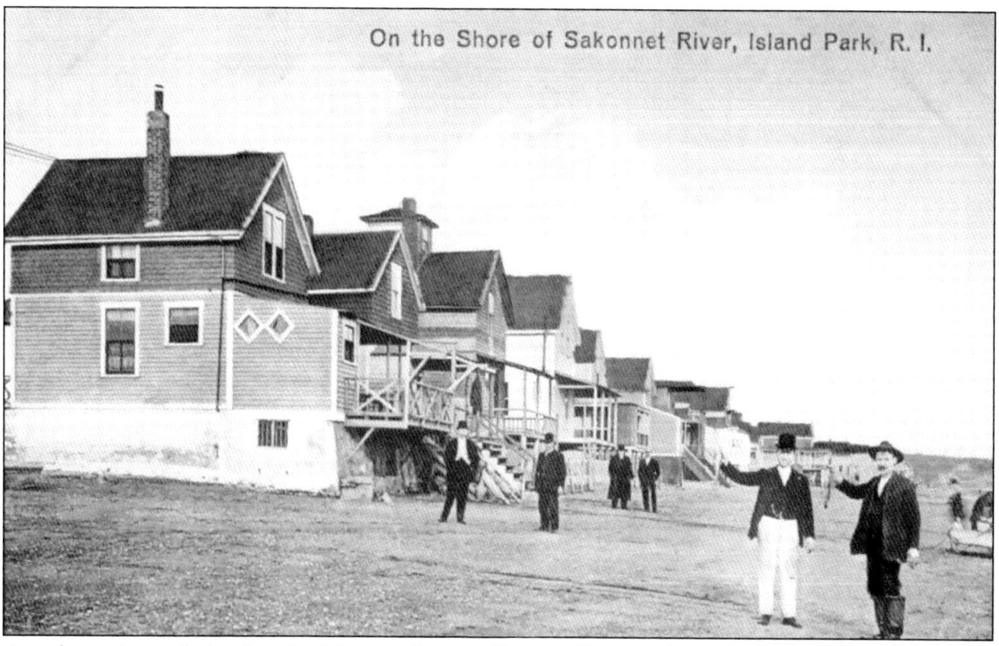

Another view of the beach. Notice the strollers—all men dressed rather dapperly for the occasion. The two gents in the foreground are holding up fish for the camera. The author of this postcard, dated August 7, 1913, complains to her mother in Fall River that the shore dinners are so good, she and her party of friends ". . . are getting fat."

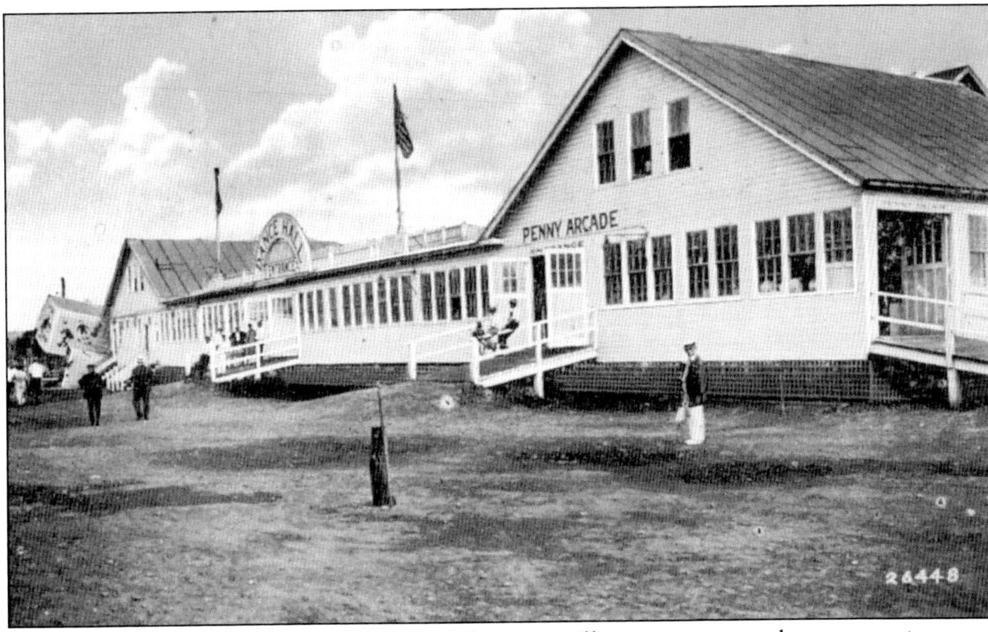

Amusements for all ages. From the original shooting gallery, amusements began to spring up as more vacationers flocked to the area for the refreshing sea breezes. To entertain the children while adults partook of shore dinners and other adult entertainment, simple glider swings and a pint-sized carousel operated.

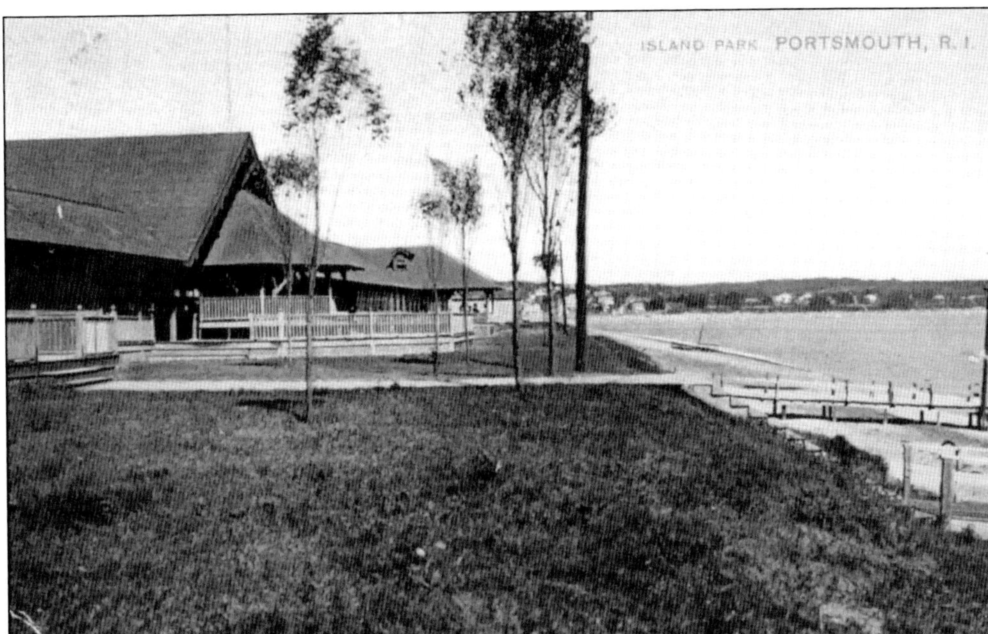

Island Park at the beginning of the 1920s. By this time, Island Park was a honky-tonk of all sorts of amusements, some more innocent than others. There were games-of-chance and of skill, fortune tellers and wheels of fortune, thrilling rides, a fun house, and souvenir concessions; on the darker side, speak-easies, fast lifestyles, and Saturday night dances were an explosive combination that resulted in many a black eye and broken nose.

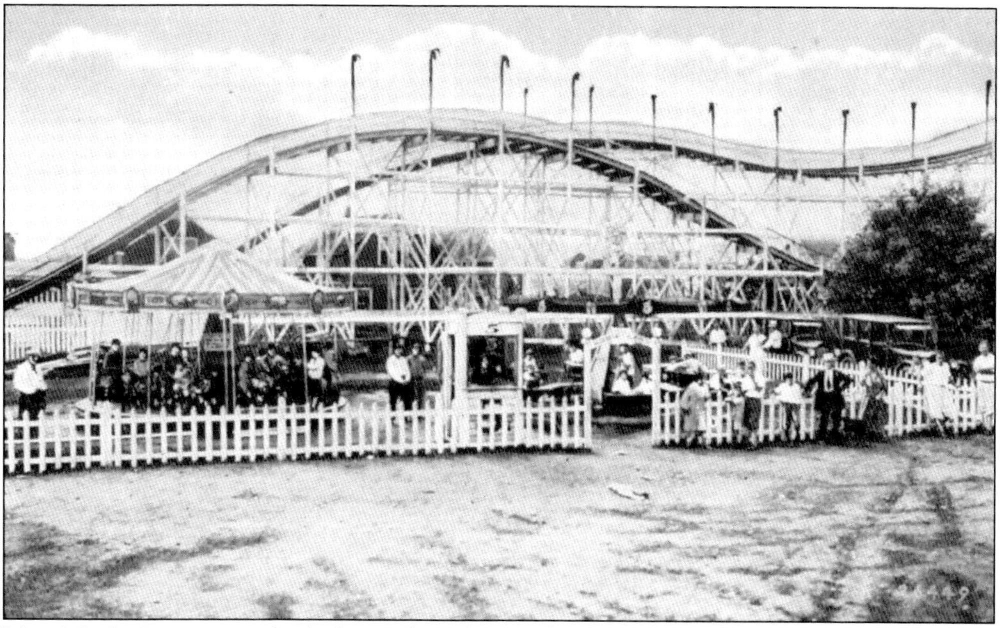

Island Park Amusement Park, located on the south side of Park Avenue at the east end. A giant roller coaster called The Bullet was built around 1926. The owners boasted that it was the second largest roller coaster in New England. The thrilling ride twisted around the park for over a quarter-mile. A few of the kiddie rides can be seen just inside the fence in this late 1920s view.

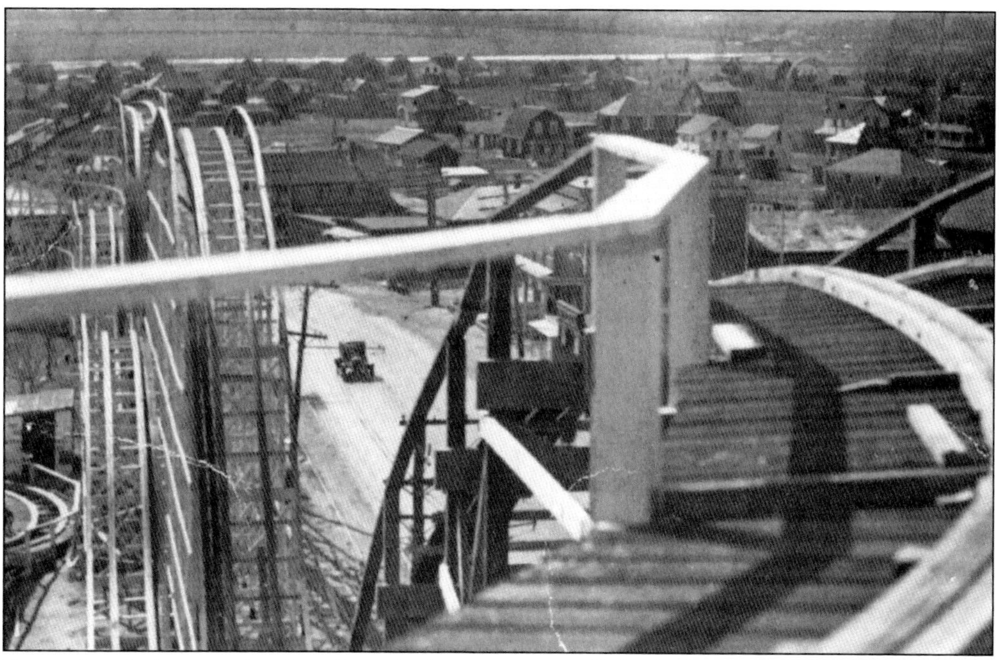

Promotional photograph taken from the highest point of The Bullet in the spring of 1926.

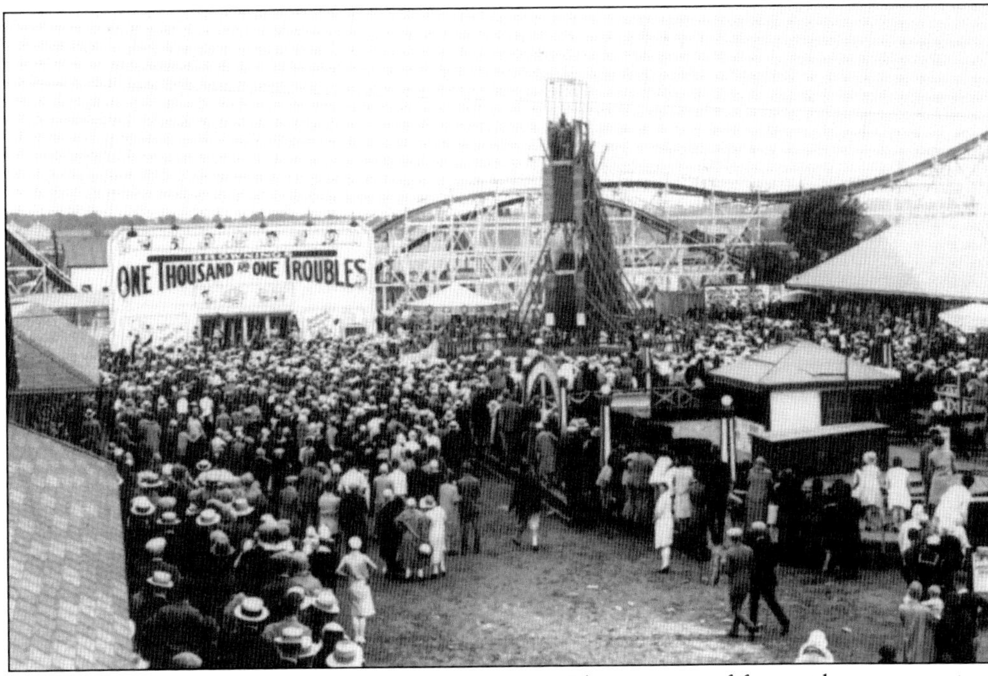

One of the so-called World Famous Diving Horses. The promise of free mid-way attractions was guaranteed to draw crowds. Vaudeville performances, famous dance bands, fireworks, and bonfires kept the crowds amused and spending money at the concessions. The horse and rider on the platform in this c. 1928 photograph are preparing to leap into a pool of water.

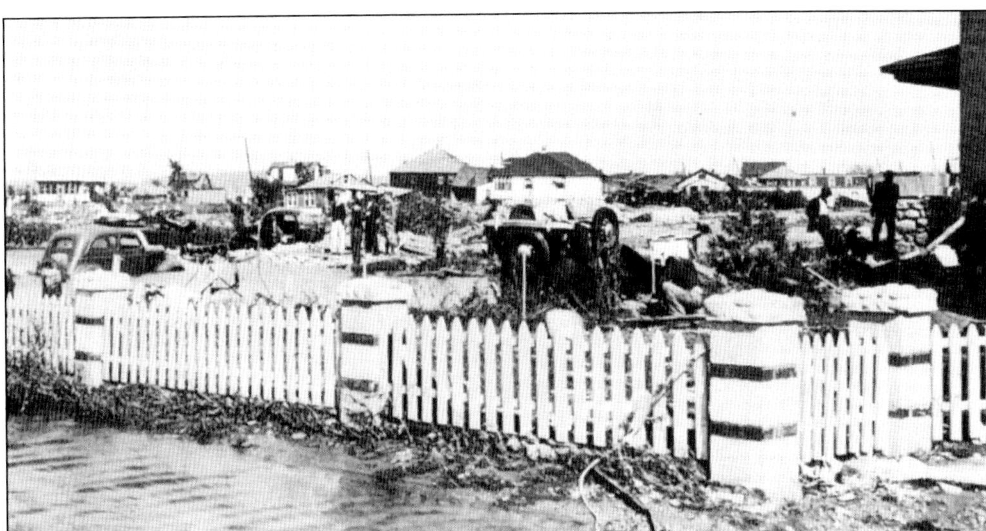

Hurricane of September 21, 1938. Late Wednesday afternoon, on September 21, 1938, the North Atlantic states were ravaged by a devastating hurricane and tidal wave. The impact on Island Park and the amusement park was a calamity from which it never completely recovered. Eventually, homes and cottages away from the shore were rebuilt. However, the amusement park is no more; those former carefree days can only be remembered through souvenirs and family photographs.

Nine

Portsmouth Park and Environs

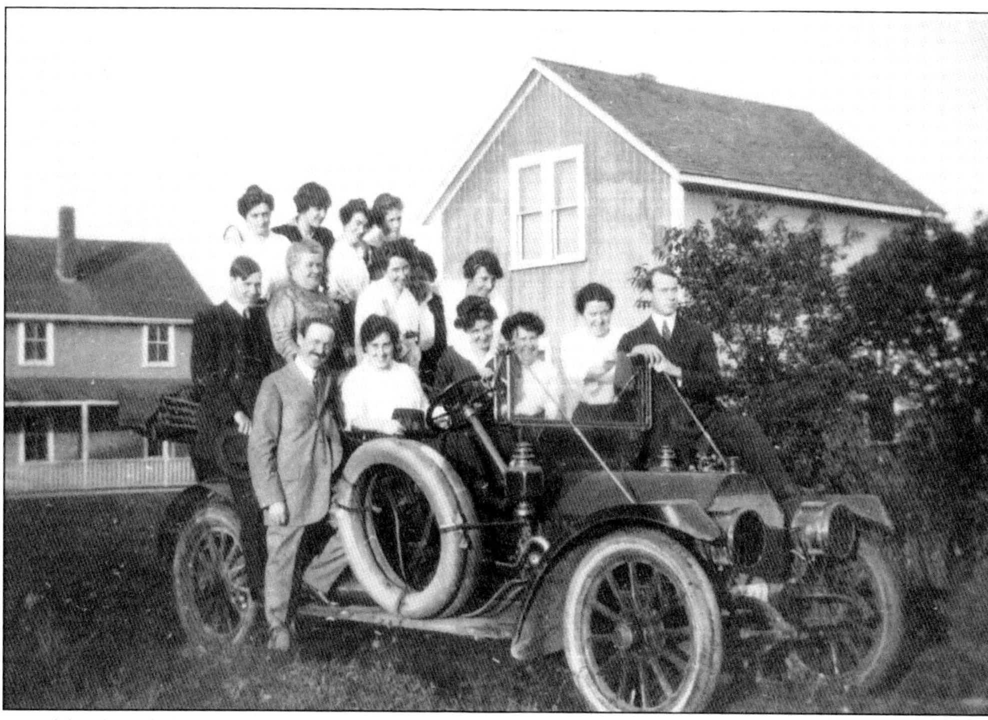

Neighborhood friends from Narragansett Avenue aboard Jennie and Charlie Dutton's new touring car, 1920. Originally a cluster of summer homes, the Portsmouth Park neighborhood matured into a middle-class suburb of the Newtown district; it remains a close-knit community, with a number of families descended from the original summer residents.

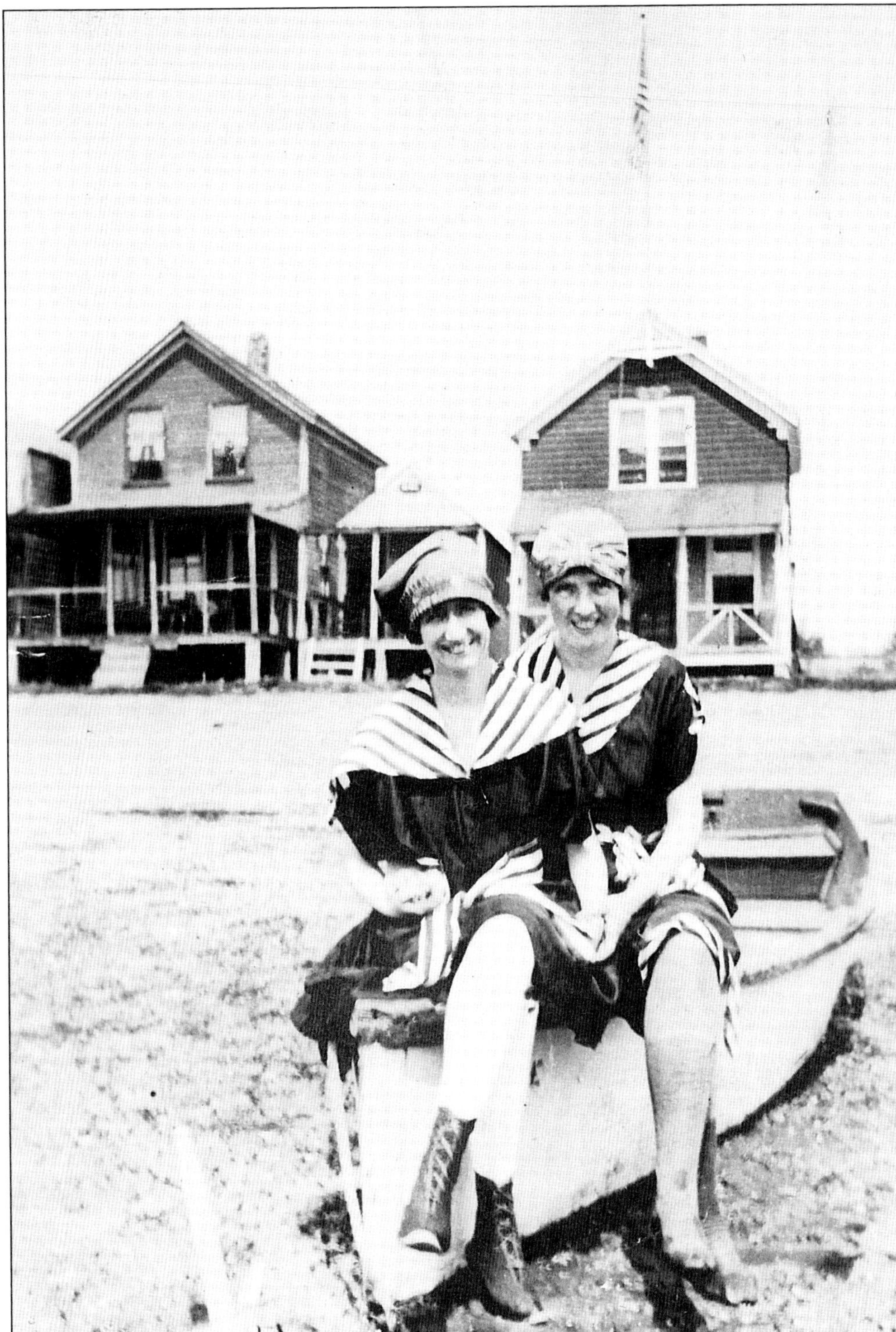

Kathy Crosson and May Hoag. Could this pair of 1920 Portsmouth Park bathing beauties be waiting for a young man to launch their skiff?

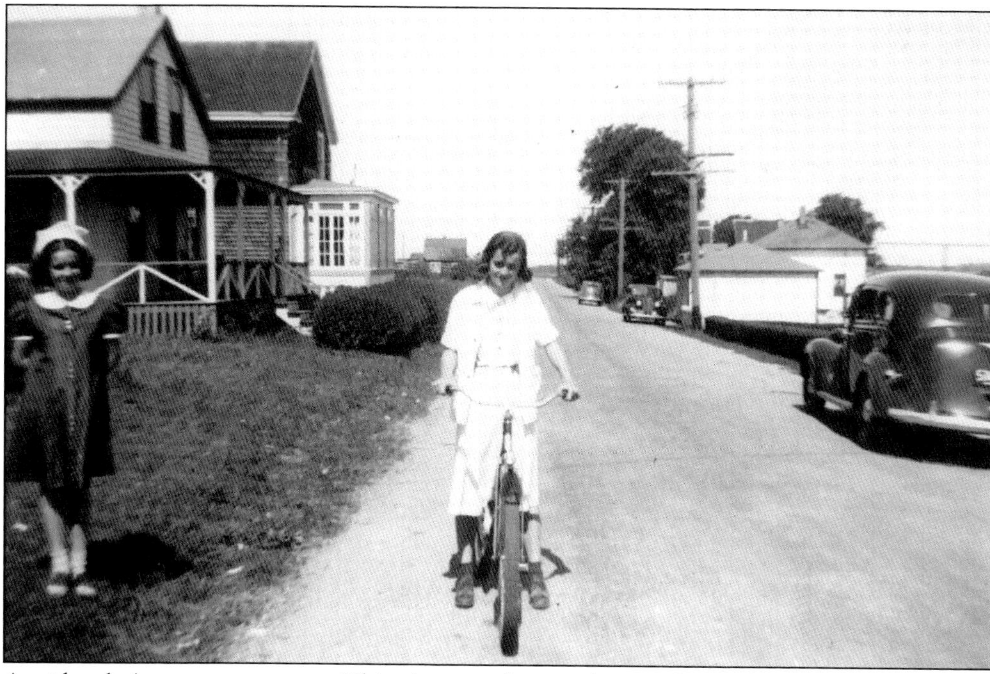

Aquidneck Avenue streetscape. This photograph was taken on September 14, 1938, just seven days before the hurricane struck. Standing on the grass is Ann Crosson Madden; Mary Regan Duffy is on the bike.

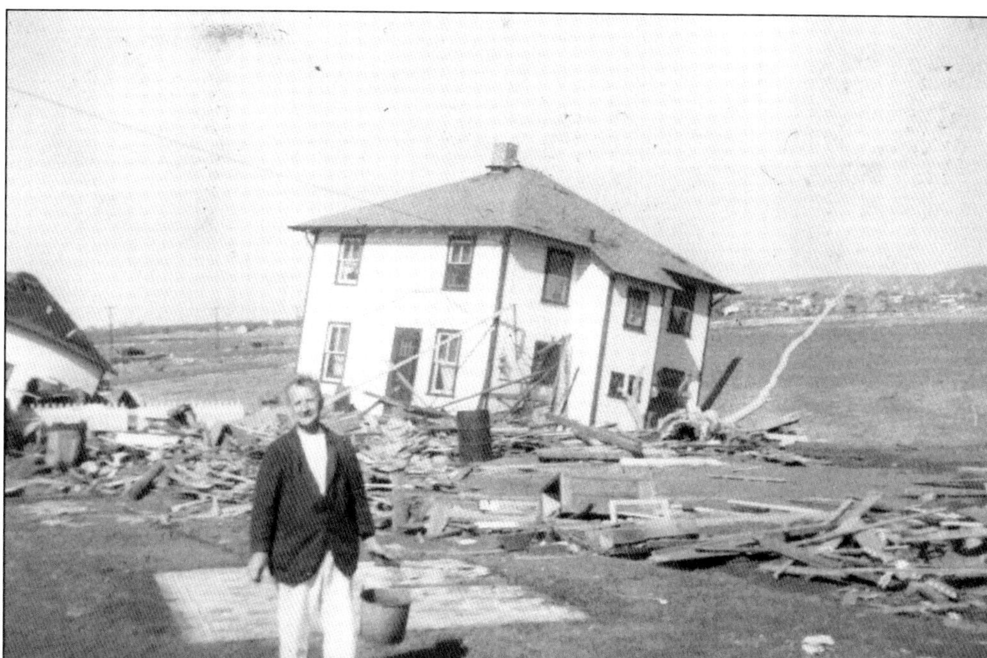

Eddie Logan's house in the same general Aquidneck Avenue area on the morning of September 22, 1938.

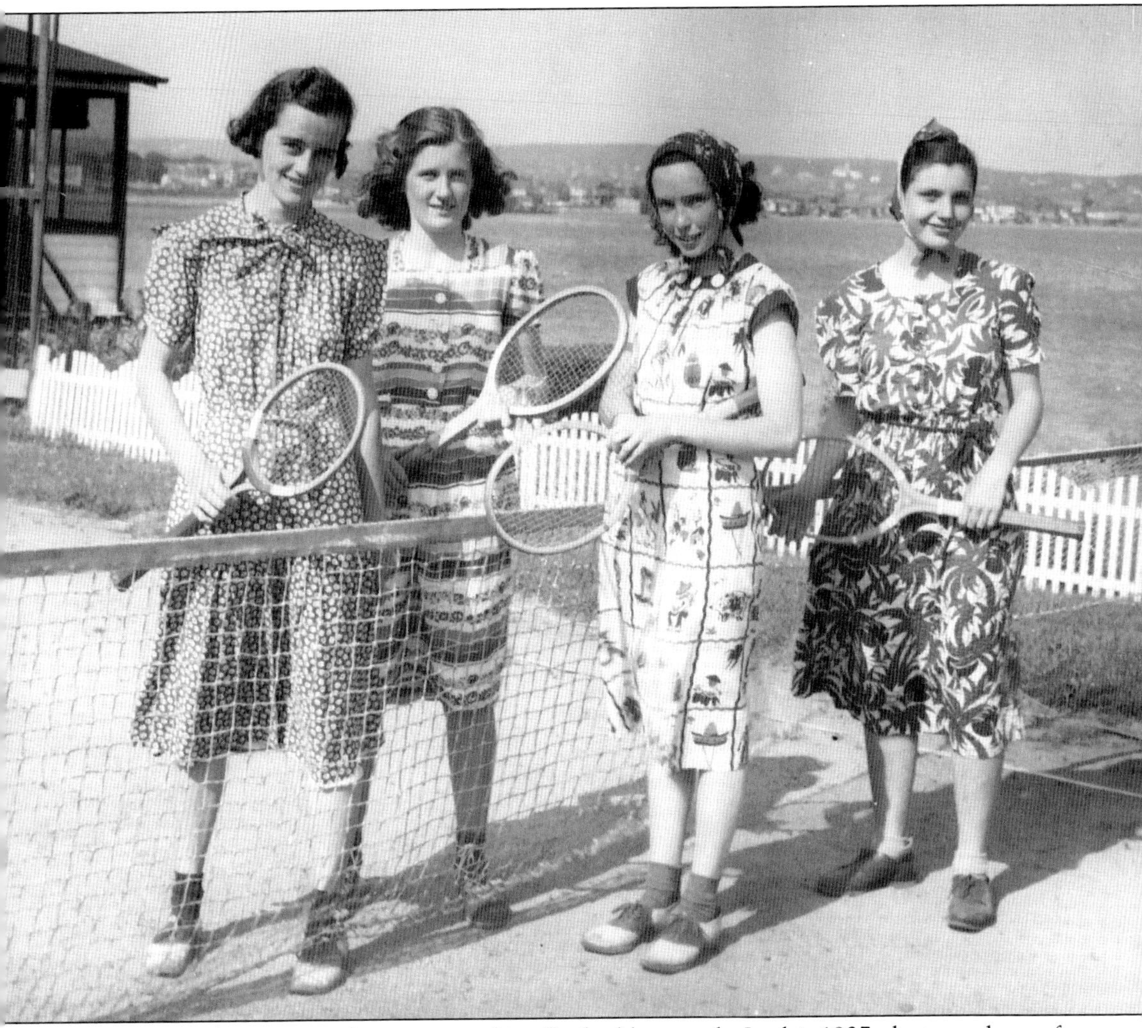

Aquidneck Avenue girls enjoying a friendly doubles match. In this 1937 photograph are, from left to right, Mary Regan Duffy, Pauline Burke Haas, Peggy Crosson Dunn, and Pat Connely Sullivan. In the background are the Sakonnet River and the Island Park shoreline.

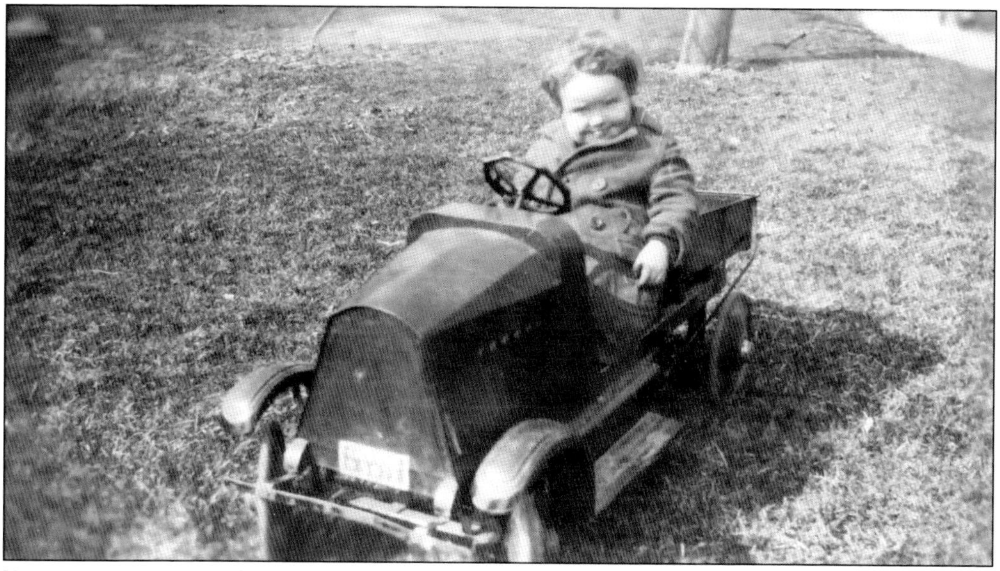

Young Jim Crosson in his new express truck, 1926.

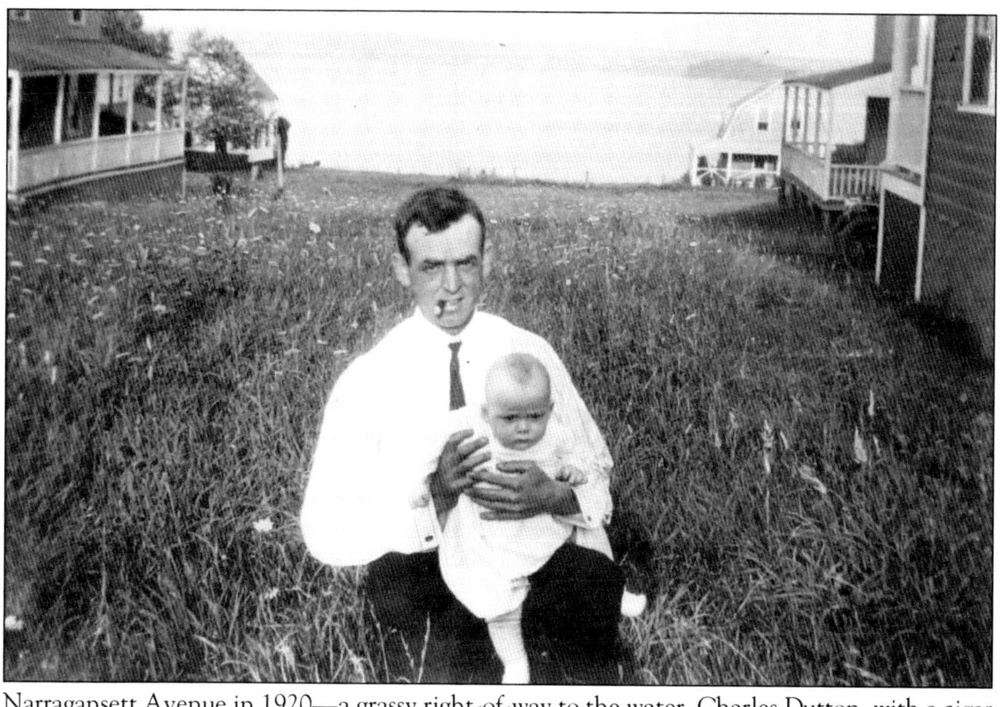

Narragansett Avenue in 1920—a grassy right-of-way to the water. Charles Dutton, with a cigar clamped firmly between his teeth, holds baby Ann Madden.

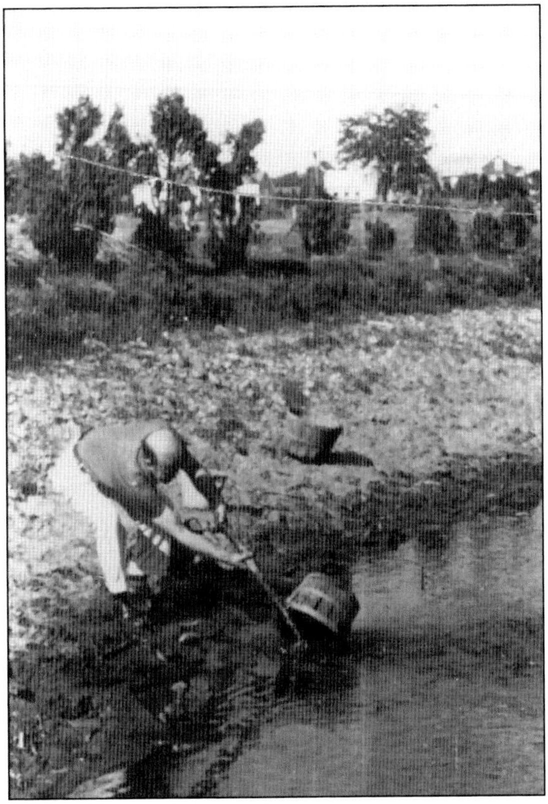

Joe Monis catching baitfish at Dunn's Beach, at the foot of Child Street, 1939.

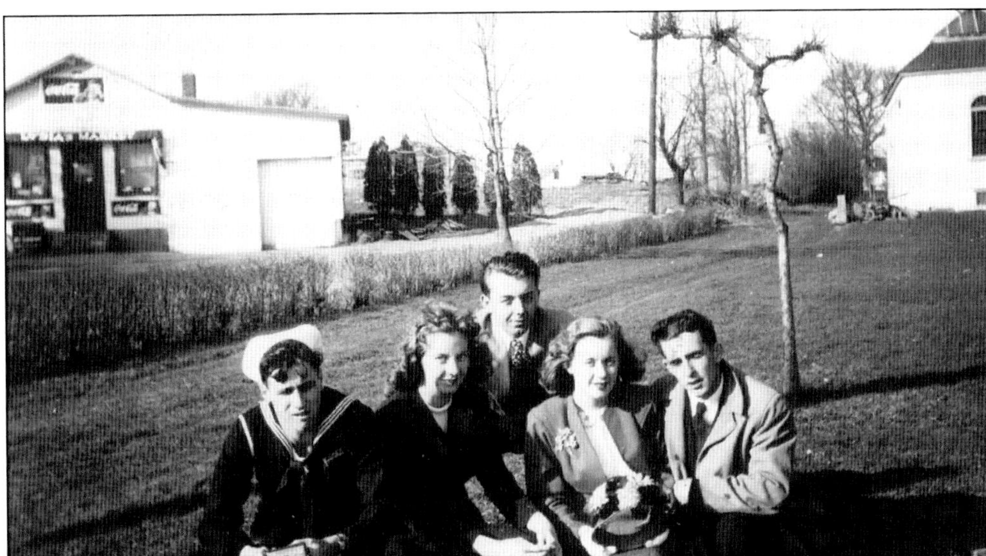

Lydia Ferreira's store, later owned by Tony Fontaine, in a 1940 photograph taken on the lawn of the town library. Judging from the leafless tree and hedge, and the Sunday-best clothing, one may date this photograph as being a Sunday outing in early April. Vernon Gorton is the young man in the back; to his left are Shirley McBride and Joe Sullivan. The sailor, and the young woman to his right, are unknown.

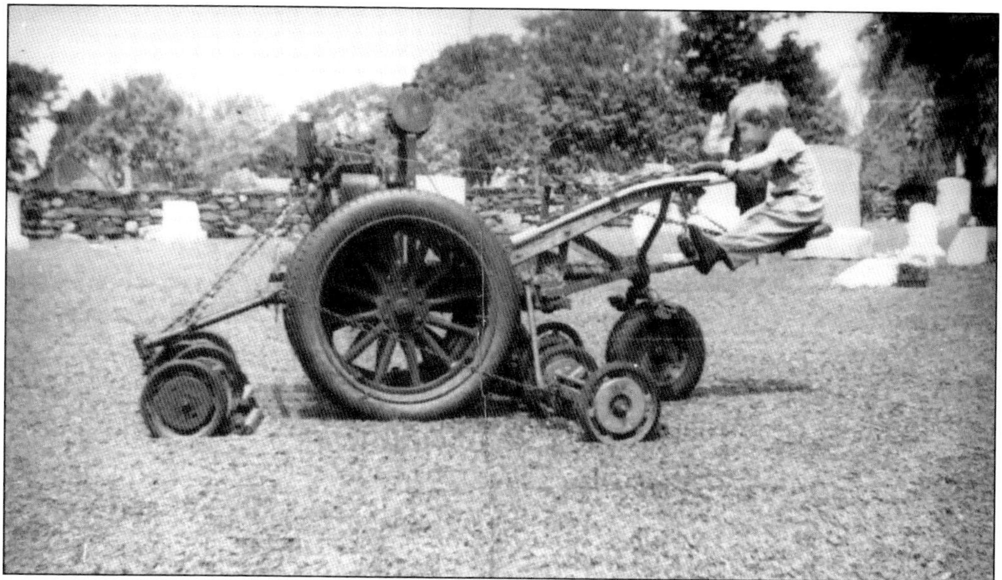

Little Peter Wilkey on his father's power lawn mower at St. Paul's Cemetery in 1938. Before Henry Wilkey joined the town's volunteer firefighters, he worked as a landscape contractor. Employing his mechanical and creative skills, Henry designed and built what many think is the first gasoline-powered, ride-on lawn mower.

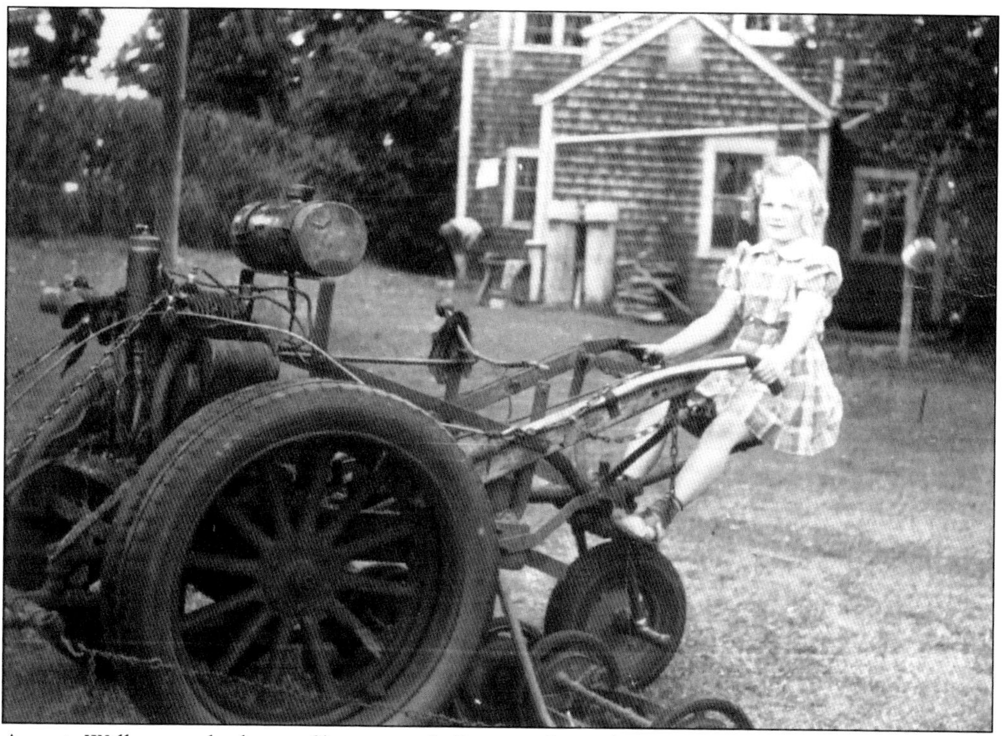

Anstris Wilkey on the lawn of her parent's Spraque Street home. Henry Wilkey added a Harley Davidson Motorcycle engine and chain drive to a Model T Ford differential. The wooden parts he needed he carved by hand, and the iron parts he made at his own forge. This contrivance pulled five mowers; it was steered by a foot on the rear wheel.

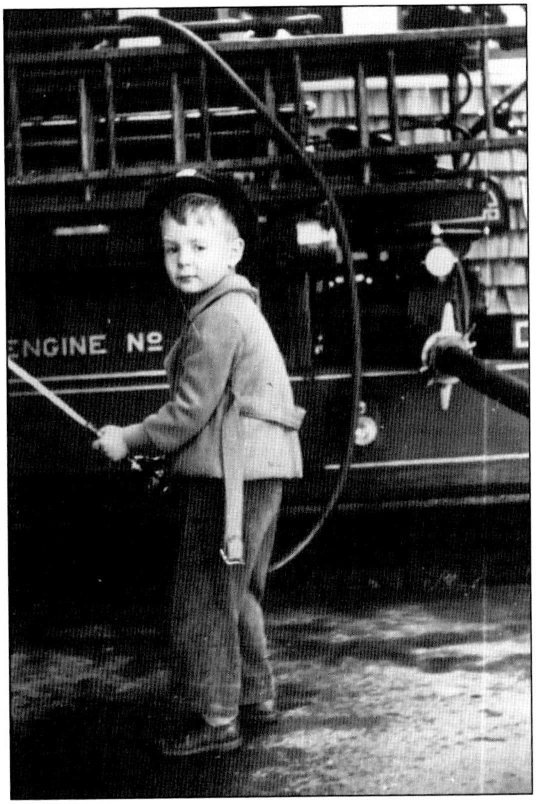

Four-year-old Peter Wilkey, destined to follow in his father's footsteps, on the town's 1935 Maxim Engine No.1 .

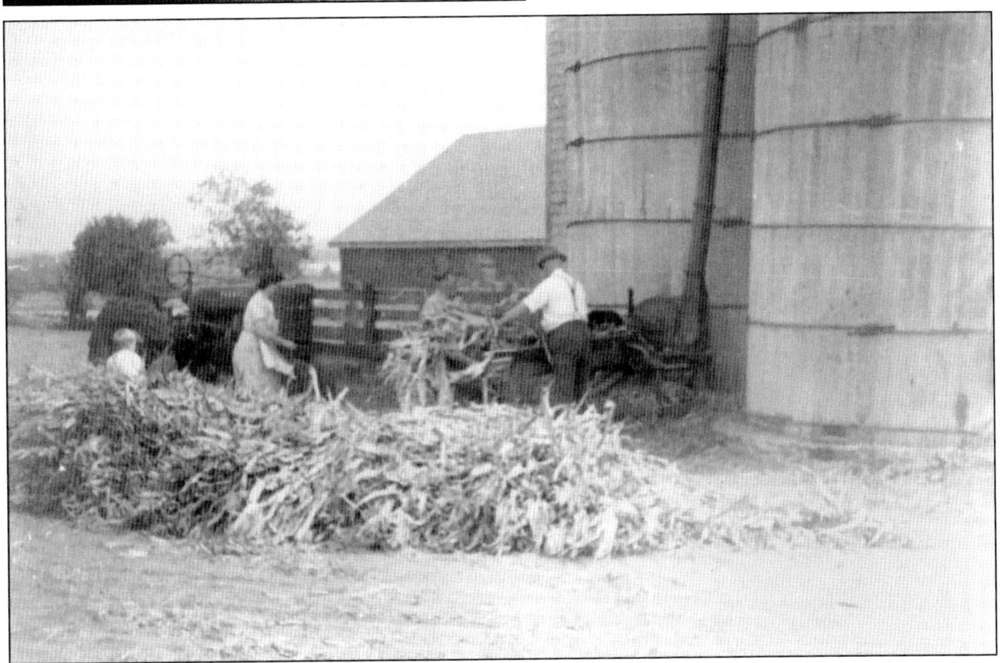

Anthony Farm, 1939. William B. Anthony and his daughter-in-law Jeannette are shown here taking in the silage. This property at the top of Park Avenue is now Viking, Valhalla, and Norseman Streets.

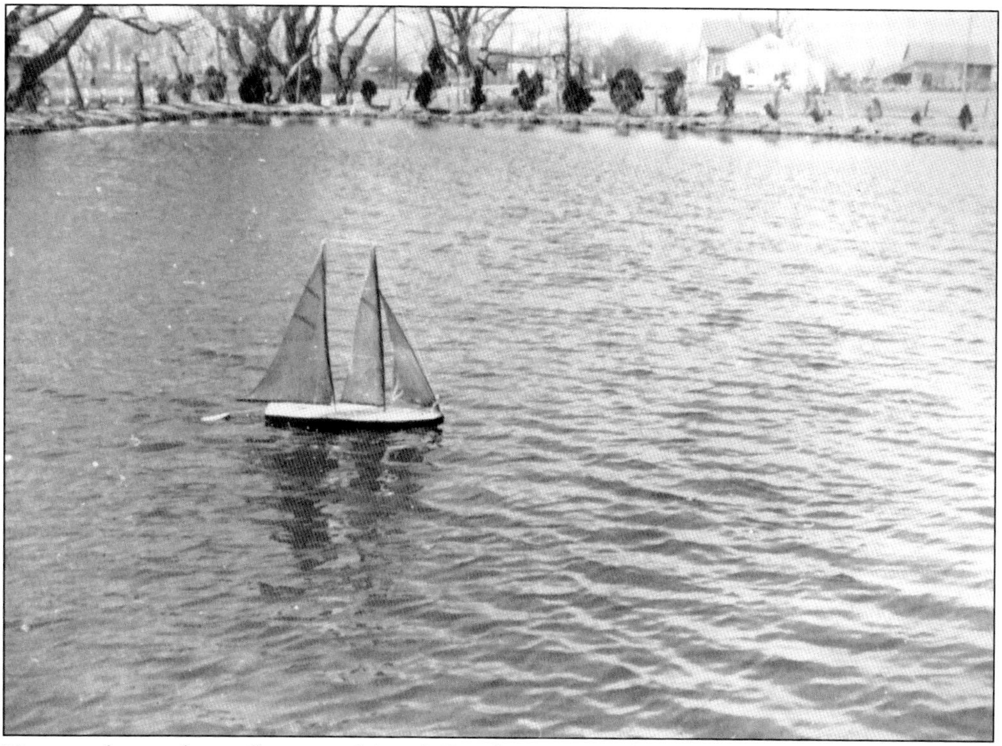

Homemade wooden sailboats on Menzi's Pond, *c.* 1940. The pond on Turnpike Avenue was filled in to make the on-ramp to Route 24. Menzi's barn can be seen in the upper right; it is this barn that the high school students paint each year.

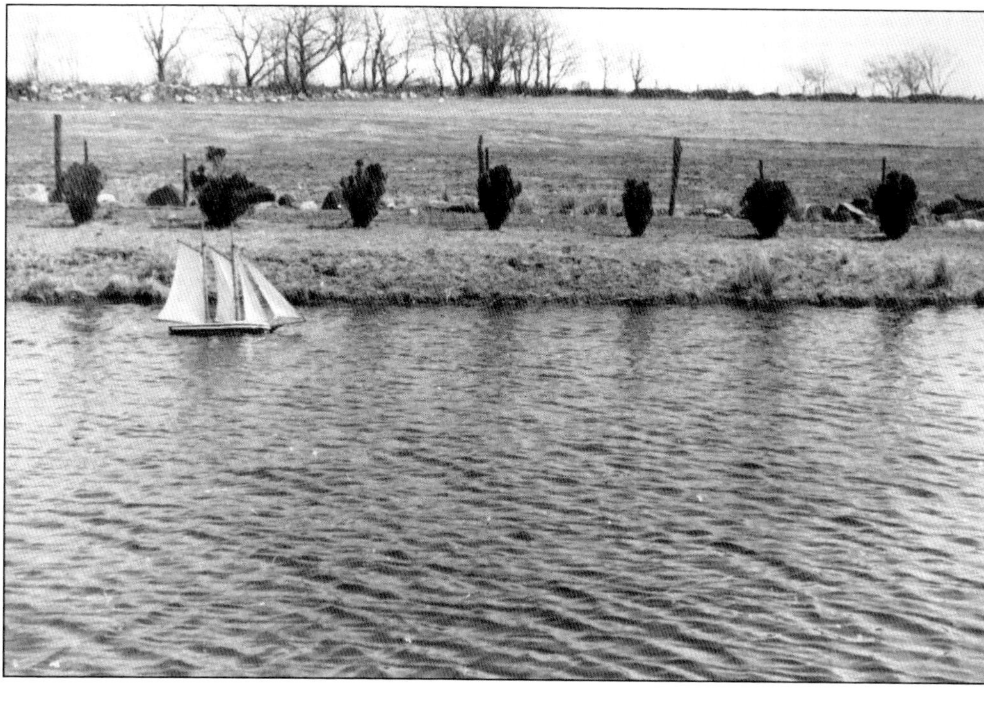

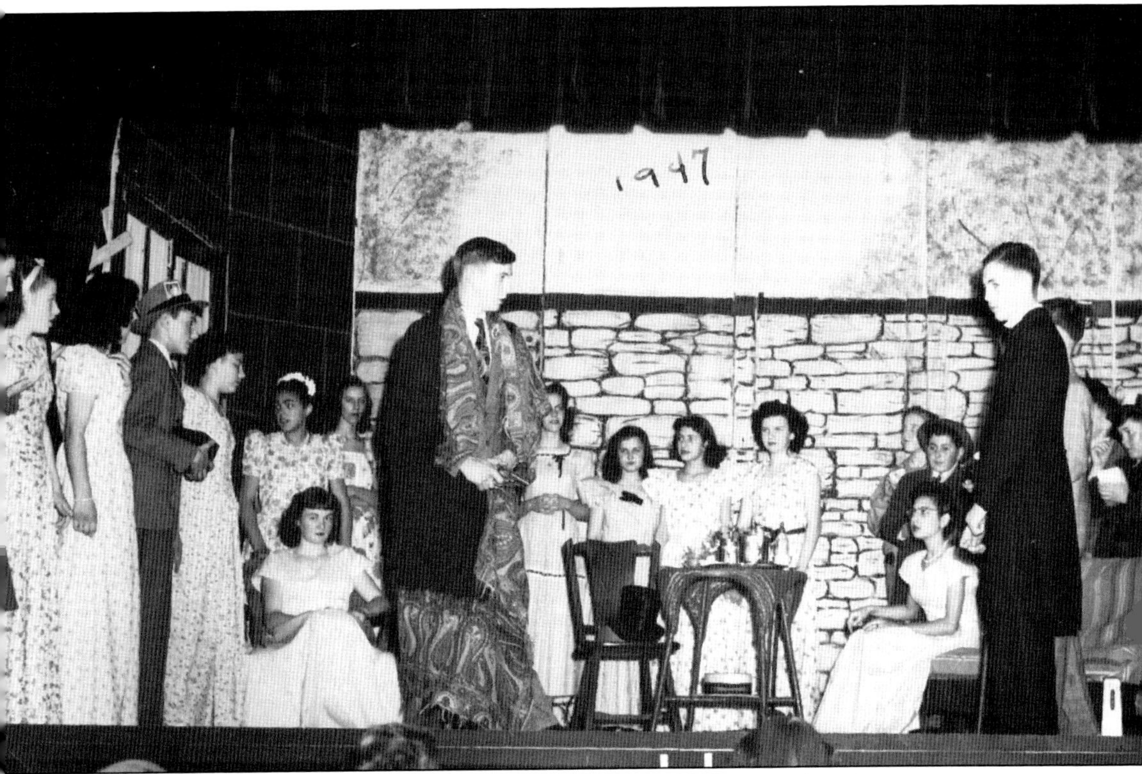

Portsmouth Class of 1947 theatrical production. The following identifications were given on the back of the photograph. From left to right are: (standing) Eileen Sullivan, Joan LaBonte, unknown, Bill Peckham, Virginia Napier, Teresa Camara, Jean McFall, Lucy Alvarnas, and Barbara Gibeau; Irene Lima, Jimmy Cosgrove, Lowell Sousa, ? Gibeau, and Ruth White; (front) Anstris Wilkey (seated), Wilbur Peckham, and Dolores Cordeiro.

Ten

Folks Who Made a Difference

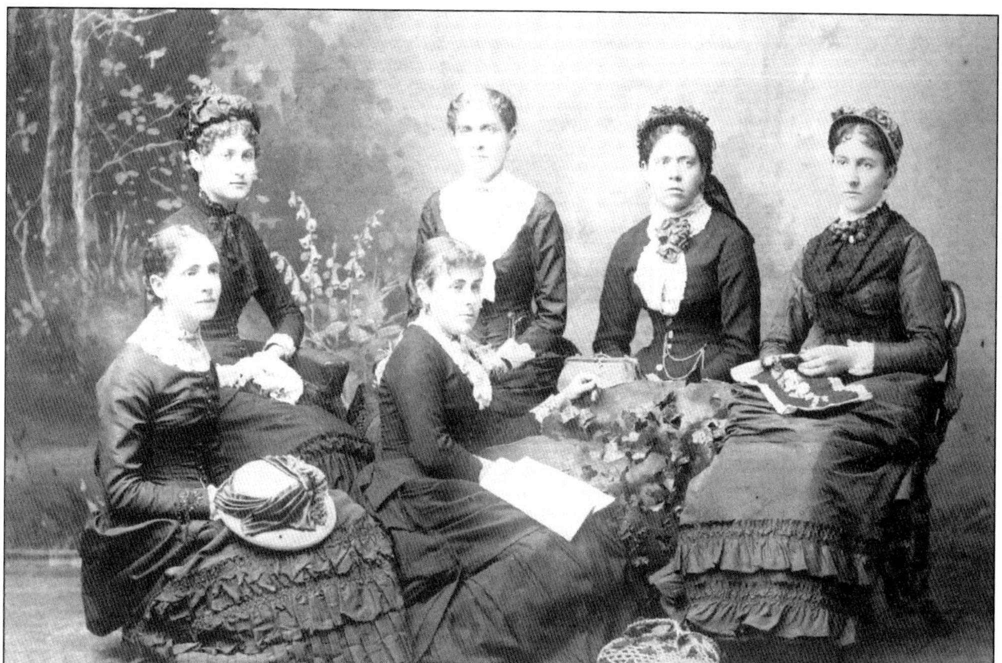

Six women, in a photograph donated to the Portsmouth Historical Society in September 1975. Gertrude Macomber, who donated this image, wrote about the sitters, ". . . I think they may have been members of the old Quaker School in Providence, the date is 1883. They do look a little 'dressy' for Quakers." The sitters are, in uncertain order, Mrs. Charles Chase, Miss Ida Pierce, Miss Mirium Macomber, Miss Kate Macomber, Miss Annie Earle, and Mrs. Arthur Weaver. The photograph is the work of Gay's Gallery of Art, J.F. Suddard, Operator, located at "Cor. South Main and Borden Streets, Fall River, Mass."

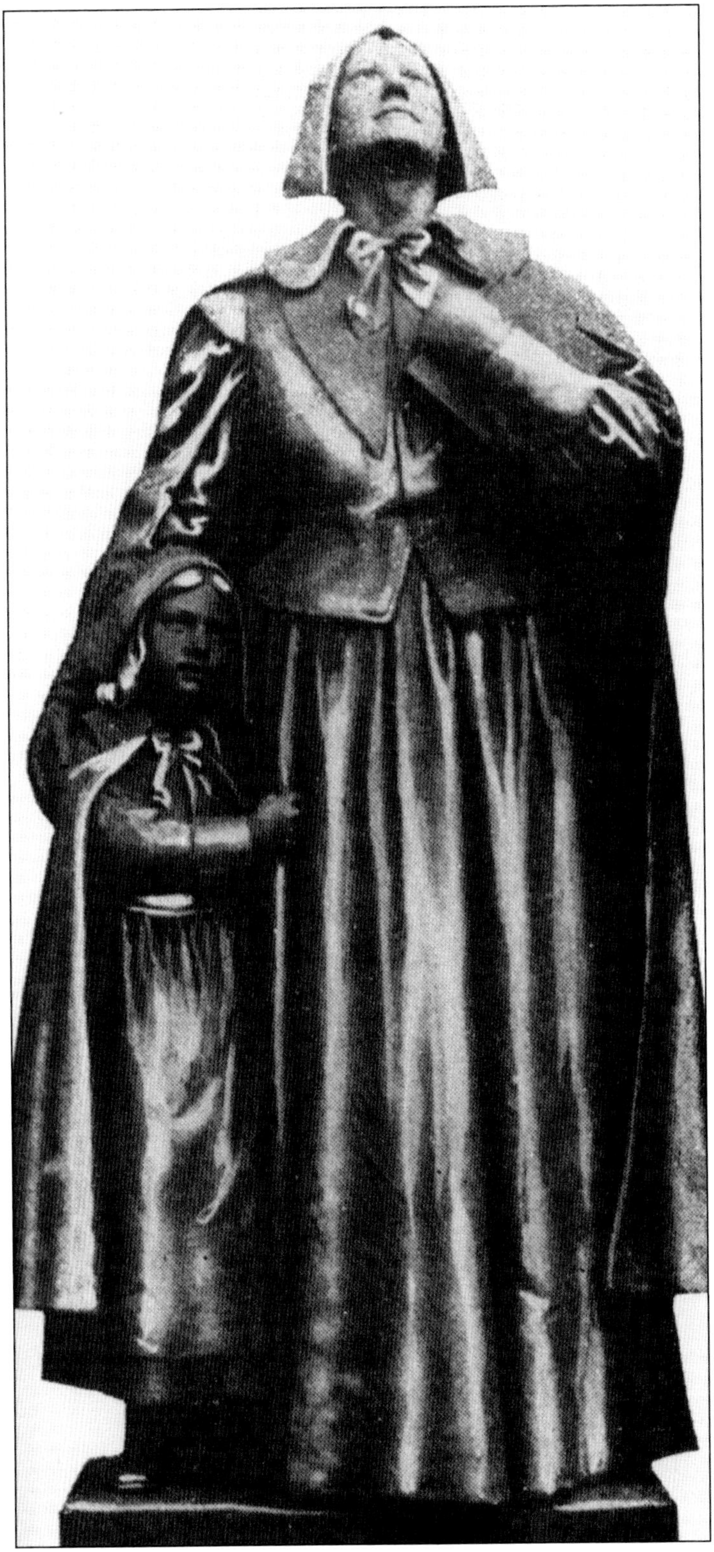

Anne Marbury Hutchinson, probably the first American champion of woman's rights. She was the first of her sex to openly challenge the inherited authorities, privileges, and prerogatives of males, and she influenced events not only in Rhode Island but in the infant nation. From her privately conceived *Covenant of Works*, she preached that all classes of people should stand as equals before the law with unabridged rights as to life, liberty, and justice. Anne, her husband, and approximately eighteen Boston sympathizers and members of her immediate family departed Massachusetts for Providence, that haven for all those distressed for conscience's sake. Anne Hutchinson has a place among the immortals of these Rhode Island shores that harbored both leaders and followers, who, with the courage of their convictions, risked all to enjoy the religious freedom that they believed to be the basic principle of a free state.

William Barton, a hatter from Warren. Barton volunteered his services to the American Army at Boston around June 19, 1775. In early 1777, he was elevated to the rank of colonel and given command of an American militia on Aquidneck. Barton's expedition to capture General Prescott started on July 4, 1777 (see pp. 13–17). Later, while defending Warren and Bristol against an invading troop of British and Hessian solders, Barton took a bullet in the leg for his effort. One of the heroes of the War for Independence, Barton died on October 22, 1831, at the age of eighty-five.

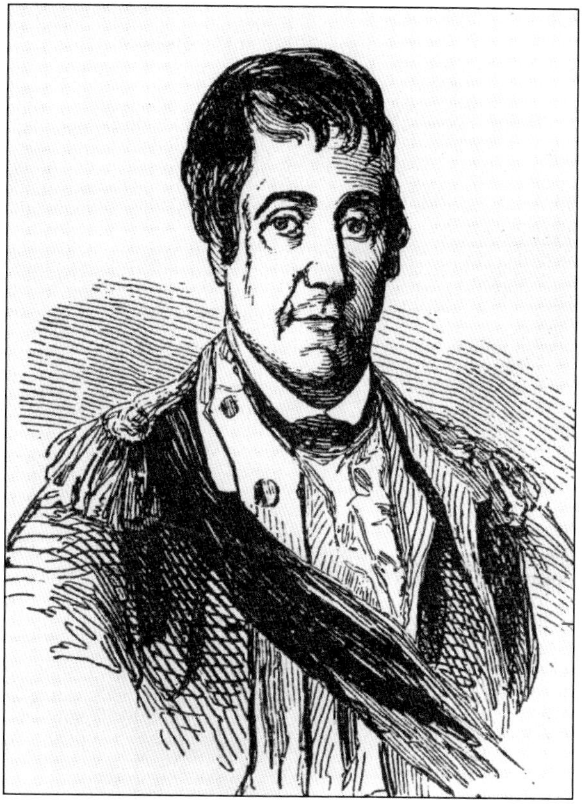

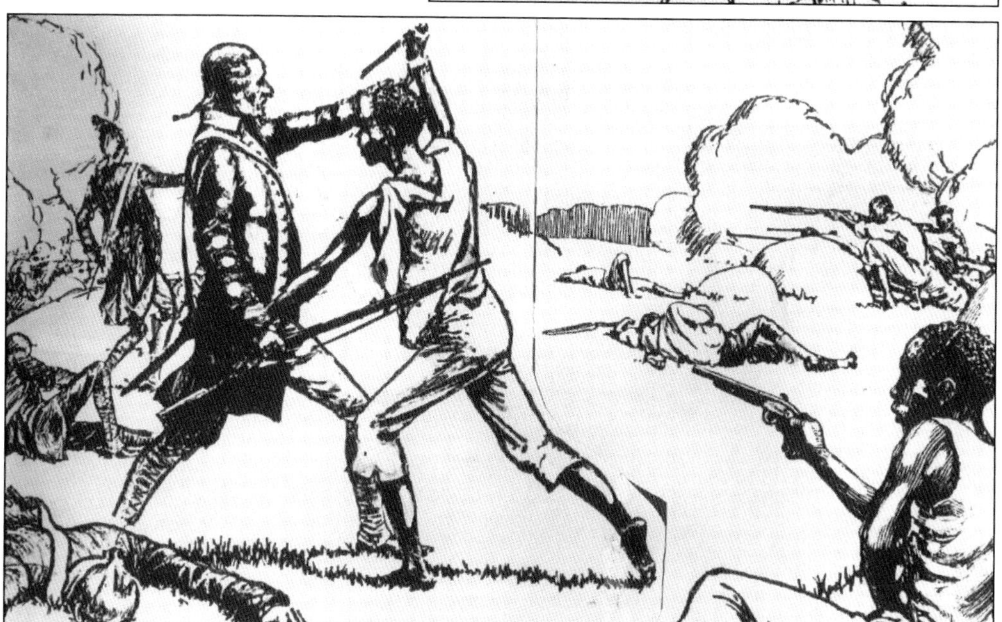

Monument at the foot of Turkey Hill near the Route 24 overpass, dedicated to the Rhode Island First Black Regiment. The Black Regiment was created in 1778 by Brigadier General James Varnum; it consisted of African-American and Native American slaves, who were promised freedom and bounties in exchange for their service.

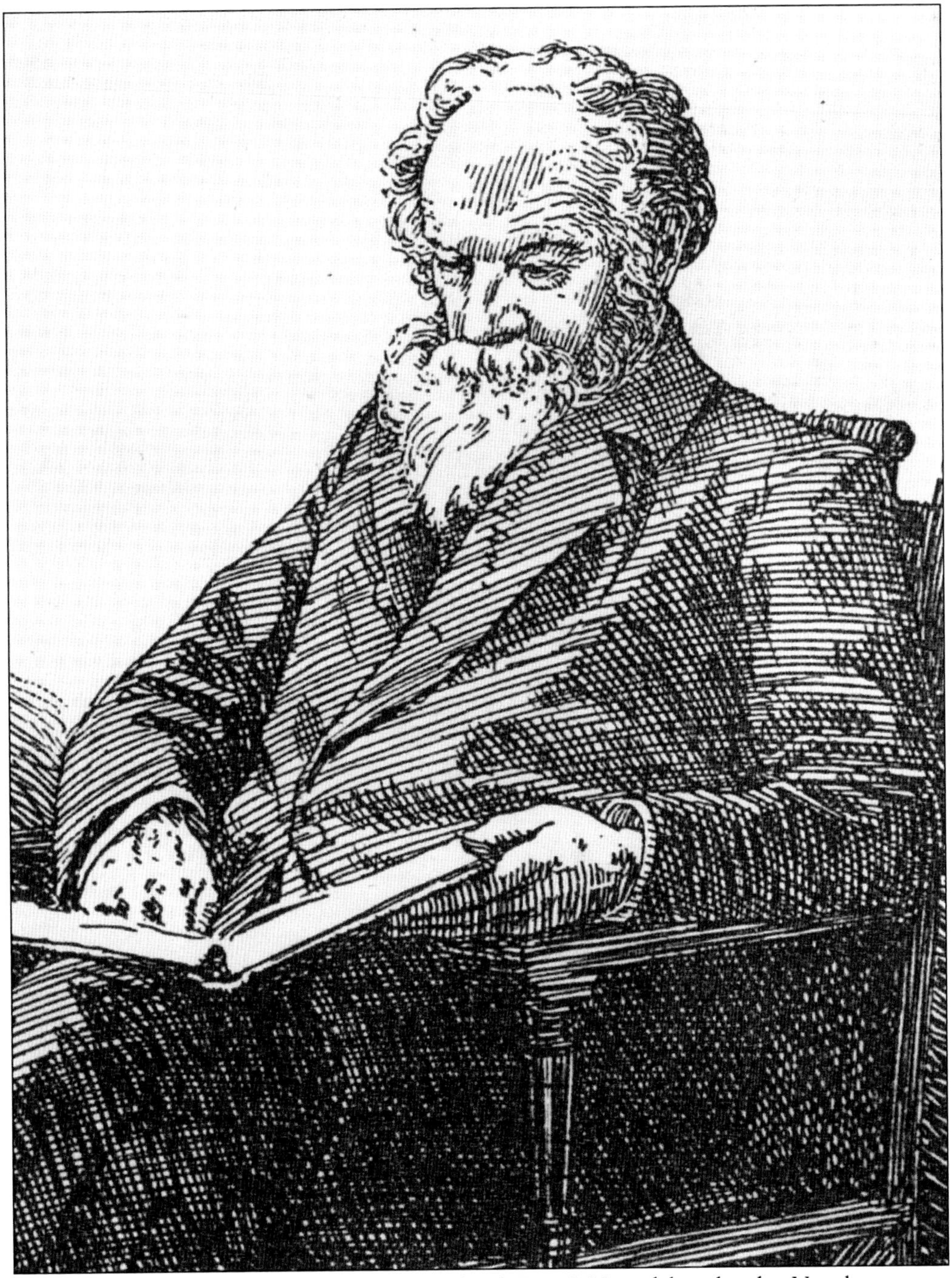

Thomas Robinson Hazard, known as "Shepherd Tom." Hazard bought the Vaucluse estate after his retirement in 1837, and lived there until his death in 1886. Shepherd Tom was one of five sons of the founder of the Peace Dale Woolen Mills. After he sold his share of the enterprise, he devoted his life to philanthropy, civic reform, and literary pursuits. An eccentric, he dabbled in the spirit world, often holding seances at Vaucluse, and he enjoyed exploring spirit materialization. All the Hazards believed spirits haunted the Vaucluse mansion, and the children were raised to believe in them.

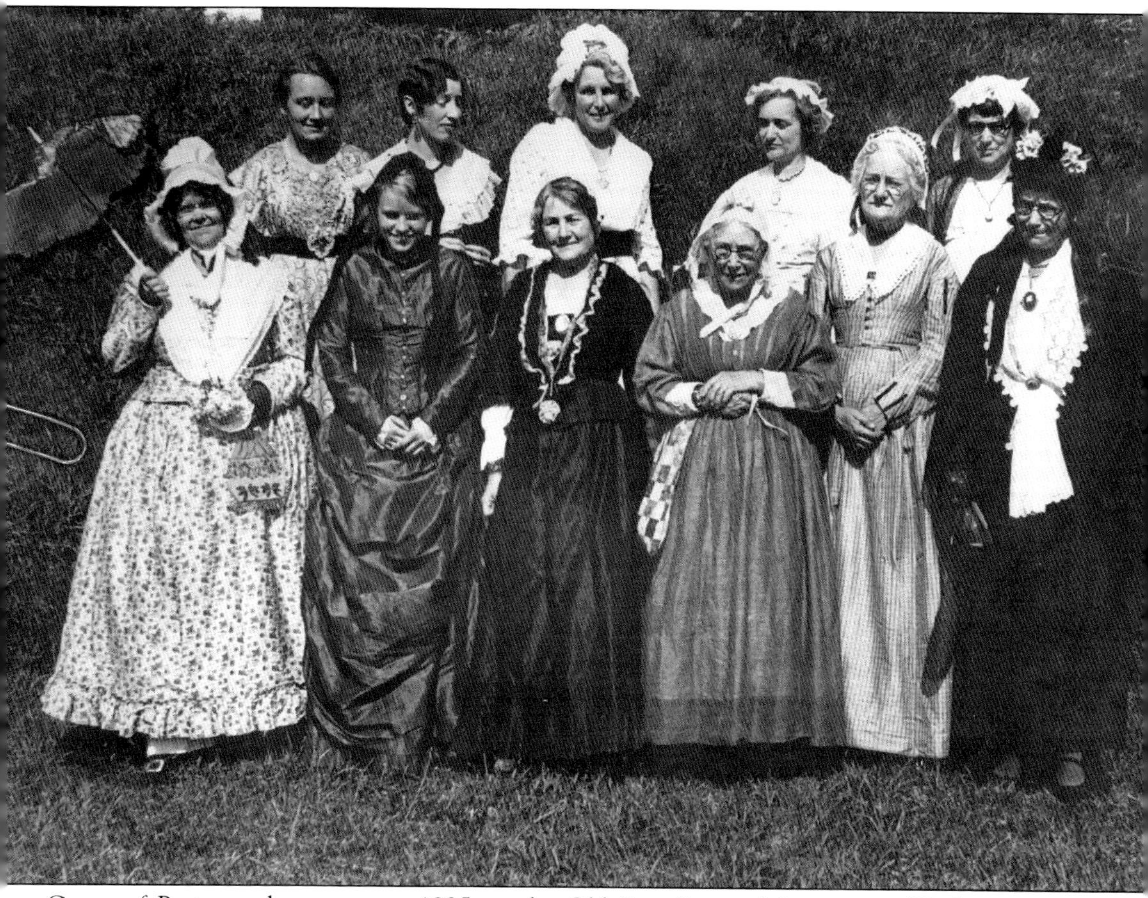

Group of Portsmouth women, c. 1925, at the Old Port Days celebration on Washington Street, Newport. A note by Elizabeth A. Wilkey attached to the photograph identifies the eleven costumed women. Additionally, she writes, "Hope Coggeshall Anthony Hathaway says the person to my left is not she. It could be Marion K. Carry, a classmate of mine who lived all her life in Newport at 12 Friendship St. We were close friends during and after our years at R.I. School of Design (1922–1926)." From left to right are as follows: (front row) Mrs. William Norton nee Hattie, Miss Nancy Chase (daughter of James and Julia), Mrs. Daniel Meader Chase nee Janet Wilcox Shaw, Mrs. Thomas J. Sweet nee Josie Coggeshall, Mrs. William Manchester nee Phoebe E.T. Weaver, and Mrs. Joseph Barker nee Julia Coggeshall; (back row) Mrs. Henry Wilkey nee Elizabeth Anthony (daughter of William and Eliza), Marion K. Carry (according to above), Mrs. M. LeRoy Dennis nee Mattie Regan (?), Mrs. Phoebe Coggeshall, and Miss Helen Coggeshall.

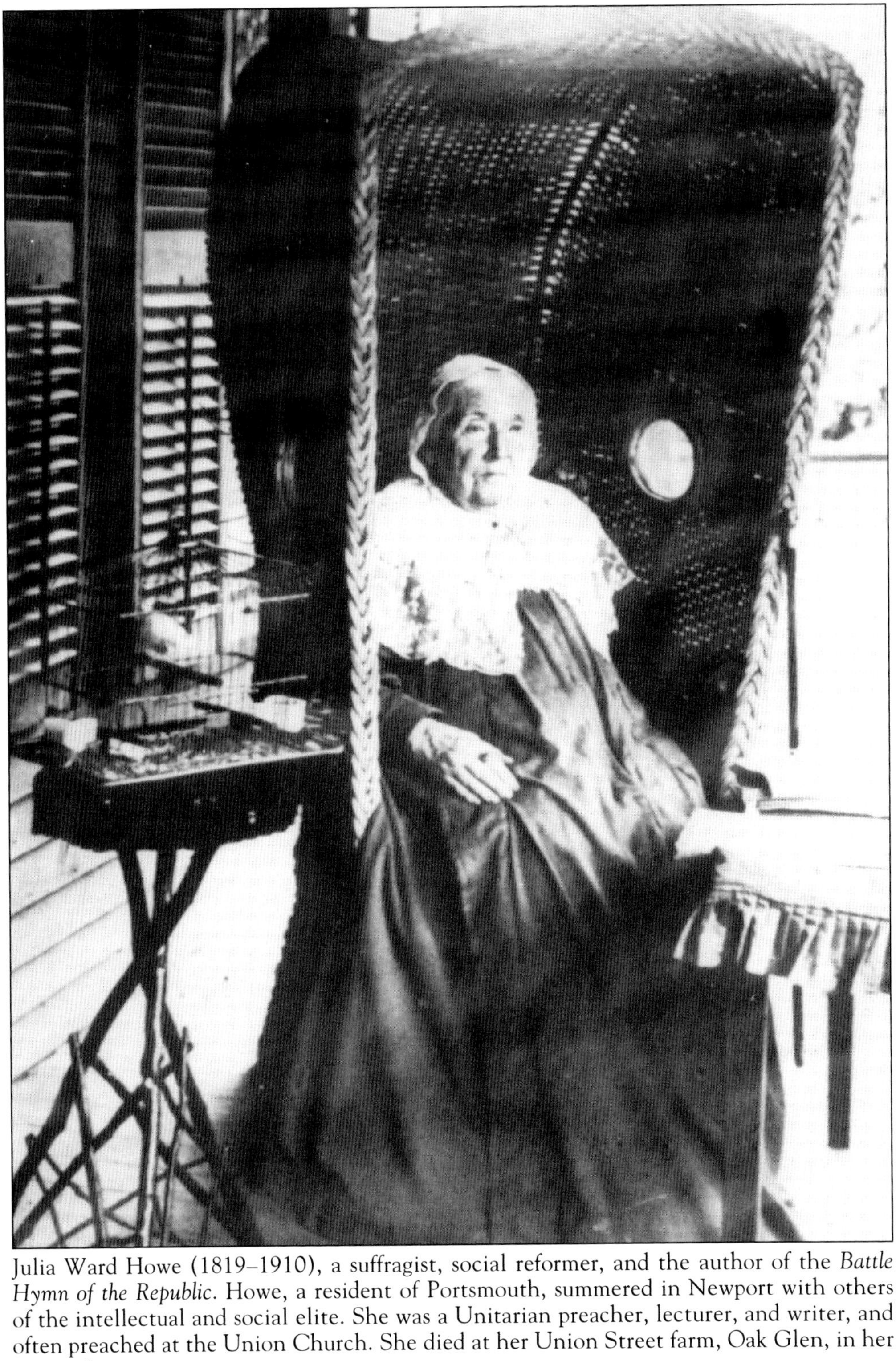

Julia Ward Howe (1819–1910), a suffragist, social reformer, and the author of the *Battle Hymn of the Republic*. Howe, a resident of Portsmouth, summered in Newport with others of the intellectual and social elite. She was a Unitarian preacher, lecturer, and writer, and often preached at the Union Church. She died at her Union Street farm, Oak Glen, in her ninety-first year.

B. Earl Anthony, c. 1913, a member of the Portsmouth Town Council and state representative from Portsmouth for three terms. For many years, Anthony was the owner and operator of the Eureka Spring Water Co. The spring, located on family land at Melville, was a principal source of income for the family. The land and aquifer that supplied the spring were condemned and seized by the federal government at the beginning of World War II.

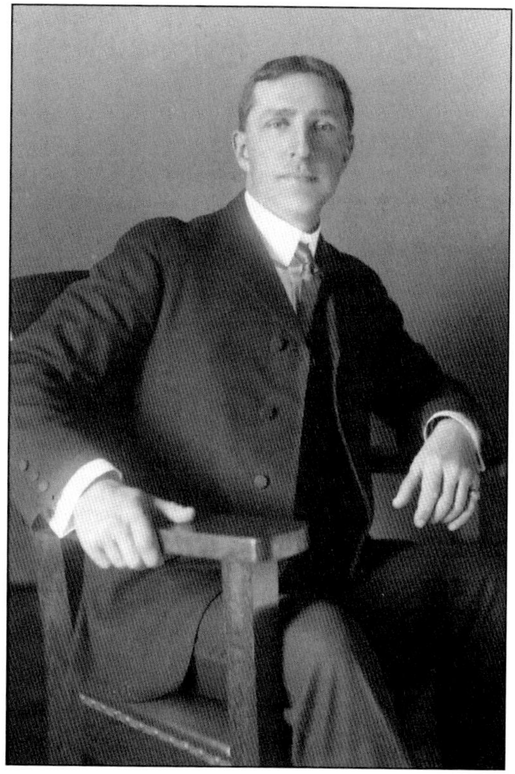

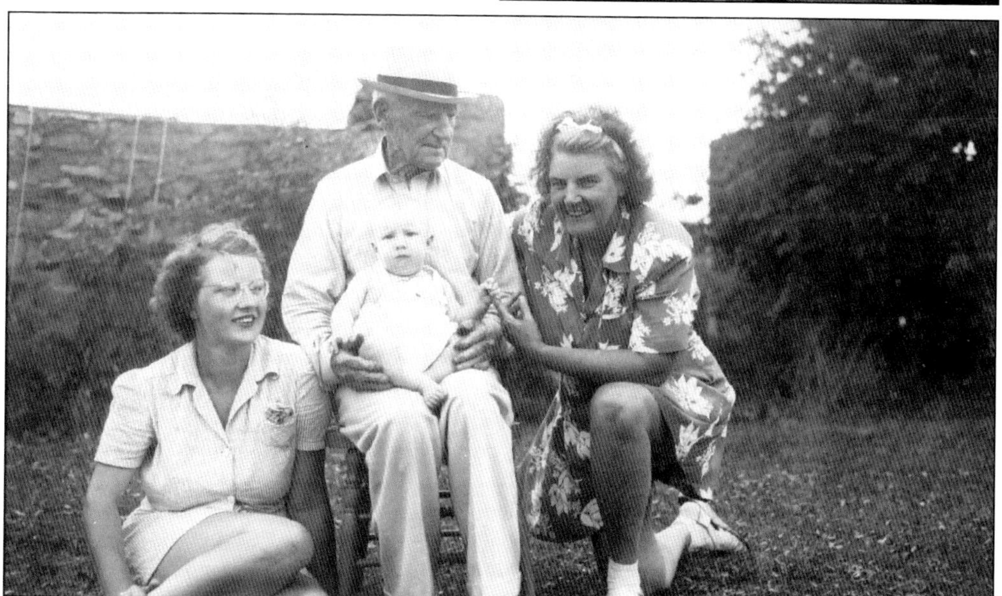

Walter Harris Knight (1858–1946) at his summer place on Hog Island in August 1942. Knight is holding his grandson, Garry Stone; his daughters, Phyllis Stone (left) and Mabel Budlong, also pose for the camera. Knight was a partner of the Bentley-Knight Company, and was one of the founders of the General Electric Corporation. He was also president of the Bridgeport Projectile Company. As a patent attorney with Knight Brothers of New York, he did considerable legal work for the Corlis Engine Works of Providence.

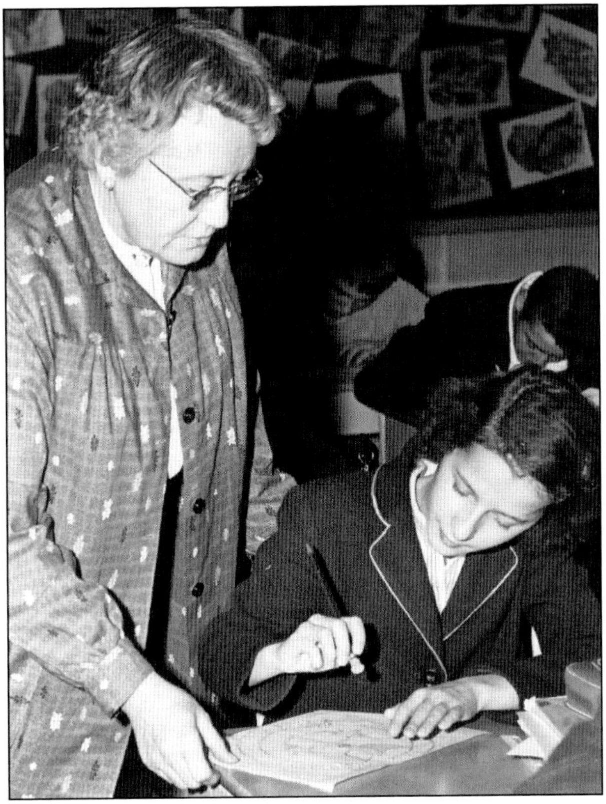

Elizabeth A. (Mrs. Henry) Wilkey, the mother of Sylvia, Astris, and Peter Wilkey. A graduate of the Rhode Island School of Design, Elizabeth was Portsmouth's roving art and music teacher; she conducted classes at all Portsmouth schools. The official Portsmouth town seal is her design.

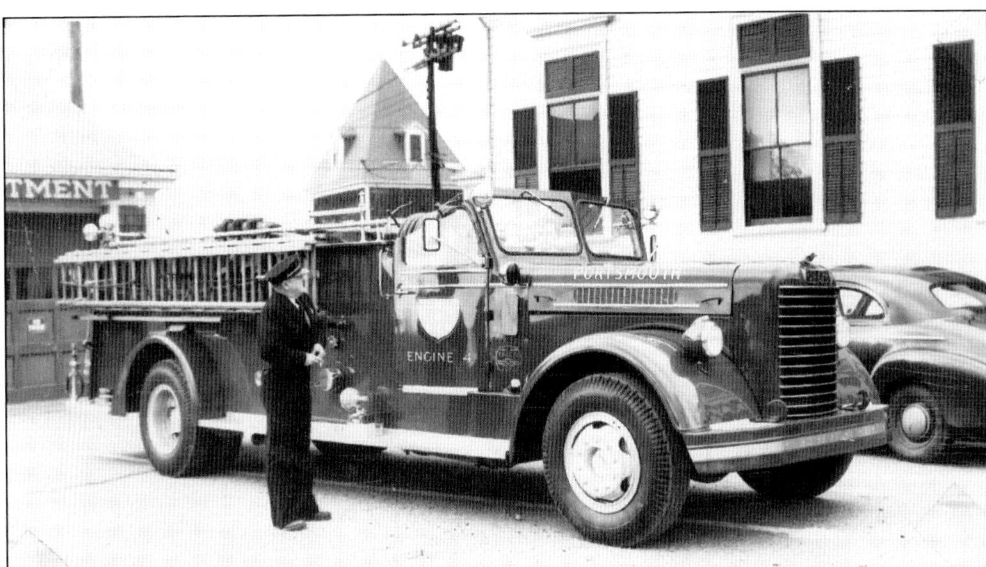

Henry Wilkey (1902–1977), the first paid fire chief of the town's all-volunteer firefighters. In this c. 1952 photograph, Chief Wilkey inspects the town's new ladder Engine No. 4. Wilkey returned from retirement for a day in 1970 for the ribbon-cutting and dedication ceremony of the new fire station on Quaker Hill.

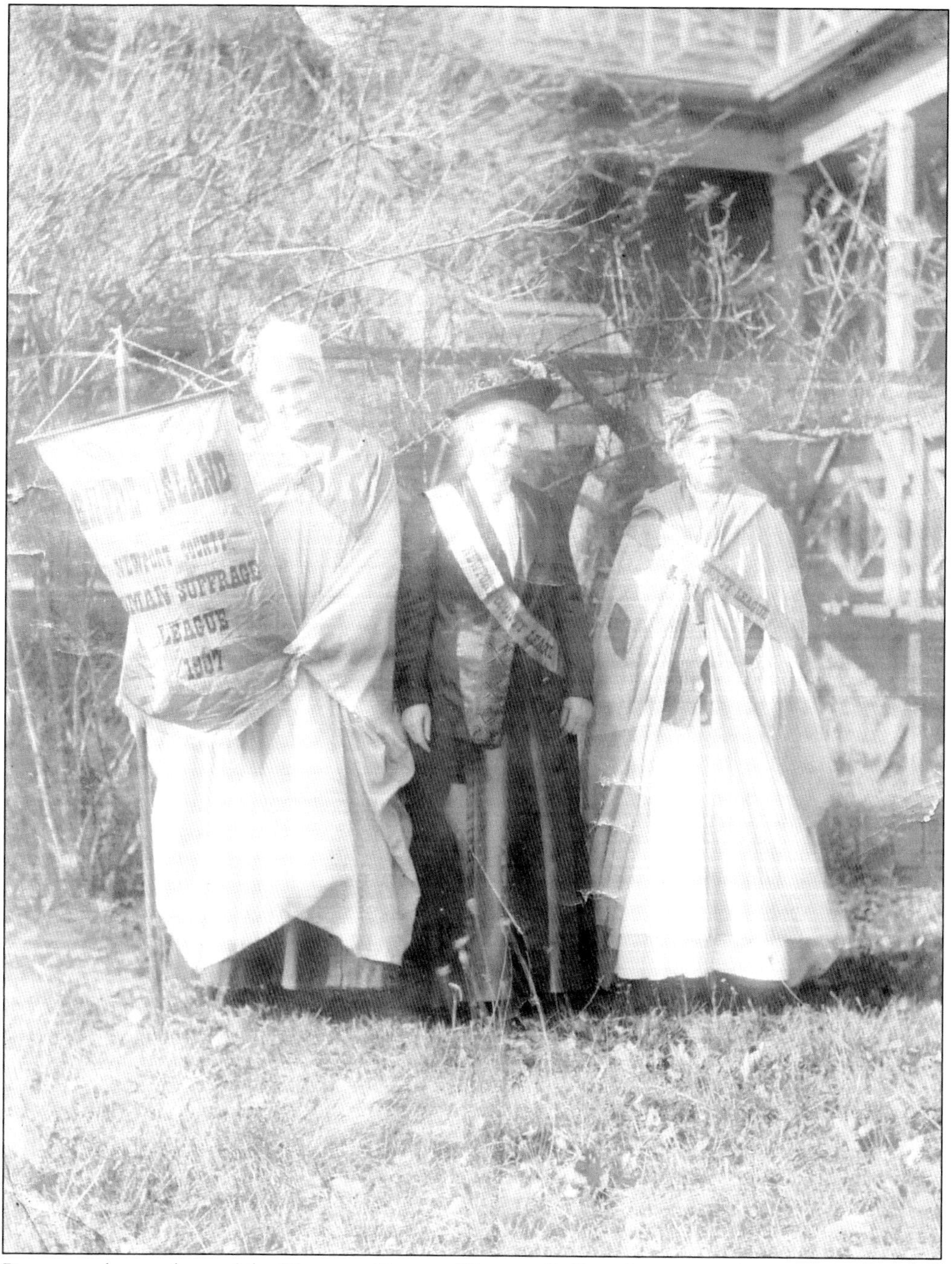

Portsmouth members of the Newport County Woman Suffrage League at the 1907 convention. From left to right are Letitia (Mrs. Abner P.) Lawton, Miss Cora Mitchell, and Emeline B. (Mrs. John) Eldredge.

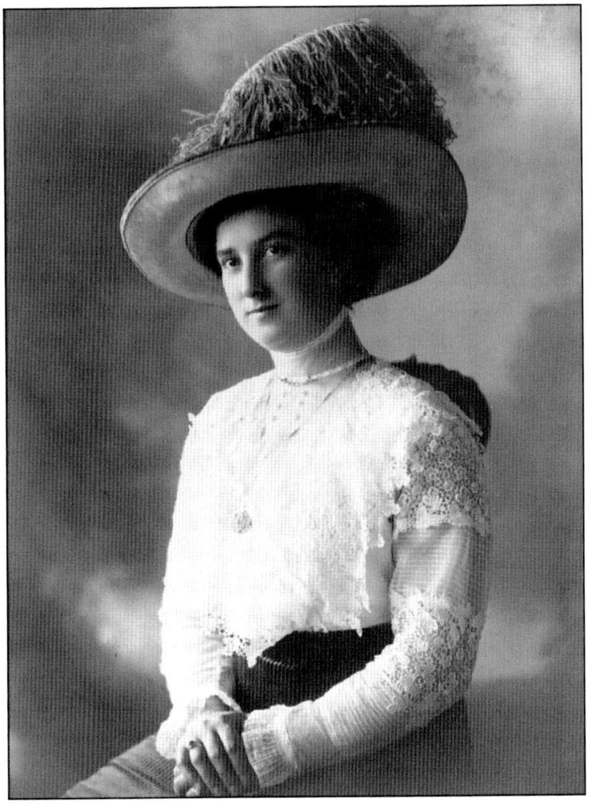

Alice Anthony Webb, the daughter of Henry C. Anthony, and the wife of Fred Webb, founder of the Cherry and Webb chain of women's clothing stores. The Webb mansion at 3352 East Main Road, now the Sea Fare Inn, is located across the road from land that was once the Anthony Farm.

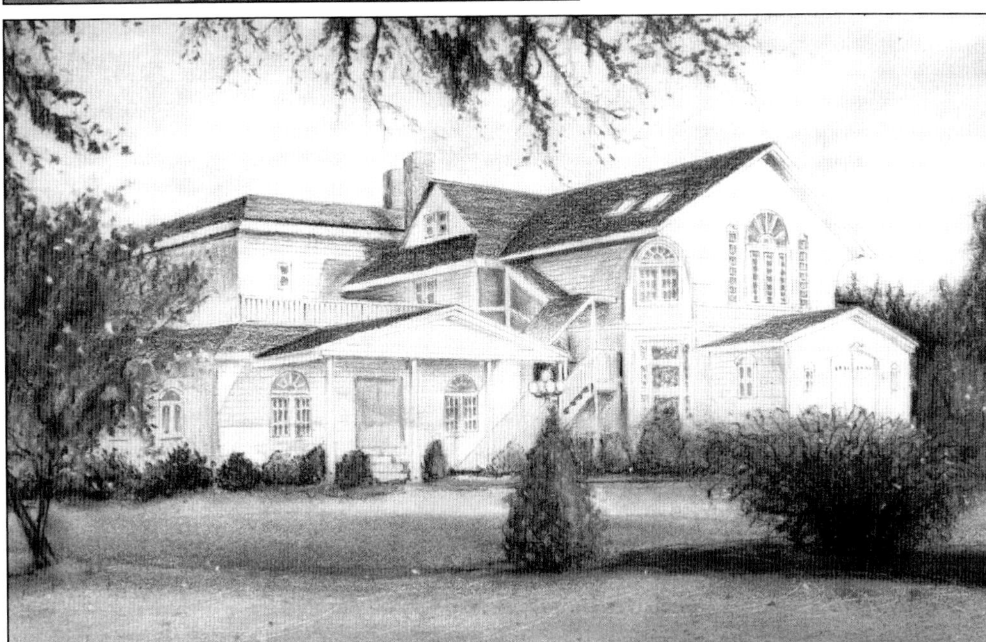

Fred Webb's 1887 mansion. Though the interior of the Webb mansion retains much of its ostentatious Victorian elegance, one is hard-put to recognize the place from its contemporary exterior.

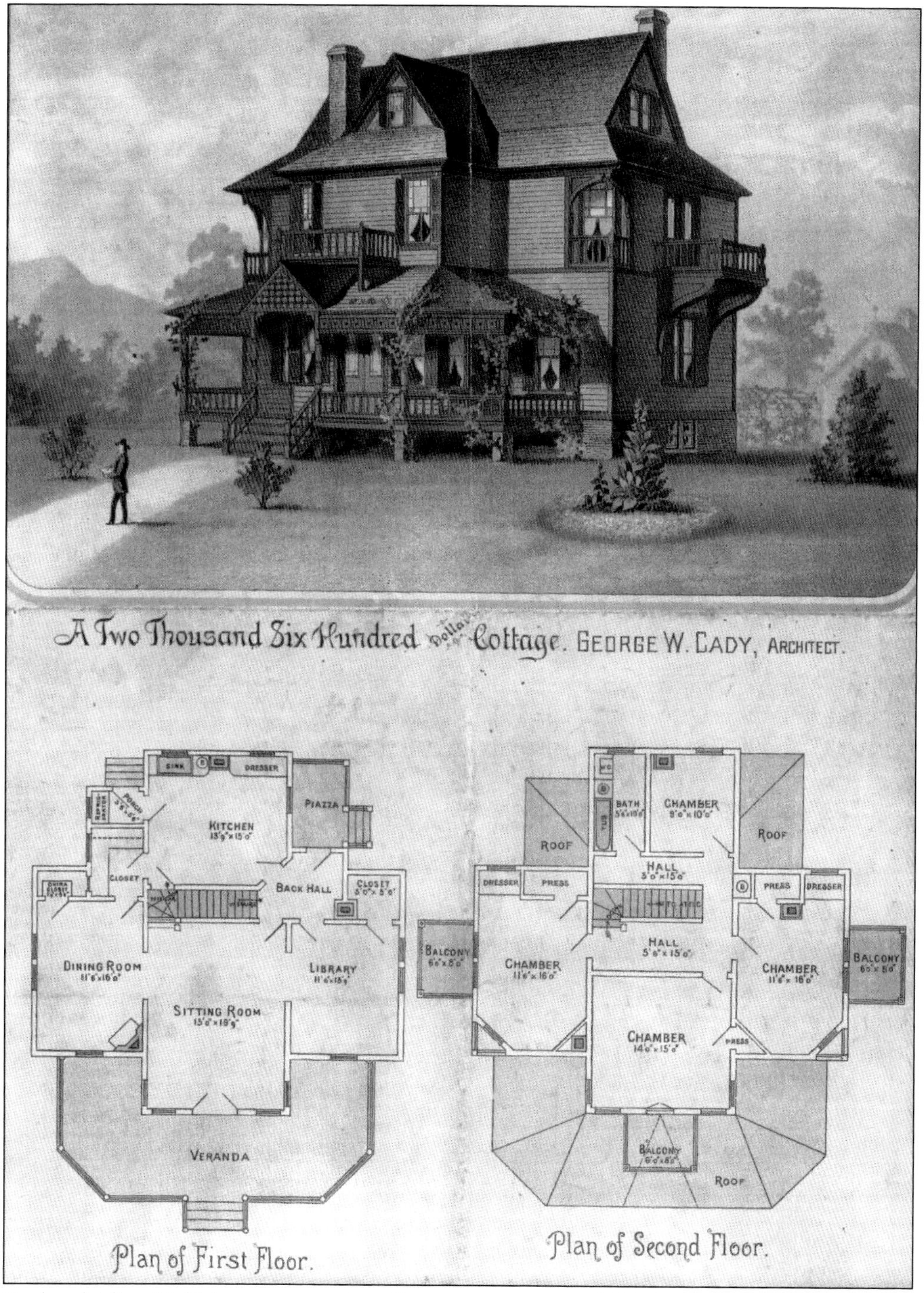

Fred and Alice Webb's spacious modern Victorian cottage at 3352 East Main Road. Fred Webb was the very model of a reserved Victorian gentleman. For exercise, each morning he walked from his home to Island Park, where his chauffeur picked him up for the drive to his store in Fall River. An interesting fact about the Webb mansion is that the garage has a turntable so that an automobile may be driven in forward, turned in place, and driven out forward.

Acknowledgments

Seldom is a book written without the assistance of numerous individuals who provide information and encouragement. It is our pleasure to salute and thank the following people who, without exception, allowed us use of precious family photographs and ephemera. Our heartfelt appreciation extends to the following: Town Clerk Carol Zinno; John T. Pierce Sr., for the postcard reprints of the town's 350th anniversary celebration; Anstris Wilkey Garcia for the Alice Anthony Webb, Elizabeth Anthony Wilkey, and 1947 class play photographs; Peter Wilkey for the motorized lawn mower, Menzi's Pond, and Dunn's Beach photographs; Dorothy Chase for the Chase Farm pictures; the Portsmouth Volunteer Firefighters for the Chief Wilkey and the DUWK amphibious vehicle pictures; George Karousos for his Sea Fare Inn and Fred Webb mansion drawings; Ann Madden for the Portsmouth Park area photographs, including Aquidneck, Atlantic, and Narragansett Avenue and several beach and cottage photographs; Nancy Peirce Lantz for the Mt. Hope Marina-Wharf Tavern photographs and menu; Charles Crouch for his Mt. Hope Marina photographs; Augusta Anthony MacLaughlin for the photograph of her father, B. Earl Anthony; Eileen Gorton Shanley for the St. Anthony's School, store, and hurricane photographs; Mario Occhi for his Lawton Valley Falls, Howe water mill, Island Park roller coaster, and Cornell Farm mansion photographs.

Without the cooperation of Joyce Almeida of Warwick, RI, for her loan of the Hog Island and W.H. Knight pictures, and Joseph Bains of Braintree, MA, for his loan of several rare postcard views of streets and farms, especially the Prudence Island and Island Park postcards, these sections would not appear in this volume.

Special thanks to Portsmouth Historical Society President Herb Hall for allowing us to rummage through the Society's image files. Thanks to Patrick T. Conley for allowing us to copy the Anne Hutchinson picture from his book, *An Album of Rhode Island History, 1636–1986* (Donning Company, Virginia Beach, VA, second printing, 1992).

Both authors supplied postcard images from their collections. Contemporary photographs are by Richard V. Simpson. Much of the historical text in this book is referenced from two books that we highly recommend for further study: *Historical Tracts of the Town of Portsmouth, Rhode Island* by John T. Pierce Sr. (Hamilton Printing Company, 1991), and *Historic and Architectural Resources of Portsmouth, Rhode Island: A Preliminary Report*, prepared and published by the Rhode Island Historical Preservation Commission (January 1979).